John Fielden's Todmorden

i

Acknowledgements

I would like to thank my friends and associates from the Workers' Educational Association local history classes held over many years in Cornholme and Todmorden, who have made learning to "do history" such fun. And most especially, my thanks go to Julian Harber, for all his teaching and encouragement, as well as for his helpful comments on the draft of this book. Thanks also to Norman Greenwood, for the loan of his ancestor's diary. To Dorothy Thompson, for a photocopy of the Gauxholme Mill strike placard. To Kit Hardwick, for the loan of Oddfellows' minute books. To Frank Stansfield, for proof-reading the manuscript, and for giving me a copy of his index to the 1851 census of Todmorden - worth its weight in gold! To Mila Caley for being so enthusiastic about the first draft of this book; and to her and John Carpenter for their generous hospitality whilst I was doing the London research. To Christine and Chris Friend also for being so hospitable whilst I was in London. To Keith Parkinson, for his wonderful work on typesetting and design. And last, but most of all, to my husband Mark for a hundred kinds of help and support; and for making such a splendid job of the photographs.

I gratefully acknowledge permission to publish some of the photographs, as follows: Calderdale Leisure Services Department, for permission to photograph the handloom (page 25) and to reproduce the cover picture, (which also appears on page 64), and the photograph of John Fielden on page viii; The West Yorkshire Archive Service, for permission to reproduce the photographs on pages 12 & 28; and Roger Birch for permission to reproduce the photographs on pages 19 and 31.

about the author

Linda Croft was born in Lincolnshire in 1953, and was educated at Cleethorpes Grammar School and the University of Durham. She has lived in Todmorden since 1974. Married with two children, she works in the Local Studies Department of Burnley Library.

JOHN FIELDEN'S TODMORDEN

**Popular culture and radical politics
in a cotton town
c.1817 - 1850**

Linda Croft

Photography by
Mark Croft

TYGERFOOT
PRESS

0630734b

Published by

Tygerfoot Press
41 Pudsey Road,
Todmorden,
Lancashire.
OL14 8NR

Tel. 01706 816407

ISBN   0 9524245 0 9

Typesetting, page layout and graphics by
Keith Parkinson Computing Services
25 Brookfield Terrace
Todmorden
Lancs
OL14 8LB
Tel. 01706 816323

Printed by RAP Ltd.,
201 Spotland Road,
Rochdale
OL12 7AF

Contents

TODMORDEN AREA c.1850
Key to some local place names

(not to scale - use in conjunction with suitable map - eg. O.S. Outdoor Leisure Map, South Pennines 1:25 000)

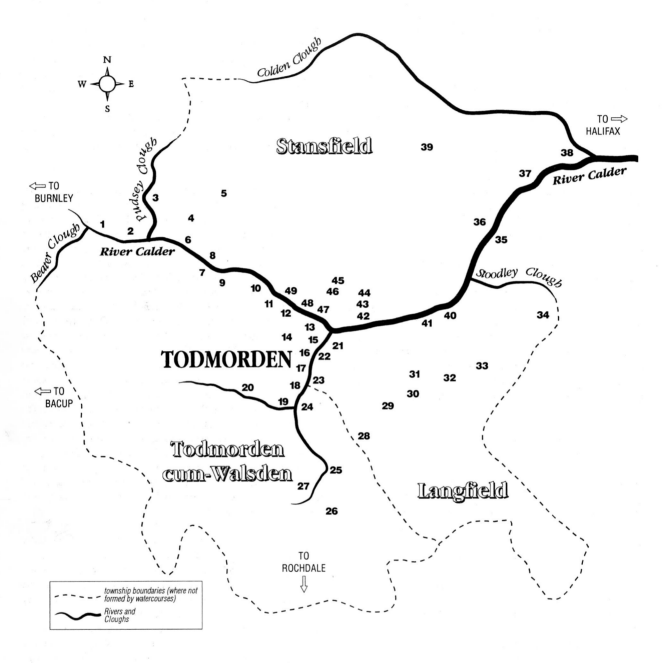

7	Barewise	13	Doghouse	32	Lumbutts	20	Stoneswood
28	Basin Stone	36	Eastwood	33	Mankinholes	34	Soodley Pike
39	Blackshaw Head	14	Edge End	46	Meadow Bottom	49	Toad Carr
48	Blind Lane	19	Gauxholme	42	Millwood	5	Todmorden Hall
26	Bottoms (Walsden)	40	Haugh	38	Mytholm	25	Walsden
23	Bridge End	29	Heyhead Green	47	Patmos	22	Waterside
37	Callis	45	Hole Bottom	1	Portsmouth	35	Wood Mill
3	Carrbottom	21	Honey Hole	43	Priestwell		
31	Causeway	6	Ingbottom	9	Robinwood		
12	Centre Vale	5	Kebcote	16	Salford		
2	Cornholme	8	Knotts	11	Scaitcliffe		
30	Croft Carr	24	Knowlwood	18	Shade		
44	Cross Stone	10	Lineholme	4	Shore		
17	Dobroyd	41	Lobb Mill	27	Square, Walsden		

vi

Introduction

When I first became interested in John Fielden and early 19th century Todmorden, about ten or twelve years ago now, I was surprised to find how little written history had been published about either the man or the town.

There was then no full-scale biography of Fielden, and the most authoritative writings about his life were a single chapter in *Chartist Portraits* by G. D. H. Cole, published in 1965, and J. T. Ward's introduction to the 1969 reprint of Fielden's pamphlet *The Curse of the Factory System*. This neglect of John Fielden was particularly surprising in view of the fact that he had two strong claims to the historian's interest. First, the Fieldens of Todmorden, as one of Lancashire's leading cotton-manufacturing families, might have expected the same degree of attention that has been accorded comparable 19th century cotton dynasties, such as the Gregs of Styal, the Turners of Helmshore, the Arkwrights of Stockport, or the Ashworths of Bolton. Secondly, John Fielden was an important figure in the radical politics of his day. His close friends and associates included reforming members of Parliament such as William Cobbett and Lord Shaftesbury; Tory radicals such as Richard Oastler and Parson Bull; working-class leaders such as Feargus O'Connor and John Doherty; and the visionary Robert Owen. Fielden, uniquely, linked such strangely assorted friends of the popular radical movement, but all of his associates had attracted far more attention from historians and biographers than had John Fielden. It was not until 1987, with the publication of Stewart Weaver's *John Fielden and the Politics of Popular Radicalism* that Fielden finally received the biographical attention that his life had so merited.

Weaver's biography is an admirable, sympathetic and scholarly study. It quite properly concentrates upon Fielden's public and Parliamentary career, but in doing so it leaves two aspects of Fielden's life seriously under-explored. One of these is the development of the firm of Fielden Brothers: a well-researched history of the firm would be a valuable contribution to both local and industrial history, and the extensive collections of Fielden family and business records now held in the archives at Wakefield and Halifax, and at John Rylands Library in Manchester, make a Fielden Brothers history a feasible project. The other aspect of Fielden's life which remains sketchy in Weaver's biography, is his career as a local political leader and in particular, the relationship between John Fielden and the local political culture. Weaver does at one point observe that "To attribute the exceptional militance of the town to the presence of the Fieldens is tempting... (but)...that the Fieldens in fact reflected the ideology of the town seems more likely".[1] Weaver's intuitive insight is impressive - but he brings no evidence to substantiate this belief. This present study makes no attempt to write a history of the firm, but it uses a detailed examination of local sources to illuminate the relationship between the Fieldens and "the ideology of the town".

If John Fielden was for a long time rather unjustly neglected by historians, Todmorden itself has fared little better. There is no substantial history of Todmorden currently in print. The standard local history by Joshua Holden was published as long ago as 1912. The appearance in 1992 of *Pennine Valley: a history of Upper Calderdale* by Bernard Jennings and Hebden Bridge W.E.A. Local History Group, has partially filled the gap; but being a general local history of all the communities of the upper Calder Valley, its coverage of Todmorden in the "Age of Agitation" is necessarily brief. There is also a short pamphlet by Edwin T. Ashworth, dating from 1901, which describes the Todmorden anti-Poor Law riots and the Plug Plot, but it scarcely ventures beyond a narrative account of the most dramatic incidents.

The relative lack of previous detailed research into Todmorden's early 19th century history has contributed, I believe, to the town being given much less than its proper due in general histories of the period, and even in specialist histories of the radical political campaigns of the 1830s and 1840s. Todmorden, small though it was, was a Chartist centre of the first rank in 1842, but this is seldom apparent from histories of Chartism. Todmorden's important role in the anti-Poor Law rebellion is better known, and the early, dramatic stages of the conflict are covered well in Nicholas T. Edsall's *The Anti-Poor Law Movement* published in 1971. Edsall sees Todmorden as a very important focus of the opposition and remarks that "no Union attempted to match its reputation as the most troublesome in England and Wales". But both Edsall and Felix Driver, in his 1993 study *Power and Pauperism* make (owing to their lack of familiarity with the local area and local sources) fundamental factual errors about the administration of the Poor Law in Todmorden - which is a pity, because such errors tend to be reproduced by subsequent historians.[2] The advantages to be derived from a much greater degree of cooperation between local history and academic history, are obvious.

This present study, then, is the first attempt to fully investigate popular culture and radical politics in Todmorden; and to explore the relationship between John Fielden and the local political culture. The sources drawn on include the records of central Government, particularly Home Office papers, the records of the Poor Law Commission, census enumerators' returns and the papers of the Board of Trade and the Registrar of Friendly Societies. Local sources used include township records, deeds, business and chapel records, maps, newspapers and trade directories. By inter-relating the information derived from these various sources it has been possible to build up a profile of the activities, occupations and sometimes even the opinions of some of the most important and interesting inhabitants of early 19th century Todmorden.

I hope that *John Fielden's Todmorden* will be enjoyed both by local people, who will discover a fascinating period in the history of their town, when the people of Todmorden played a small but significant part in shaping an emergent new world; and also by those who have a more general interest in 19th century history, who will find in Todmorden the unique case of a town whose leading employer was also a Radical Reformer.

John Fielden
1784 - 1849

Chapter 1

John Fielden: Cotton Lord and Radical Reformer

The Fieldens and Todmorden

The Fielden family virtually created Todmorden. As the spinning and weaving business that they founded in the late eighteenth century grew to become one of the largest cotton enterprises in Lancashire, so the town of Todmorden grew and expanded also. It was the Fieldens who first brought gas to the town, using it to light streets and houses as well as their Waterside Mill. When the Leeds to Manchester railway was in the planning stages, it was they who lobbied to ensure that it would pass through Todmorden, and so provided Todmorden with a rapid link to Cottonopolis. The Fieldens promoted Sunday and day-school education for poor children. They built and endowed the Unitarian church. Fielden money paid for Todmorden's magnificent Town Hall and eventually the family allowed the town to acquire, for a nominal sum, the beautiful Centre Vale estate for a public park.

But a similar story might be told about a dozen industrial dynasties in a dozen manufacturing towns. What makes the Fieldens and Todmorden different, and indeed unique, is that in the early 19th century the Fielden brothers, and John Fielden in particular, proclaimed themselves to be Radical Reformers. By this they meant that they supported a thorough reform of Parliament, universal manhood suffrage, and the introduction of legislation to limit the hours of work in factories and so protect factory workers and domestic handloom weavers. It is as the Parliamentary promoter of the Ten Hours Act of 1847 that John Fielden is chiefly remembered today. But his radicalism also led him, much more controversially, into strident opposition to the New Poor Law of 1834, and public support for Chartism (the working-class movement for the vote). After Todmorden rioted in defiance of the Poor Law, John Fielden came under the scrutiny of the Government which hoped to secure enough evidence to convict him on the very serious charge of instigating a riot.

No other leading industrialist went so far, or risked so much, as did John Fielden in his advocacy of the political rights of the people. Todmorden between about 1820 and 1850 can truly be called "John Fielden's Todmorden", not only because, as the leading partner in the town's largest employers, he played a major part in building and developing the town; but also because he identified so closely with the struggles of the local people to improve their living conditions and gain their political freedom.

The Fieldens Embark upon Cotton-spinning

John Fielden was born in 1784, in one of the cottages at Laneside near Todmorden in which his father Joshua had recently set up business as a cotton spinner.

Todmorden was, at that time, a mere village. Situated at the meeting-point of three steep-sided valleys, it consisted of just Todmorden Hall, St. Mary's church, two or three inns, and a scatter of cottages. Less than twenty years previously the three valleys themselves had been marshy and choked with vegetation, until they were drained and turnpike roads linking Todmorden with Burnley, Halifax and Rochdale were driven through them. Now small communities were beginning to form alongside the new roads in the valley bottoms - Toad Carr in the Burnley valley; Millwood and Charlestown in the Halifax valley; Dobroyd, Gauxholme, and Square at Walsden in the Rochdale valley. But the real life and activity of the district was in the hills. The uplands around Todmorden were divided into scores of small farms which, as the soil was poor and the climate cool and damp, offered only a very thin living. But there was a long-established textile trade and the farmers eked out their meagre returns from agriculture by producing cloth for the market. The farmsteads reverberated to the pounding of the shuttle in the loom, and each week hundreds of pieces of woollen and worsted

Clothiers on their way to market, c. 1814

cloth were loaded on to the sturdy backs of pack-ponies, and carried off to the Piece Hall at Halifax, or to more distant markets and fairs.

The Fielden family had for generations been engaged as entrepreneurs in this textile trade, and some members of the family had been very successful. Amongst those who prospered were the five sons of Joshua and Martha Fielden of Bottomley - Joshua, Nicholas, Thomas, Samuel and John - who, around the beginning of the eighteenth century, were all successful clothiers. John married an heiress as well as succeeding in trade, and became a substantial landowner who lived in style at Todmorden Hall. His brother Nicholas, meanwhile, established himself as a "stuff-maker" (or master worsted manufacturer) at Edge End farm, and it was here that he trained several of his nephews to the business. One of these nephews was Joshua; and it was his son, also named Joshua, and also trained to the family business, who in 1782 took the momentous step of abandoning the hills for the valley, and the worsted trade for the cotton business, and so laid the foundations of what eventually became one of the largest cotton firms in Lancashire.[1]

But when Joshua Fielden first set up in the cotton business, it was in a very small way indeed. Each week he walked the twenty-five miles to Manchester, returning with a hand-cart full of raw cotton. The family then set to work, carding the fibre by hand, and then spinning it on a small hand-operated "jenny", and the following week Joshua would sell the spun cotton in Manchester and return with a fresh supply of the raw material. In 1783, shortly after Joshua set up in business, the end of the American War of Independence liberated the supply of cotton and prepared the way for a great expansion of the infant English cotton industry; and the following year, John Fielden was born, Joshua's sixth child, and third son.

John Fielden's Childhood

During John's infancy, the Fielden family business was slowly expanded and mechanised. Joshua had already sunk all his available resources into the business, and had to mortgage the Laneside cottages to obtain the capital necessary for expansion.[2] First he added another storey to the cottages, and installed carding-engines. By 1794, when ten year old John started work in the mill, there had been added a waterwheel and some throstles, or water-powered spinning machines. But John started work on the old hand-operated billies and jennies, which were still used at Laneside, and which employed some of the children of neighbours as well as the younger Fieldens.

John's transfer from school to cotton mill came very suddenly. His parents, Joshua and Jenny Fielden, were Quakers, and members of this sect generally tried to give their children as much schooling as their circumstances allowed. But there was little on offer in Todmorden in the 1780s; the only proper schools were the two endowed schools - Clegg's School near

St. Mary's Church, and a school at Cross Stone. The Fielden children were not sent to either of these, probably because Joshua and Jenny objected to the close association between these schools and the Church of England. Instead, John received his education from a local character who went by the name of "Long Sam", and of whom it was said that, although he was himself illiterate, by getting his pupils to read out loud from the newspapers to one another, and discuss what they read, he turned out pupils who were excellent readers and writers! At the time when John Fielden was one of Long Sam's pupils, the papers were dominated by reports of one colossal event - the French Revolution. The revolutionists' ideals of Liberty, Equality and Fraternity fired radicals throughout Europe. Long Sam declared himself a Jacobin, and subscribed to the radical *Leeds Mercury* newspaper for his pupils to read from. But when Britain went to war with revolutionary France, a crack-down on British Jacobins and Radicals began and Joshua Fielden, in alarm, withdrew his son John from the dangerous influence of Long Sam and set him to work in the factory. But it was already too late. Joshua was later to complain that his sons were "as arrant Jacobins as any in the Kingdom", and John especially, had already wholeheartedly embraced the democratic and egalitarian beliefs that were to underpin his life's work.

Nor did John Fielden ever forget his early experiences as a child labourer in a cotton mill. Many years later, when he was a wealthy businessman and Member of Parliament, some Oldham businessmen solicited his support against a reduction of working hours for factory children, and in reply he wrote:

> "I well remember being set to work in my
> father's mill when I was little more than ten
> years old; my associates, too, in the labour
> and recreation are fresh in my memory......I
> shall never forget the fatigue I often felt
> before the end of the day, and the anxiety of
> us all to be relieved from the unvarying and
> irksome toil we had gone through before we
> could obtain relief from such play and
> amusements as we resorted to when
> liberated from our work". [3]

From his own experience he knew that children in cotton mills were cruelly overworked. And as he himself admitted, conditions at his father's mill were relatively benign. The hours of work were ten a day - fewer than many factory children worked then or later - and Joshua and Jenny Fielden were more able than most parents to allow their children occasional indulgences. Of the children who worked alongside Fielden in the mill, very few were still living, he said, when he was beginning his Parliamentary career. Some had died very young, and most of the others had appeared to age prematurely, and died before they reached the age of fifty years. He believed that their early deaths were attributable to the nature of the employment in which they had been brought up. But, a few years after John started work in the mill, his father found he had to increase the daily hours of labour. He had had a new 5-storey steam-powered mill built adjoining the Laneside cottages, and had equipped it with spinning mules - the latest improvement in machinery. But he found that to run it profitably, he had to increase working hours, as other firms using the same kind of machines were working 77 or even 84 hours a week. The hours at the Fielden factories were increased to 12 a day from Monday to Friday, and 11 on Saturday - a total of 71 hours a week.[4]

Fielden Brothers of Todmorden

As the Fielden boys grew up, they were increasingly taken into the management of the business, until, from 1803, Joshua just kept a supervisory eye on the business and left its day-to-day running to his three elder sons. Samuel was in charge of the spinning mill at Lumbutts which the Fieldens leased from 1794, and bought outright in 1803.[5] The second brother, Joshua, became the firm's mechanic; and John was trained by his father to buy and sell cotton on the Manchester Exchange. In 1811, Joshua, the founder of the firm, died. After his death the firm became known as "Fielden Brothers", and the two youngest brothers were taken into partnership, James taking

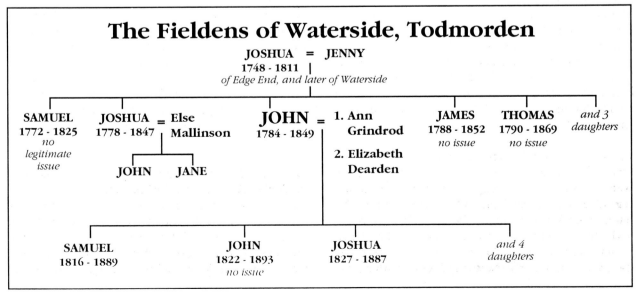

The Fieldens of Waterside, Todmorden

JOSHUA = JENNY
1748 - 1811
of Edge End, and later of Waterside

SAMUEL	JOSHUA = Else	JOHN =	1. Ann	JAMES	THOMAS	*and 3*
1772 - 1825	1778 - 1847 Mallinson	1784 - 1849	Grindrod	1788 - 1852	1790 - 1869	*daughters*
no				*no issue*	*no issue*	
legitimate	JOHN JANE		2. Elizabeth			
issue			Dearden			

SAMUEL	JOHN	JOSHUA	*and 4*
1816 - 1889	1822 - 1893	1827 - 1887	*daughters*
	no issue		

over the general management of the workpeople, and Thomas acting as the firm's agent in Manchester. John Fielden took over his father's role as general manager and under his guidance, the firm went into a long period of profitable expansion. Soon after his father's death, John married and moved into the new house which he had had built at Dawson Weir, just across the road from the Waterside factory. Surprisingly little has been recorded about his wife, beyond the facts that she was called Ann, her father's name was John Grindrod, and she was an Anglican in religion.[6]

John Fielden and Religion

John Fielden had been born into a family with an exceptionally strong Quaker tradition. Many of the Todmorden Fieldens became Friends in the very early days of Quakerism, and there is a strong possibility that the family had a tradition of religious radicalism that dated back to before the Civil War period.[7] But, as a young man, Fielden became dissatisfied with the Quaker religion. The sect had once been a radical one but by the early nineteenth century had settled into a rather quietist and conservative stage of its history. Fielden tried first Methodism, and then the Church of England. Anglicanism might seem an unlikely choice for a radical industrialist of Jacobin political opinions, but Todmorden Anglicanism in the early 19th century was a broad and populist church. The curate of St. Mary's was the Rev. Joseph Atkinson, who was an unpretentious man, much-liked in Todmorden. He was a farmer as well as a priest, whose parishioners were as likely to see him leading his cattle or pushing a wheelbarrow as preaching from the pulpit. He deliberately fostered a close and harmonious relationship between the church and the chapels. But the Church of England, even under Atkinson's benevolent and tolerant curacy, did not offer what Fielden was looking for.

There was in Todmorden at that time, a small Bible Reading Society, made up of ex-Methodists who had split off from the main body in 1806 when Joseph Cooke of Rochdale had been expelled from the local Methodist Circuit for heresy. In a typical Pennine manner (rather reminiscent of the early Quakers), this small independent group met at regular intervals in earnest enquiry after religious truth. John Fielden began to attend some of their meetings. The visit of the Rev. Richard Wright to this little group in 1818 was a turning point in Fielden's life. Saying afterwards that "These views harmonise more with my ideas of what Christ Himself has taught than any other I have yet heard", he became a convert to the Methodist Unitarians (as the followers of Cooke and Wright were now calling themselves). At last, in this small, radical and free-thinking sect he had found his spiritual home, and a religious creed that meshed well with the Jacobin political ideals that he had adopted during his school days with "Long Sam".

St Mary's Chapel, Todmorden, in the early 19th century

4

Factory children, c. 1814

Todmorden and Cotton

By the time that John Fielden took over the management of the family firm in 1811, Todmorden had become firmly established as a cotton manufacturing town. Whereas it had once looked eastwards, towards Halifax, Yorkshire and the woollen trade, it now looked south and west, to Manchester, Lancashire, and cotton. The water of the many fast-flowing cloughs that tumbled into the Calder in and near Todmorden had been channelled and harnessed to power cotton spinning machinery. There were 35 spinning mills in the Todmorden area, containing a total of 237 mules and 88 throstles, which carried between them more than 60,000 spindles. The Fieldens' main mill at Waterside, with 10 mules and 6 throstles, was only the fifth largest in the area and considerably smaller than the largest local mill at Lineholme in the Burnley valley, with its 19 mules. But the Fieldens also had another 10 mules at their Lumbutts factory,[8] and interests in several smaller spinning mills at Dobroyd, Stoneswood, Smithyholme and Waterstalls.

As a predominantly cotton-manufacturing town, Todmorden's trade suffered relatively little from the economic uncertainties of the long war with France which lasted, with only one short break, from 1793 until 1815. It is true that there was still some worsted cloth being made in Todmorden, at the huge Callis Mill in the Halifax valley, and at nearby Lobb Mill and Eastwood. This type of cloth was mostly exported to the continent of Europe, and during the war the manufacturers suffered from the loss of their

markets, from blockades and embargoes, and not infrequently, from the loss of ships and cargoes at sea. But worsteds accounted for a relatively small and declining proportion of Todmorden's textile output, as many local firms changed over to the cotton trade which (except for a short period from 1811-1812 when England was at war with America), enjoyed a long period of relative prosperity in the early years of the 19th century. The Fieldens' trade was nearly all with the New World and during the Napoleonic Wars their business expanded phenomenally. They added Causeway Mill in Lumbutts Clough to their assets in 1815,[9] and at the end of the war were said to be employing 3,000 handloom weavers to turn into cloth the yarn produced by their several spinning mills. At the peak of the wartime boom, their weavers' wages reached 8s for a cut of 30 yards[10] - a quantity that a hard-working and skilful weaver could produce in a single day.

But if this was a good time for the weavers, it was an even better one for the manufacturers, and the easy profits to be made enticed a flood of new entrants into the cotton business. It was relatively easy to set up as a cotton spinner or manufacturer, and not a great deal of capital was required. The water-powered spinning mills situated in the local cloughs were small, several of them, including Strines, Holme, Staups, Cross Lee, Hough Stone, Burnt Acres and Hudson Mills, having only two or three mules apiece. It was even easier to set up in business as a manufacturer of cotton cloth, as the weavers usually owned their own looms, and so the would-be manufacturer needed only a stock of warp and weft which he weighed out to the weavers one week, and took back in the form of cloth the following week. It was then but a short time till the master sold the cloth, and made his profit. There was even a back-door mode of entry to the trade via the black market in "range" or "moulter". This was warp and weft that the weavers fiddled from that allocated to them by the master. At this time the profits the cotton manufacturer made were so good that a blind eye was turned to the weavers' small embezzlements, and the weavers boosted their wages by abstracting some of the yarn and then skilfully dampening the cloth so that it would weigh in correctly when returned to the manufacturer. There was a well organised system of collecting "range" from the weavers, and selling it on to small manufacturers, at a price considerably less than that commanded by cotton fresh from the spinner, and several local cotton firms are said to have started off by using "range", during and just after the Napoleonic Wars.[11]

So long as the economic boom of the war years continued, the cotton industry could accommodate all these new and aspiring capitalists. But when the war ended, economic crisis was not far behind. Lucrative Government contracts came to an end and markets contracted at the very same time as thousands of returning soldiers flooded the labour market. It soon became apparent that many of the new manufacturers had borrowed too freely and were in deep financial trouble. They tried to salvage their situation by increasing working hours, cutting wages, and trying to undercut their rivals in the marketplace. The Fieldens, along with some others of the longer-established and more humanitarian employers, joined a campaign initiated by Nathaniel Gould of Manchester for a factory act to limit the hours of work in cotton mills, and in 1816 a petition was sent from Waterside Mill to the House of Commons, signed by the Fielden brothers and all their workpeople. This campaign eventually resulted in the Factory Act of 1819, which made it illegal to employ children under 9, and restricted young people aged between 9 and 16 to a 12 hour day, or 72 hour working week. The hours at the Fieldens' factories had been 71 hours a week - less than the new legal maximum - for many years, and no further reduction was made.

Paper, Gold and Reform

The demand for shorter working hours was only one of the Radicals demands in these difficult post-war years. They also took issue with the Government's economic policy, particularly the decision to return to the gold standard in 1819. The Government considered that a return to the gold standard would increase confidence in the currency: the Radicals argued that it was monumentally unfair, because debts contracted during wartime in paper money, would now have to be repaid in the much more valuable gold currency, and that if there was to be a return to gold, there should be an "equitable adjustment" of all contracts that had been made in wartime currency. This was an issue with very wide popular appeal, because some of the main beneficiaries of the return to the gold standard were the bankers and financiers who had lent the Government money with which to pay for the war against France. An enormous National Debt had been incurred, and the repayments, in gold, were being met by very heavy taxes on articles of common consumption.

William Cobbett, the great Radical journalist, led the attack on these "tax-eaters" in his *Political Register*, and John Fielden, who was by now an industrialist of some standing, with a growing reputation as a Radical Reformer, came to Cobbett's attention when he declared himself a strong opponent of paper money, and equally opposed to the Government's plans to bring back the gold standard. So began the long association between John Fielden and William Cobbett. Over the next fifteen years, Fielden was to take an ever greater part in local and regional politics, always portraying himself as a disciple of Cobbett. It was Cobbett who published Fielden's first pamphlet (on the subject of currency reform) and in 1832 when Fielden was invited to stand as one of the Parliamentary candidates for the two-member constituency of Oldham, he agreed only on condition that William Cobbett was invited to be his running-mate.

The agitations of these post-war years, encouraged by Cobbett's biting journalism, built up into a demand for a reform of Parliament. During the French wars the popular democratic movement had been forced underground by severe Government repression, but once peace was re-established, it quickly welled up to the surface. Reform missionaries came to Todmorden and summoned a mass-meeting by putting out a handbill calling for "Parliamentary Reform, Peace, Unanimity and Order". Melville Horne, then the curate of Cross Stone, was roused to deliver a blistering sermon:

> "As Jacobins have invaded your township of Stansfield", he thundered "to spread their pernicious principles among its peaceful inhabitants, and are to take to the field on the 23rd instant, to discuss the subjects of Parliamentary reform, I feel it is my duty to God and the country to fire guns of alarm, and to light up a beacon to warn you of your danger, and to call all honest men to the defence of Old England."

He castigated all the Radical leaders, recommended the transportation of Jacobins, and called upon each member of his congregation to reform *himself*, and leave the reform of Parliament to Parliament[12]. There can have been little sympathy between the curate and his parishioners. Todmorden was overwhelmingly in favour of reform. Melville Horne did not stay long in the town, and was spoken of by a late nineteenth century local historian as "an able man but withal much calumniated"[13].

Scaitcliffe Hall, home of the Crossleys

The part played in the local agitation by John Fielden and his brothers will never be known, but it is very likely that the Fieldens, as early converts to the Radical cause and lifelong supporters of universal suffrage, were prominently involved. They must have shared the general sense of outrage, too, when a peaceable public meeting in favour of reform was brutally dispersed at Peterloo. The Government followed the Peterloo massacre with the Six Acts which limited such political freedom as the people did possess, making it more difficult to hold mass meetings, to criticise the Government, or to publish cheap newspapers. In the face of such repression, hopes for a radical reform of Parliament had to be postponed. Not until 1830, eleven years later, did another opportunity to press for a reform of Parliament present itself, and in the meantime, John Fielden's attention and energies were chiefly concentrated upon two objects. One was the firm of Fielden Brothers, which was entering boldly upon such new ventures as silk-manufacturing and powerloom weaving. The other was his small band of Unitarians, and the chapel and school that they were setting up at Honeyhole.

Fielden Brothers Expands

The Fieldens' main factory at Waterside was the site of almost continual innovation and expansion in the 1820s. First, a small silk-spinning department was established. New buildings were added at frequent intervals and a huge new weaving shed opened in 1828. Two years later Waterside had its own gas works, the first to be established by a private company, and as surplus gas was sold to light houses in the vicinity of the mill, Todmorden had a gas supply many years before most major towns and cities. It was mostly thanks to the efforts of the Fieldens, too, that Todmorden got an early rail link to Manchester. The Fieldens were major subscribers to the Manchester and Leeds Railway Company, formed in 1825 with the object of building a trans-Pennine rail link, and John Fielden became a director of the company. In 1831, he successfully argued the case for the line to pass through Todmorden (and within yards of the Waterside factory) rather than taking an alternative route through Huddersfield. Without this rail link to Manchester, Todmorden, which was already on the periphery of the cotton district, would have been severely disadvantaged against other cotton-manufacturing towns.

By now, with interests in railways as well as mills, the Fieldens were very wealthy indeed. The total assets of Fielden Brothers in 1833 was £300,000 - of which John's share was £100,000 and Joshua's, £80,000, with James and Thomas each holding a £60,000 share. This was exclusive of land or interests in mills and railways that were held by the brothers as their individual property, which in John Fielden's case amounted to a further £60,000.[14] Most of this wealth had been generated in the preceding decade. When Samuel Fielden, the eldest of Joshua and Jenny's five sons, had died in 1822 his mother had affirmed that his personal wealth amounted to less than £5,000 - a tiny proportion of the resources that his brothers could command ten years later.[15]

7

John Fielden and the Handloom Weavers

The late 1820s were a time of great distress for the handloom weavers, and it was Fielden's attempts to do something to help them that first that first made him a figure of regional, rather than merely local, influence.

In 1825, Todmorden and its immediate district was producing each week 7,000 pieces of cotton calico cloth, and several hundred pieces of fustians, satteens and velveteens, every yard of which was woven entirely by hand. But a great change was imminent. New and improved powerlooms had recently become available, and firms throughout Lancashire were investing in the new machinery. In Todmorden, Buckleys were planning a powerloom shed at Ridgefoot Mill, Firth and Haworth were setting one up at Albion Place, and Fielden Brothers had the most ambitious plans of all - a weaving shed covering an acre of ground and holding 800 powerlooms, powered by a 60 horse-power steam engine. When competed, it would be the largest weaving shed in the world.

The handloom weavers of Lancashire saw the new powerlooms as a terrible threat to their livelihood. Already they had suffered repeated reductions in their wage-rates, as the manufacturers who had crowded into the cotton trade during the boom years tried to secure markets for their products by undercutting one another. The better manufacturers had been forced to follow suit, and the wages of the Fieldens' weavers, for instance, which, as previously noted, had at one time been as high as 8s a cut, were by 1825 down to about 2s 6d. This gave a weaver (if he was conscientious, hard-working, in good health and had a constant supply of work), a weekly wage of about 15s - about the same as a male adult labourer in a factory, but less than most skilled workers. In November 1825, a new round of reductions began, and by mid-April 1826, the situation was truly desperate. Weavers' earnings, at 1s 6d a cut, were now below subsistence level, but were still being pushed down and many weavers had little work, or none at all. The resources of parish overseers and local charities were soon exhausted. Petitions were sent off to Parliament, begging for help for the distressed weavers, but the Government did nothing.[16] Fielden decided to seek the co-operation of other manufacturers in an attempt to help the weavers.

On 14th April, 1826, Fielden chaired a meeting of calico manufacturers at the Black Bull Inn in Burnley, at which a plan to raise the wages of the handloom weavers was adopted. The calico manufactures agreed to a list of minimum wages for weaving provided that the townships would agree to support via the poor rates any weavers who could not get work at the agreed rates. Four days later the scheme was endorsed in Manchester by 48 manufacturers and 53 printers and purchasers of calico, and ten days were allowed for the townships to hold meetings to consider the plan. Todmorden-cum-Walsden township voted on 27th April to adopt the proposals

Todmorden Unitarian Chapel. Built in the 1820's, it can still be seen above Longfield Road.

provided other townships did likewise[17] but the scheme was already a dead letter: the hungry and frustrated weavers had attacked the powerlooms.

On the very day that Fielden and his fellow manufacturers had met in Burnley, a crowd of weavers had attacked the factory of Mr. Sykes at Accrington. Then all was quiet for a few days until April 24th, when they returned and completely destroyed Sykes' powerlooms. Over the next few days the weavers systematically destroyed the power-looms of Lancashire. They visited Accrington, Black-burn, Over Darwen, Helmshore, Haslingden, Old-ham, Edenfield, Chatterton and Bacup, and there were similar outbreaks in Ashton-under-Lyne and Bradford. At least 3,000 powerlooms were destroyed, and between fifty and sixty people killed in the rioting. When the rioters reached Bacup they an-nounced their intention of coming on to Todmorden next.[18]

Fielden Brothers were the obvious target. They were at this very time installing powerlooms in their Waterside factory. John Fielden had already foreseen the possibility of violence and instructed his brothers that if the rioters reached Waterside they were to "offer no resistance...something to eat and drink I fancy would do them more good than destroying the looms, and I should offer it them".[19] His brothers took a more pragmatic line, and sank all their new powerlooms in the mill-dam, and Buckleys of Ridgefoot Mill did the same.[20] But, as it turned out, the precaution was unnecessary as the loom-breakers were turned back by the soldiers, and the destruction ended at Bacup.

The riots called the attention of the nation to the distress in the North. The Government sent meal to be doled out to the near-starving operatives, and a London committee raised cash to aid the distressed. Amongst the sums it voted to be sent immediately were £700 to Burnley and its surrounding villages, and £150 to Todmorden. The money was desperately needed. There was still a shortage of work, and what little was available was at starvation wages. There were local distributions of clothing and clogs to the poor in the autumn, but this helped only a few. Wages never fully recovered from the depression of 1826 and from this time on the calico handloom weavers were unable to earn more than a pittance.

The sufferings of the handloom weavers, and the refusal of the Government to take any significant action to alleviate their distress, was to John Fielden's mind, yet one more indication of the urgent need for a Radical Reform of the country's political institutions.

The Unitarian Chapel and School

One of the small ironies of John Fielden's career is that, whilst Unitarianism appealed to him because of its liberal, humanitarian and above all, democratic values, within a few short years of joining the Todmorden Unitarians he had assumed total personal control of the Todmorden Unitarian chapel and all its affairs.

The little band of Unitarians that Fielden joined in 1818 was made up of men and women from comparatively humble stations in life. The most active members included a wharfinger, a grocer and draper, a timber merchant, a beershop keeper, a whitesmith, a shoemaker, a wheelwright, and several factory workers and handloom weavers. They met in a small room in Hanging Ditch where they kept a few books and religious periodicals. In 1823, thirty-six of them, including John Fielden, organised themselves into a Unitarian Society and opened a chapel at Cockpit, near Honeyhole. But they were soon in financial difficulties. Having paid off £408 of the £990 that the site and building had cost, they found themselves overwhelmed by the remaining debt. There were only two members of the congregation who were men of substance, John Fielden and George Ash-worth, and it was proposed that they should purchase the chapel and pay off all its debts. But Ashworth dropped out of the scheme, and in 1828 John Fielden bought the meeting house and became its sole owner and thereafter managed all the chapel's affairs himself.

The ownership of and responsibility for the chapel gave him the opportunity to accomplish simultane-ously two objects dear to his heart - to advance the cause of education for poor children in Todmorden, and to find a suitable minister for the Unitarian congregation. Fielden had been actively promoting education for poor children since about 1803 when he and his brother Joshua were two of the teachers at a Sunday school held in the workhouse at Gaux-holme. In 1816, he had been one of the main movers in the Todmorden Sunday School Union - a co-operative effort between the Church of England and the Methodists which set up several non-denomina-tional Sunday schools. Now he saw the opportunity to do more, and arranged for a Thomas Stewart to come to Todmorden and help start a school at Waterside factory. This was about five years before Parliament legislated that children employed in cotton mills should receive two hours education a day. Shortly after Stewart's arrival, it was agreed that he would also act as minister to the Todmorden Unitarian congregation. Fielden also organised and personally superintended a Sunday school for about a hundred children in the Unitarian chapel, in which a rather wider curriculum than was usually offered by Sunday schools included writing, mathematics and history. He also began a day-school in the chapel for children from the age of four until they were old enough to start work in the factories.

Shortly after this, John Fielden found himself champi-oning local non-conformity, in a clash that brought him into head-to-head conflict with John Crossley, hitherto accepted as Todmorden's leading citizen.

The Growth of Religious Rivalry

After the death in 1819 of Joseph Atkinson, Todmorden's farmer-curate, the easy accommodation that had existed between the local Anglicans and Methodists was soon transformed into a jealous rivalry. The Rev: Joseph Cowell arrived as the new curate of St. Mary's in 1821 and energetically set to work at improving the local standing of the Church of England. Within a few months of his arrival the pulpit in St. Mary's had been raised, a new cemetery obtained, and the building of a new sacristy begun. The upper room of the sacristy was intended for use as a Sunday school.

The Anglicans and Wesleyans had been competing for some time to attract the largest congregations, and in particular, the greatest number of children to their Sunday schools. The Anglicans' new sacristy could accommodate two hundred children; but the Wesleyans - not to be outdone - countered by building a large and handsome chapel, with room inside for 1,200 people, in a prominent position on York Street, which they opened triumphantly in 1827.

The "New Church" Dispute

The Anglicans took the new York Street Methodist chapel as a direct challenge. Their church of St. Mary's was in a very poor state of repair, and they decided that a new church was needed. But the necessary funds would have to be voted by the payers of the church rate or "ley", who were the owners and occupiers of the farms in Todmorden-cum-Walsden township, many of whom were non-conformists and already paying towards the support of their own chapels and ministers.

The "new church" dispute led to heated arguments in vestry meetings, with John Fielden as the champion of the non-conformist rate-payers, and John Crossley, Churchwarden, as the champion of the "new church" party. At times, the animosity between the two men was very personal. Crossley once taunted Fielden, in open vestry meeting, with working his hands long hours for low wages, the children especially, and Fielden replied that they paid the standard prices for the work done. (Or, according to another version, that "but for the work so provided and the wages paid, people would not have the wherewithal to purchase the products of the scoffer's farms").[21] But the conflict between Fielden and Crossley was more than personal. It had a symbolic element as well.

John Crossley of Scaitcliffe represented one of Todmorden's very few "gentry" families. The Crossleys had been a leading family in the district for generations and could trace their ancestry back to "John del Croslegh of Todmordene", who had lived in the reign of Edward the Third. John Crossley was a landowner on a very large scale, who also had considerable interests in canals and turnpike roads, was the Treasurer of the Rochdale Canal Company, a Provincial Grand Master of the Freemasons, and served in 1827 as Deputy-Lieutenant for the County of Lancashire. He maintained homes in both Todmorden and Rochdale and drove between them in an ostentatious carriage with the horses decked out in silver-mounted harness. Fielden, by contrast, spoke for the class of small independent farmers and industrialists. Todmorden's isolated situation, poor climate and soil, small farms, and diffused pattern of landownership had all conspired to create a sizeable group of small property owners and businessmen, who, being geographically isolated from families of great wealth or power, were accustomed to running their own local affairs. Plain, austere, pious and careful men for the most part, they were not given to extravagance either in their private lives or as a public body.

They saw no need for a new church - especially if it was they who had to pay for it - but allowed that the churchwardens could apply to the Commissioners for Building Churches, provided that they incurred no expense in preparing or presenting their case. A new church - Christ Church - was built in 1832, and as one of the "Million Churches" built in the industrial North out of the indemnity money paid by the French after the Napoleonic Wars, it cost the ratepayers nothing.

In the "new church" dispute, both sides could claim victory. Fielden and his party carried their object of paying nothing towards a new Anglican church. Crossley and his party got their church - but only because the Government made the necessary funds available. But the dispute was far from insignificant. John Fielden had emerged as the natural spokesman for Todmorden's middle class, for its small owner-occupiers of farms and larger tenant farmers, as well as for those mill owners and industrialists who were emerging into affluence and beginning to feel their own potential power. Soon, this class would challenge the old elite for a share of national Government, and John Fielden would be the natural and accepted local leader of that agitation. A little later, the Fielden and Crossley families would again clash as local political leaders - and this time, with a very different result.

Within the image: Christ Church & Sacristy About 1842 Todmorden — from an Old Oilpainting

Christ Church, Todmorden, built in 1832.

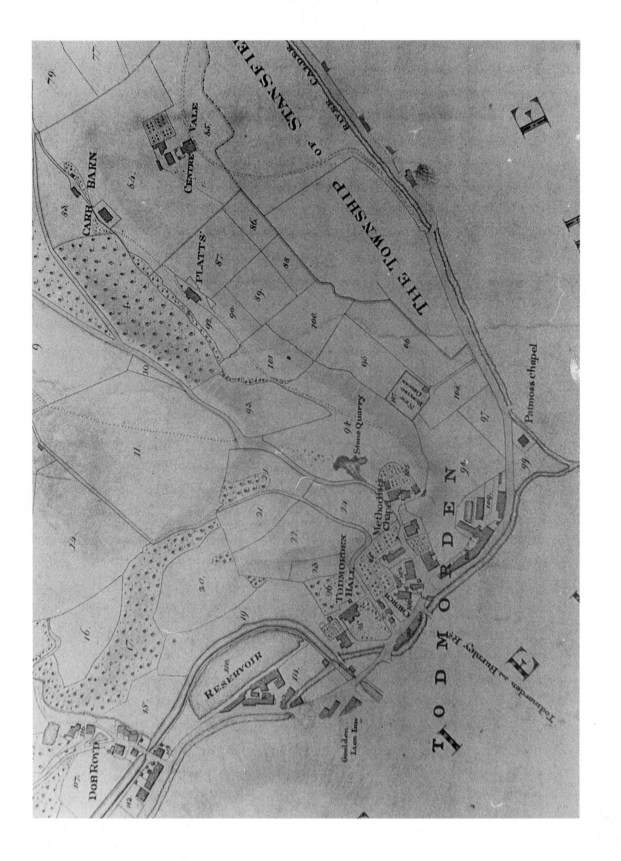

Part of Todmorden-cum-Walsden Township, 1823

Chapter 2

Working Class Life and Culture

The Handloom Weavers

It was not until the late 1820s, when the Fieldens and other local manufacturers opened their new power-loom sheds, that the working lives of most people in Todmorden began to be significantly changed by the effects of the Industrial Revolution. Until that time, the main textile process to be mechanised was cotton spinning, and the resultant demand for hand-weavers had actually reinforced traditional modes of work. Throughout the first quarter of the nineteenth century, local peoples' working lives continued to a pattern that would have been very familiar to their parents and grandparents.

Yet there were some important differences between the Todmorden handloom weavers of the early 19th century, and their predecessors of twenty or thirty years earlier. First, their numbers had greatly increased. The local population grew from 8,453 in 1801 to 14,329 in 1821,[1] and with few, if any, extra hands being required in agriculture, the increased population was mainly absorbed into weaving. Secondly, they were weaving a different type of cloth. The worsted cloths - stuffs, Russells and Florentines - that had been the staple local article of production in the late 18th century, had been largely replaced by calico, which was a coarse, narrow cotton cloth used in the home for making sheets, shirts etc. And thirdly, a significant proportion of the weavers were now women. Unlike worsted production, cotton manufacture offered no domestic out-work to women spinners, and so a lot of women who had previously been employed in this way turned to weaving "narrow cally", alongside the men.

Weaving calico did not in fact require great strength or extraordinary skill. Children were very often apprenticed to a master handloom weaver at the age of eight. The apprenticeship lasted for eighteen months. For the first year, they received no pay. During the final six months, they would be set a daily target of work to be done, and be paid for whatever they could achieve beyond that. At nine years old, their apprenticeship finished, they were self-support-ing.[2] At this point, a few of the children went to work in the new factories, but most stayed and swelled the ranks of the handloom weavers. Local handloom weaving was probably at its peak in the years around 1820, when, of the men from Stansfield and Langfield townships who married at Heptonstall Chapel, three out of four gave their occupation as weaver - and since there were as yet no powerlooms operating locally, they were all weaving on the handloom.[3]

This extraordinary degree of reliance on a single trade demonstrates the extent to which in this locality, handloom weaving was not so much an occupational category, more the way of life of a whole community. At its peak employing three out of four men as their main occupation, it also employed unknown but very considerable numbers of women, and most of the children and young people who were not otherwise occupied. Small farmers kept a loom or two in the house for when there was little to do on the farm; paupers and the aged could contribute to their upkeep by weaving as much as they were able. Those who were too old, too infirm or too unskilled to weave, could still make themselves useful by winding the weft onto bobbins for the weaver to replenish his (or her) shuttle. Even the poor Baptist pastor of Lineholme chapel, refusing an offered increase in salary from his even more poverty-stricken congregation, declared that it was not necessary, because "My daughter can weave, and I can wind bobbins".[4]

William Greenwood: Handloom Weaver [5]

Few handloom weavers left any record of their lives, but by extraordinary good fortune, a single volume has survived of a diary kept by a local weaver. William Greenwood lived at Carrbottom near present-day Cornholme, and his diary for the year 1825 gives a fascinating insight into the life of an early 19th century Todmorden handloom weaver.

Pudsey Mill, c1825. William Greenwood's cottage can be seen behind the mill.

William was then aged about 28 and living at home with his elderly parents. He was the last remaining child, his older brothers and sisters having married and left home. The Greenwoods lived in a pleasant cottage overlooking Pudsey Clough, where a little community was growing up half-way between the valley bottom and the ancient upland settlement of Shore. A number of cottages had been recently built and most of them were occupied by handloom weavers. William's father was a little better off than most and owned his own cottage.

William's main occupation was weaving 70s calico - a plain cotton cloth made with a warp and a weft of equal thickness. He delivered his finished pieces to Joseph Firth, who paid him 2/6d a cut. (John and Joseph Firth made the transition from being employed as book-keepers for Fielden Brothers, to engaging in business as cotton spinners and manufacturers on their own account in about 1825 or early 1826: it is uncertain whether Greenwood was working for the Firths or the Fieldens). The amount of weaving William did per day varied enormously. Many days he did none at all, and quite frequently he would weave just a few yards. But on one occasion he wove as much as 30 yards. It took him about half an hour to weave a yard of cloth, so on that day he must have sat in his loom for about 15 hours. Over the whole year, William earned something between £11 and £12 at weaving, giving him a weekly income of about 4s 6d. This was not very much, but he was able to supplement this with earnings from other sources.

One of these was "twisting in" or joining on new warp threads for other weavers who could not or did not want to do this job themselves. William had several regular customers, whom he charged 5d a time, and he also used to twist-in for his father. He also taught some of the local children to read, write, and do simple accounts. A school at his house on Sunday mornings was attended by about 12 or 14 children - mostly boys aged about 11-14, who paid him 2d or 3d for a month's tuition. Other scholars came on Thursdays in winter and on Wednesday evenings in the summer months. His total income from teaching was at least £2 10s for the year, and he made a few pence more from the sale of copy books, quills and ink. It is rather more surprising to find that William was also a moneylender. There are frequent references in the diary to sums ranging from 6d to £6 being lent out for periods varying from a few days to three months, and to interest being charged on these transactions. At one time, William had at least £13 out on loan. All in all, William's by-occupations could have brought his annual income up to nearly £20 a year, or about 8s a week, which would have been a sufficient sum for a young man with no dependants.

William Greenwood's diary illustrates very well that, even as late as 1825, a handloom weaver could enjoy a relatively relaxed, easy-going and varied style of life. William worked at his own pace and in his own time. From his diary you can tell that he often got up from his loom, went to the cottage door, stopped to chat with this neighbour or that. He often left his work entirely, perhaps to follow the hare-hunt, to walk, to go swimming in a mill-dam with friends, or attend a "tiping" (or knur-and-spel contest) on the moor. His work left him plenty of time to further his education and to take a leading part in a local friendly society. William was the organiser of a small band of students who studied one afternoon a week with the pastor of Shore chapel. He referred to this as the grammar or "lodgic" class, and so it seems that they were studying Latin grammar and perhaps philosophy, and William, as shown by his accounts, collected 1d a week from each scholar, and paid the Rev. Midgeley 6d. a week for teaching them. He was a member of a friendly society which met at the Roebuck Inn at Portsmouth in the Burnley Valley, and in the early part of the year was evidently acting as treasurer or clerk to the society.

The year in which William was writing his diary was the last in which a handloom weaver, even one with no family to support, could live so congenially. On November 24th, 1825, he wrote: "Joseph Firth pulled down 3d per calico yesterday". He was recording the first signs of the impending crisis in the handweaving trade - the same crisis that John Fielden tried to resolve with his plan for a minimum wage for handloom weavers, and which culminated in the powerloom-breaking riots of April 1826.

Food and Clothing

In his diary , William Greenwood reports buying apples at 2½d a pound, pears at 3d a pound, veal at 4½d a pound, and beef at 5d a pound. Prices mean little until compared with earnings, but here, the calculation is fortunately very simple. William was paid 2/6d a cut, or 1d a yard, for weaving calico; and it can be calculated that it took him about half an hour to weave one yard. His earnings, then, in 1825, were 2d an hour. So to buy a pound of apples he had to weave for an hour and a quarter; for a pound of pears, an hour and a half; for a pound of veal, two and a quarter hours; and for a pound of beef, two hours and a half. Food was, in terms of labour, very dear.

The fact that William records an occasional purchase of fruit or butcher's meat in his diary, confirms that these kinds of food were unusual and rather special. The staple diet of the local working people was oatmeal, made into porridge with skimmed milk and sweetened with a little treacle. This was at least cheap. Oatmeal cost about 1s for 10 pounds, milk about 3d a quart, and treacle was just over 2d a pound.[6] Eaten three times a day this could be rather dull, so to introduce a little variety the oatmeal was cooked in different ways. "Waff" was made by melting a tablespoon of bacon fat in a saucepan, adding oatmeal until it was thickened by boiling, then adding half a cup of milk, a spoonful of sugar and a pinch of salt. "Stirabout" was similar to "waff", but made with syrup instead of milk. "Aver bread" or oatcakes were made rather like a thick oaty pancake, and were hung from the ceiling on a "bread fleygh" to dry. Pieces of oatcake would be broken off and eaten as an accompaniment to the inevitable porridge, or, as a special treat, with a bit of cheese, red herring or bacon.[7]

The bacon was often home-grown, and many of

Cottage interior with woman making oatcakes, c.1814

William Greenwood's friends and neighbours kept a backyard pig. The family pig was a big investment. The one that his brother John bought cost him £3 12s 6d, a sum that it would have taken him about 400 hours to earn at the handloom. The growth and progress of the local farmers' and cottagers' pigs would be a matter of absorbing local interest, until, at the end of November or beginning of December, the local pig-killer did his rounds, and the final weights of the rival pigs could be compared. The day after the pig was killed, its carcass was cut up, and friends and relatives were invited to a great feast or "liver-eating", at which all the non-preservable parts of the animal would be consumed. This was followed by busy days of smoking or curing the meat, and making black puddings from the blood and the fat.

For drink, people brewed their own weak beer, or made tea from garden herbs such as mint, balm or pennyroyal, often sweetening it with treacle. Imported tea and sugar were too expensive for everyday consumption.

If food was dear, clothing was even more so: When William had his shoes soled, it cost him 4s, and a black silk handkerchief which he bought (probably to wear at the funeral of a fellow friendly society member) cost him 5s. This was the equivalent of 24 and 30 hours at the loom respectively.

Working-class Education

We do not know where William Greenwood learned to read and write, but it is very unlikely that he ever attended school. Todmorden's two endowed schools took mostly fee-paying pupils and so they served those parents who were sufficiently well-off that they could not only pay school fees, but also forgo their children's labour or earnings; and this was only a small minority of the local population. Between them, the two schools had just ten free school places for the children of the poor, and so most people had to look to the Sunday schools for their children's education.

Most of the Todmorden non-conformist chapels had their own Sunday schools. The first is believed to have been started by Eastwood Congregationalists (then at Bent Head) before 1807, and other early ones were Mankinholes Wesleyans in 1815, Zion Hill (Doghouse) Methodists in 1816, Lineholme Baptists in 1818, Shore Baptists in 1819, Cornholme Methodists in 1820, the Unitarians in 1824, Patmos Methodists by 1825, Millwood Baptists by 1826, and Knowlwood Primitive Methodists in 1826.[8] A school at Lanebottom, Walsden, built by a public subscription initiated by the friendly society meeting at the Waggon and Horses Inn, opened in 1818 or 1819 as a Sunday school but later became a day-school also.

More day schools were opened in the town in the 1820s; and these encompassed a very broad spec-

Cross Stone schoolhouse, which also served as a meeting-room for the ratepayers of Stansfield.

trum, from genteel academies for young ladies, to factory schools and dame schools. Their teachers and their abilities were as varied as the schools. When the Government surveyed educational provision in 1833, most local children still got as much education as they could - or as much as they could not avoid - on a Sunday, the only day they had free from work. There were 3,746 children in the Sunday schools, and only 669 children attending day-school in the Todmorden area.[9]

The inadequacy of formal provision for the education of the poor and the children of the poor had never stopped heroic attempts at self-improvement. Samuel Law, a handloom weaver who lived at Barewise in the Burnley valley, published in 1772 a long pastoral poem that he had written as he sat in his loom. One very important source of information and education for the working class was the press, and the education that the newspapers gave was in the main a political one - just like John Fielden's education in the school of "Long Sam". The Stamp Duty Act of 1819 tried to combat the spread of radical ideas by imposing a government surcharge on the price of a newspaper. This made newspapers expensive, and so groups of working men would often club together to buy a paper. William Greenwood belonged to such a group, paying his contribution over at quarterly intervals to his friend William Jones. Sometimes the subscribers would meet regularly to read and discuss the news. Of three such discussion groups meeting in Walsden, one comprised a labourer, a weaver, a mason and two others: another was made up of handloom weavers; and the third comprised a handloom weaver, a quarryman and an old man of independent means. Another reading circle was held at the home of John Dean, a handloom weaver of

Upper Ashes in Stansfield. He was illiterate; but he took newspapers and got others to subscribe and read them aloud, and he ardently followed all the political arguments of the day until his death in 1848. Alternatively the news could be followed and discussed by subscribing to a news-room (James Fielden was the treasurer of one which was held in premises near the Golden Lion in 1830), or in a public house such as the Wellington in York Street, where James Suthers, the landlord, was never so happy as when reading aloud to his customers the latest political news, paper in one hand, and his churchwarden pipe, half as long as himself, in the other.[10]

Another potential source of knowledge was the various libraries which were set up in Todmorden in the early part of the 19th century. Some of these were attached to Sunday schools or chapels; others were subscription libraries open to all. The oldest and longest-running of the subscription libraries was the Todmorden Old Book Club, which started meeting in 1798 at the Golden Lion Inn. It was run along the same lines as a friendly society, with a monthly meeting - in this case held on the Monday nearest the full moon - at which the members paid a subscription of 8d, which included 2d for the room and refreshments. The membership was drawn from both the middle and working classes. From time to time attempts were made to set up a library in the Toad Carr area, but none of these met with the kind of success that the Old Book Club enjoyed.[11] Most of Todmorden's non-conformist chapels had a library of

some kind, though they must have varied widely in scope and quality. But some ranged far beyond religious tracts and morally-uplifting works and attempted the general education of the scholars. The proposals for book purchases put before the Todmorden Methodist Sunday School teachers in 1822 included *The Wonders of the Heavens, 100 Wonders of the World*; Goldsmith's Histories of England, Rome and Greece; Cooper's Poems; and a selection of travel books.[12]

Yet another potential source of learning was the non-conformist pastor. Some of these men were quite considerable scholars, and nearly all of them were poor and only too willing to boost their small stipends by doing a little teaching on the side. William Greenwood and his fellow-students - about twelve young men and two young women - studied one afternoon a week with the pastor of Shore Baptist Chapel.

These sources of learning were small and informal. They consisted of a few working men, and occasionally women, gathering round a newspaper, or meeting one evening a week in a public house, a chapel vestry, or somebody's home. They were scarcely noticed by middle-class contemporaries, and left only the faintest traces of their existence. Yet their collective importance as informers and educators of the working class can scarcely be overestimated.

The same spirit of self-help, or rather, mutual assistance, that ran through these little reading circles, libraries and study-groups, was evident also in contemporary friendly societies, trade unions and co-operatives. The earliest of these associations of mutual assistance were the friendly societies.

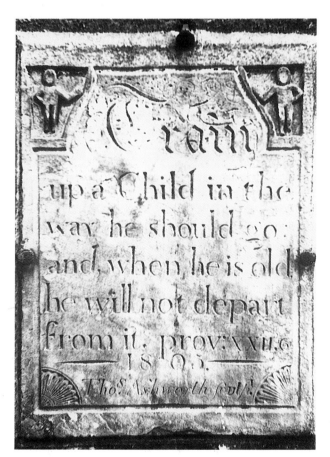

**Inscription over the door of
Cross Stone schoolhouse**

Friendly societies [13]

The purpose of friendly societies, as expressed by a society meeting at Blackshawhead, was "to raise a fund by subscription for us and our Families in the forlorn and desolate Times of Old Age, Infirmity and Disease". When a working man became too ill or too old to follow his usual occupation, his only source of aid was the township overseer. But the overseer only assisted the truly destitute, and besides, many people were ashamed to go on the parish, and in particular, dreaded the final indignity of a pauper's funeral. By joining together into small societies of perhaps fifty or a hundred members, and paying a small subscription into the society's box at the monthly meeting, people could insure, in some degree, against illness and provide their relatives with a sufficient sum to bury them in decency when the time came. Some societies also provided pensions to their aged members, or a small payment on the death of a member's spouse.

The first friendly society in Todmorden was the Friendly Society of Workmen which met at the

Early Todmorden Friendly Societies

Location	Public House	Men's Societies	Women's Societies
Todmorden	Golden Lion	1763-1823	1817
Lumbutts		1794, 1796, 1806	
Lobb Mill	Sportsman's	1813-23	1809, 1812
	(White) Swan	1787, 1793, 1799, 1814	1821, 1827, 1840
Bottoms	Freemasons	1799, 1818-1825	1810, 1826
Portsmouth	Roebuck	1809, 1825	1810, 1813, 1825
Cross Stone	Bay Horse	a) 1821-6, 1829	1825
		b) 1824	
Toad Carr	Shoulder of Mutton	1823	1825, 1832-76
Walsden	Waggon	1810, 1818	
Blackshawhead		1797	1810, 1818-27
Blackshawhead	Old Blue Ball	1819	
New Delight	Sportsman's		1808, 1840
Todmorden	Royal George		1816-23
Holme	New Inn (Hare & Hounds)		1820-33
Kebcote	Sportsman's		1825
Woodend		uncertain, prob. 1793-1815	

Sources: see Notes and References, Chapter 2, nos. 13 and 14
(Existence not necessarily continuous across the whole span of dates given)

Golden Lion from 1763. Between then and about 1830, friendly societies were established at most of the major public houses in the district.

The rules of the local working men's societies were all very similar. They were open to men aged (usually) from 18 to 35, who were approved by a ballot of existing members, and who were not engaged in any particularly hazardous occupations. Most societies cancelled or suspended the membership of anyone who joined the army or navy, and the Union Society meeting at the Sportsman's Arms at Lobb Mill banned miners, too, decreeing that: "If any member leaves his trade to work in the mines without necessity, and gets damage thereby, he shall have no benefit from this Society". The monthly contribution was almost universally 6d for the box, and 2d to be spent "for the good of the company". Only two societies dared set a higher rate of contributions. The men of the Cross Stone society, founded in 1821, paid 10d for the box as well as the traditional 2d for drink, and the Golden Lion society revised its rules in 1823, putting the monthly subscription up to one shilling, out of which the stewards spent £1 on drink to share amongst the company. A year or eighteen months after joining, a man became a "free member", entitled to sickness benefit, which was 4 or 5 shillings a week.

Several local societies tried to provide their aged members with old age pensions. The sum offered was 2s a week, which was about the same amount as the overseers of the poor usually granted to old people who were incapable of work and destitute. The friendly society members were of course free to supplement this by working if they wished. The age at which this pension became payable varied from society to society. The White Swan offered it from the age of 60, the Blackshawhead society at 62 but only to men who had been members for 25 years. The Freemasons Arms society and the Golden Lion, both promised 2s a week to men aged 70 and over, but even setting the pensionable age higher does not appear to have overcome the inherent problems of a society of only perhaps fifty or a hundred people attempting to provide for the old. None of the men's societies formed in the 19th century in Todmorden offered pensions to the aged, and when the Golden Lion society revised its rules and greatly increased the members' contributions in 1823, it nonetheless abolished pensions. The aged were of course able to draw on the society's funds when they were sick, just like the other members, but automatic payments to the aged was a dream that could not be fulfilled by small, voluntary, local agencies.

Women's Friendly Societies [14]

Women were not usually eligible to join the men's friendly societies, but they soon began to form societies of their own. In the closing years of the eighteenth century and the early years of the nineteenth, a number of women's friendly societies were set up in Halifax and its satellite townships by philanthropic ladies, who wished to improve the morals of working women as well as their living standards. These societies were not emulated in the upper Calder Valley, where there were relatively few leisured ladies to engage in this kind of project; but the working women of Hebden Bridge, Heptonstall, Todmorden and Sowerby began before very long to set up their own independent societies, without any middle-class assistance. By the 1820s, places like Todmorden and Heptonstall had nearly as many friendly societies for women as they had for men. These societies are particularly interesting for the light they shed on the lives of ordinary working-class women of the early 19th century - a group of people who are all too often hidden from history.

The first female society in the Todmorden district was formed at "the house of John Eastwood" at Lobb Mill in 1809. Over the next few years, women's societies were formed at the Freemasons Arms, at the Roebuck Inn at Portsmouth, at the Royal George, at Black-shawhead, at the New Inn (now the Hare and Hounds), at the Bay Horse (now the Berghof Brandstatter), at the Shoulder of Mutton (now Jack's House), and possibly also at the Sportsman's at Kebcote.

A female member of a friendly society, like her brother or husband, enjoyed the monthly meeting in the public house and the annual club feast. She paid over each month her 6d for the box and 2d to be spent on liquor. She served her turn as Stewardess, and drew from 3s 6d to 5s a week if she was ill. The payments made to her family at her death were similar to those promised by the men's societies, and some of the women's societies offered small pensions to aged members. The Portsmouth society paid 2s a week to members over 70, whilst the Royal George society promised 2s 6d. The Blackshawhead Society also offered 2s a week at 70 in its original rules, but rescinded this provision four years later.

The women's societies were governed so very much like those for men, that it was in fact very uncommon for them to make any provision for women's special needs. The Royal George society was the only local one that made any allowance in pregnancy or childbirth. It allowed 8s to a woman in childbirth towards the expenses of a midwife - a very progressive provision, but the society stipulated that this applied only to children born in lawful wedlock, and from one husband only. Usually women were

The Hare and Hounds Inn. Originally known as the New Inn, it was the home of a women's friendly society from 1820

barred from all benefit for the forty weeks of pregnancy and one month of lying-in, and any woman who did draw sick pay during this time had to pay back the money, or be permanently excluded.

The women's friendly societies sometimes found it difficult to decide how much housework a woman might do whilst drawing sick pay from her club. They all agreed that she might suckle her own child. The Portsmouth society allowed in addition only "giving orders to those who wait upon her, or other persons in the house, or signing her name to deeds and papers, or walking out for health, or other trifling business", but the Lobb Mill society permitted her to cook for her family. The Blackshawhead society laid down exactly what a member on sick pay must not do. She must not "lead an irregular life by attending at sports, weddings, pastimes, fairs etc., and shall not do any kind of work or housewifery whatever such as cleansing the house, washing, brewing, baking, knitting, sewing, or any other kind of woman's business with respect to housewifery whatever".

It would be interesting to know the occupations of the members of the female friendly societies. Were they occupied mostly with housework, or were they perhaps hand-loom weavers, or employed in the new cotton factories? The local women's societies were mostly founded between about 1810 and 1825; so they date from a time when large numbers of women were employed as handloom weavers, and probably earning almost as much as men in the same trade. But whatever their members' occupations, the widespread existence of female friendly societies testifies to the importance of women's work and wages in early industrial Yorkshire and Lancashire, and also shows that they must have had considerable control over the disposal of their own earnings. It was often held to be a barrier to the establishment of women's societies, that married women had no legal right to their own earnings and that husbands could prevent their wives from paying their contributions, or could appropriate any benefits due to them. This does not seem to have retarded the growth of women's friendly societies in the textile areas, where they quickly spread to become the earliest independent associations of working women.

Trade Unions

Trade Unions were wholly illegal until the repeal of the Combination Acts in 1824, and even after that, their legal position was so marginal and uncertain that they often disguised themselves as friendly societies. So it is not surprising that there should be very little information available about early trade unions in Todmorden. But there is enough to demonstrate that local trade unions did exist and were active at this time.

In the summer of 1818 the operative cotton spinners of Manchester attempted to establish a "General Union of Trades" to support them in their dispute with the Manchester masters, and to form a united front to resist any future wage reductions. Todmorden was chosen as an ideal venue for the secret meetings of delegates because, as the magistrate John Crossley reported to the Home Secretary, "it lays out of view, in a central situation between Manchester, Halifax, Blackburn and Bolton, and is in a very retired situation".[15] Delegates travelled to these meetings from as far afield as Liverpool, Nottingham and Birmingham, and even Somerset weavers sent their representatives.

It is probable that a Todmorden trade union was represented at these meetings, and the most likely candidate is the Spinners' and Weavers' Union which was certainly active in Todmorden during the following decade. William Helliwell was an official of this union. By 1825 the Spinners and Weavers had started a co-operative building venture, putting up a row of cottages - known as "Union Buildings" - on Doghouse Lane. There was a large room over the cottages which was let to Buckley's of Todmorden as a "twining room", or place to operate hand-driven machines to prepare cotton for spinning. By 1830, the union had entered co-operative retailing. The Leeds Directory notes the existence of a shop on York Street, selling flour, groceries and drapery, which was run by "William Hallowell" acting as agent for the "United Spinners' Co.".[16]

In 1832, as Todmorden celebrated the passing of the Reform Act, the Society of Whitesmiths, the Mechanics' Trades Society, and the Loyal Free Mechanics all marched in the procession alongside the friendly societies. Like the friendly societies, these organisations provided sickness and death benefits for their members, but as they drew all their members from a single trade, they were also able to act as trade unions.

The question of whether a workmen's organisation was a trade union or merely an innocent friendly society, was one of the contentious issues during a dispute in March 1840 between the contractors and the bricklayers building the Summit tunnel. With rumours circulating that the bricklayers intended striking for more pay, the contractors had been to Newcastle, South Shields, Hull, Kendall and other places, and recruited a new set of workmen, offering them 5s a shift instead of the 6s the old hands were getting. When the new workmen arrived, the old hands were dismissed, but they countered this by successfully bribing the new recruits to strike, offering them £1 15s a man. The unfortunate new recruits were hauled before the magistrates for breaking their contract. Seven of them were given 3 months imprisonment with hard labour, one got one month, and the other eight were sent back to work. A man called William Hall who was the provisional secretary to the bricklayers' committee, wrote to the Northern Star, putting their side of the case: if the contractors had dismissed them because they were "In Society" (i.e. unionists), that was a disgraceful

Summit Tunnel. 2,869 yards in length, its construction employed 1000 men for 2 years and 4 months

Early Co-operatives

A third type of working-class organisation of the early nineteenth century was the co-operative. These sometimes grew out of friendly societies or trade unions, as happened in Todmorden when the Spinners and Weavers Union decided to open a co-operative shop. A shop of this type was always known locally as "t'union". Todmorden had a very strong co-operative movement in the late 1820s and early 1830s.

When, in 1832, a Congress of Co-operative Societies was held in Liverpool, thirty-eight societies sent their delegates. Amongst them was John Mitchell of Blind Lane, Todmorden, representing a co-operative society of which he was the secretary. This Todmorden society had 250 members, had funds to the value of £200, and employed 150 people manufacturing calicos, fustians and velveteens. This was by far the largest society represented at the conference, in terms both of membership and of numbers of people employed. Some of the other societies represented were from large towns and cities, such as Huddersfield, Birmingham, Leicester, Halifax, Sheffield, and even districts of London; but, apart from Todmorden, only one society could boast more than 200 members, and none of the others employed more than a handful of workers. The Huddersfield society, with twelve employees, had the greatest number. This Todmorden co-operative was also one of the earliest of the societies represented at the congress. It had been formed in 1828, (the month is not given), and so only William Lovett's First London Society, formed in 1827, and possibly the Birmingham society, founded in November 1828, had preceded this Todmorden one.[20]

John Mitchell, the secretary of this Todmorden co-operative, gave his address as Blind Lane, but must be the same John Mitchell of nearby Toad Carr who is listed in an 1830 trade directory as a cotton manufacturer, and who had been a wheelwright of the same address in 1825 and 1828. The area around Toad Carr and Blind Lane was at that time a typical handloom weavers' colony - a busy suburb of artisans' cottages, whose inhabitants were unusually prominent in Todmorden's radical religious and political associations, including the Unitarian Chapel, the Political Union, and, at a later date, Chartism.

It is easy to imagine that such a neighbourhood would be fertile ground for the co-operative ideas that were circulating in the late 1820s. The idea of co-operation was not in itself new, but had newly become associated with the visionary and anti-capitalist ideas of Robert Owen. All over Britain, co-operatives were being set up, often with the intention of circumventing the capitalist system by encouraging direct trading between co-operative enterprises, or of using the profits of trade to set up self-contained harmonious communities. The handloom weavers of Toad Carr, who had recently suffered a severe drop in wages, decided in 1828 to

excuse, "as our society is only formed to keep us from the frowns and disgrace of being compelled to apply to the parish for relief". He claimed their society paid 12s a week to accident victims, £8 for funerals, both of the man and his wife, and 5s per week to those too old to work, and utterly repudiated the rumour that they had been planning to strike for a 50% advance in wages.[17]

Local trade unions remained highly secretive. The Todmorden Iron Moulders sent a delegate to the National Conference of Trades, or "Labour's Parliament" which met on Easter Monday, 1845, in preparation for the Chartist Convention: but neither the name of the delegate, nor the contents of any speech he may have made, is recorded.[18] The local Society of Free Mechanics, which had marched in the Reform celebrations in 1832, was still in existence in 1850, when a dismissed member summoned another member for the £4 0s 3d which he claimed he had invested in the society. Although the society was still illegal, the magistrate supported the dismissed member and ruled that he be given his equal share of the society's funds.[19] Strikes in the cotton industry happened quite frequently, but it seems that any unions that were formed amongst the spinners and weavers were either temporary, or else a very well-kept secret. If they existed at all, they had long since faded away by 1878, when it was agreed to form a Todmorden Weavers' Association, but even in the circumstance of a 10% wages cut it took two years to get it off the ground.

go into business on their own account. As they already owned their own looms, the capital required was not too large to be raised from their own resources, with the help of other small investors. But this handloom weavers' co-operative was not the only local co-operative society in 1832.

John Mitchell, at the Liverpool Congress, said there were three co-operative societies in his neighbourhood. One of these was the Toad Carr co-operative which he represented. One may have been the Spinners' and Weavers' Union, which ran a co-operative shop at about this time, and the third I cannot identify. But just a few days later, an ambitious scheme for a network of co-operative stores in and around Todmorden was agreed at a meeting of operatives held at the White Hart Inn on October 13th 1832.

The minutes of this meeting turned up a hundred years later in a secret drawer in a desk which had been inherited by a Todmorden man, and were given to the then secretary of Todmorden Industrial and Co-operative Society. They recorded the formation of the "Todmorden Co-operative Society", which proposed to establish a central warehouse in Todmorden, and a store in each of four districts of the town, and to sell both eatable and wearable goods, - the wearable goods to be, so far as was possible, the products of co-operative enterprises. The funds for this were to be raised by issuing £1 shares. Members would pay 1s as an entrance fee, and then weekly contributions until, by November 1833, the full £1 would have been subscribed. The meeting was presided over by John Lord of Blind Lane, and the plan adopted was proposed by a Mr. Hirst.[21]

Mr Hirst can be confidently identified as Thomas Hirst of Huddersfield, a paid co-operative missionary. Hirst had been at the Liverpool Congress, representing ten co-operative societies in and around Huddersfield. He then came to Todmorden to promote the setting up of a new co-operative society here, and by 10 November he was in Ripponden where a meeting in a public house led, two weeks later, to 24 people paying a shilling each as their first instalment in the new Ripponden Co-operative Society. R.C.N. Thornes writes that: "Of all the Co-operative missionaries who were active in West Yorkshire in this period Thomas Hirst was, undoubtedly, the most tireless. He devoted himself to the cause of co-operation with a single-mindedness which, ultimately, was to cost him his life. He travelled, often on foot, throughout Yorkshire and the surrounding counties, lecturing and advising on Co-operation".[22]

Many of these "Owenite" co-operatives collapsed in 1834 amidst the general debacle that saw the end of the Grand National Consolidated Trade Union. Some - including the Ripponden Society and several in the Huddersfield area - did manage to survive; but it is almost certain that the Todmorden co-operatives, which were not represented at the Fifth Co-operative Congress at Halifax in 1835, were casualties.

The Culture of Chapel and Pub

One local friendly society, explaining the reasons for its formation, called attention to "the many great hardships and sad Necessitys labouring men now are subject to, who have nothing to support themselves withal but the fruits of their labour", and explained that its members came together "in tender regard to each other, and for the better support and maintenance of every Member of this Society".[23] This working class ethic of mutual assistance, which found expression in the friendly society, the trade union and the co-operative, was very strong in the Todmorden area and the upper Calder Valley generally. But there were other strong influences upon the local "labouring men". One was culture of the non-conformist chapel: the other we might call the culture of the public house. The two were utterly opposed.

The chapels had much to offer their members. Many of the local chapels were small and more or less congregationalist in organisation. They formed close-knit communities of mostly working-class people, who built their own chapels and ran their own affairs. They might invite visiting preachers, or they might join together to support a regular minister. They helped one another with spiritual dilemmas, and gave charitably to their poorer members in times of trouble. Their Sunday schools educated the local children, and talented working men could become known and respected in the community as deacons or lay-preachers, or even train for the ministry. But in return for the fellowship they offered, the chapels expected their members to set themselves apart from the temptations of the world. They had to conform to rigorous standards of behaviour. A small offence might bring an affectionate admonition: a more serious one would mean being called before the elders, who might forgive the truly penitent, but the serious or persistent offender would be excluded from the church.

The Baptists of Shore, for instance, were expected to keep the Sabbath and attend Church regularly. They were not expected to lie, steal, embezzle, sell ale without a license, drink excessively, join "secret societies" or strike their husbands or wives; nor go to horse-races, join hunting-parties, or stay over-late at Todmorden Fair; nor go to fortune-tellers, or "apply to witches to remove maladies from their or their children's bodies".[24] But many of these activities that were forbidden to the Baptists were quite usual behaviour in the wider community, and not generally regarded as improper or unethical.

The Baptists were forbidden to join friendly societies, or "secret societies" as they called them, but in the community at large membership of a friendly society was seen as meretricious. It was the mark of a steady man who was making provision against his own possible sickness, as well as helping those other members of his society who had become sick or

Shore Chapel. Originally built in 1777, it was extended in 1853 and again in 1871

lame. But the Baptists of Shore gave it as their opinion in February 1831 that "it is not consistent with the principles of Christianity for any one to enter the Society of foresters, Orange boys, Odd lads or Free masons", and although there seems to have been some disagreement amongst the chapel-members on this point, within a few months a consensus was reached, and one of their members left the Baptists under censure for having entered into a secret society.

One of the highlights of the local year was Todmorden Fair, which was traditionally held on Maundy Thursday and Good Friday. The Baptists were allowed to attend the fair, but they were disciplined if they stayed excessively late. A Todmorden man, recalling the fairs of his childhood around 1830, remembered the swinging boat, which was set up in front of Todmorden Hall and which was a big attraction for the children, and he recalled that all along the roadside were stalls selling jewellery, knives and toys, or where you could have a "lucky dip". Along Shop Lane (now Water Street), the meadow was covered with an immense spread of pots and crockery, all laid out on straw, and interspersed with stalls selling gingerbread and brandysnaps. But the biggest attractions of all were to be found at White Hart Fold: "it was here the tight-rope dancers performed; it was here the little shows with the big giants, the fat women, the waxwork figures, Toby the sapient and learned pig, and the man that

used to swallow the long sword and belch from his mouth the fancy barber's pole, were congregated". Here too, you were tempted by the sellers of treacle toffee, and hot pies and gravy, or could decide to spend your last coppers seeing the mystery of "Maria Martin, or the Murder at the Red Barn" at Old Wild's booth on Smith Hill - even though it had already played three Todmorden fairs in succession. People often held weddings and christenings at fair time, when the district was on holiday and gifts and the things needed for setting up house could be got from the fairground stalls.[25] With so much going on and everybody in a holiday spirit, the fair often got quite rowdy - which is, no doubt, why the Baptists were forbidden to stay late.

Nor were the Baptists supposed to have any dealings with witches, astrologers or wise-seers. Again, this set them apart from the majority who readily consulted these reputed wise men and women. James Standing, the Cornholme poet, wrote in the 1870s that: "Twenty years ago the inhabitants of our rural districts, and perhaps more especially those of our Lancashire and Yorkshire hills, were generally believers in magic", and he tells how if something were lost - a sheep, a handcart, a wheelbarrow or even a mug or a mop - people would go to the "wise-seer" or "glass-reader" about it. He would question them at length, then take out his glass (which was generally about the size and shape of a duck's egg), and peer solemnly into it. At length he would pretend to see the lost article. If a sheep, he might send the owner to seek within a few miles of a certain spot, as by the time he got there it could have wandered off again; if a wheelbarrow or a mop, he might know very well where it was, having himself set some mischievous lads to hide the article. These wise-seers were sometimes also believed to be able to work cures by magic.[26]

John Holgate, who lived at Ingbottom near Friedhurst in the Burnley valley, was a fortune-teller who also claimed to be able by his art to prevent bleeding and cure burns; and these claims were widely believed by his neighbours, as the following incident demonstrates. A child living nearby fell against a heated oven and burned its hands severely. A neighbour, hearing its cries, rushed in to see what the matter was, and immediately volunteered to go to Old Holgate, saying she was sure he could cure the child instantly and without medicine. She went to Holgate, paid the fee, and was told that when she returned she would find the child fast asleep, entirely cured. It was to her extreme surprise that she returned to find the child crying more pitifully than ever.[27] The neighbour seems credulous to us; but at the time, belief in witchcraft was general. An 1825 entry in the records of the Shore Baptists says that "All present, with the exception of three who were neuter, thought it was sinful for Christians to apply to witches to remove some malady out of their own or their Children's bodies, or on any other account". There is no suggestion that they disbelieved in witchcraft - only that they thought it unchristian. In later years, too, the Baptists sometimes spoke out against their members having to do with wise-seers. One member of the church was criticised but forgiven for having applied to a fortune teller in 1839, and in 1850, the members expressed their disapproval of "people going to Howgate to have their fortunes told". It is likely that "Howgate" is a reference to the same John Holgate. Ingbottom was at no great distance from Shore chapel. John Holgate appears in the 1851 census as a 64 year-old cotton twister, but was said in 1847 to have made a living for many years as an astrologer and fortune-teller.

Over the twenty year period from 1820 to 1840, twelve men and eighteen women were excluded from the Baptist chapel at Shore. It is striking that the offences that brought about the exclusions were quite different for the two sexes. Of the women, eight were excluded for fornication, and eight for neglect of, or disobedience to, the church. One woman was excluded for drunkenness, and one for railing. No men were excluded for fornication, and only one for negligence; but five were excluded for drunkenness, and the remaining six for various offences including Sabbath-breaking, buying embezzled weft, and selling ale without a licence. The high rate of exclusions of women for fornication illustrates in a particularly vivid way the clash between the social mores of the Chapel, and the mores of society at large. For chapel members, sexual irregularity was, in women, a serious offence. There is no record in the Shore chapel minutes of a woman making a successful plea of innocence or penitence against a charge of fornication. It was an offence for which the only possible sentence was exclusion. But in society at large, no particular stigma was attached to a woman who bore an illegitimate child. Illegitimacy simply was nothing unusual: from 1st July 1837 to 1st

Riding the Stang c.1814 as depicted in Walker's "Costumes of Yorkshire"

April 1839, there were 1748 births registered in Todmorden union, and 201, or more than 1 in 9 of them, were illegitimate.[28]

If such a high proportion of *all* births were illegitimate, then clearly, the proportion of *first* children born outside marriage must have been even higher. In fact, it was quite usual for a couple to delay marriage until the first child was expected or even born. William Greenwood mentions in his diary four cases of young women whom he knew finding themselves pregnant by their sweethearts in the course of a single year. In one of the cases, the woman took out a warrant against her boyfriend, and a week or two later, the diarist reports that the couple "went off - it is supposed to be married - yesternight about 6 o'clock". In a face-to-face society like Shore in the 1820s, where everybody knew everybody else, the pressure of public opinion would be brought to bear on the father of the child, and if this did not get him to the altar, the mother could affiliate the child before the magistrates. They would generally order the putative father to pay a shilling or two shillings a week towards the child's upkeep, the money being collected by the overseers who passed it on to the mother.

The New Poor Law of 1834 took a much more punitive attitude towards the mothers of illegitimate children and this, as much as the spread of the more respectable and moralistic values of the chapel, contributed to the hardening of attitudes to illegitimacy later in the century. But the New Poor Law was never implemented in its full rigour in Todmorden, and in the economic circumstances of the early Victorian age, delaying marriage until after conception had many advantages. The young couple delayed the expense of setting up their own home. Their parents kept the advantage of their grown children's labour or wages. And the courting couple could enjoy for a little longer the relative freedom and affluence of their young adulthood: an all-too-brief interlude between a childhood spent at the loom or the jenny, and the full responsibilities of parenthood in almost certain poverty.

The chapels demanded that their members conform to very rigorous standards of behaviour. But that more vigorous popular culture which centred on the public houses was not merely anarchic. It also had its own code of conduct, and its own ways of punishing transgressors. One of these was "Riding the Stang". John Travis records an incident in about 1830 when a tradesman had been drinking and neglecting his work, and his friends paid a group of lads to "ride the stang" around the public houses, yelling, collecting money, and calling out the miscreant's offence in the traditional semi-nonsensical rhyme:

> "I diddle, diddle, dang! It's noaather my fort
> nor yo'ers that I ride this stang, but for old
> Bawtry's wife, who's lick'd her good man.
> It's noaather for eitin beef puddin', nor yet
> pig souse, but all for drinking a glass o' gin
> and waater at George Eccles' hewse".[29]

This customary way of shaming someone who had offended against the unwritten social code might be employed against hard-hearted employers, nagging wives or drunken husbands.

These three great strands that made up working class culture in the early nineteenth century - the ethic of mutuality, the culture of nonconformity, and the force of custom and tradition - can be seen as having their respective homes in the friendly society, the chapel, and the public house. In practice of course, most people participated in all three, to a greater or lesser extent. William Greenwood belonged to a friendly society, but not, from the evidence of his diary, to a co-operative or a trade union. Although not a chapel member, he went sometimes to Shore Baptist chapel and rather more frequently to the Inghamite Chapel at Toad Carr. And he enjoyed drinking in public houses, following the hounds, and staying late at Todmorden Fair.

Handloom Weavers and Factory Workers

In 1829, the handloom weavers, who had scarcely begun to recover from the 1826 depression in their trade, suffered yet another crisis. Again there was a shortage of work. Wage rates fell back until local weavers were earning so little that by the time they had paid their rent and bought fuel and candles, they were left with, on average, less than 3d per head per day to buy food for themselves and their dependants. The Fieldens were applied to weekly by scores of handloom weavers seeking work in their factory, and had to turn most of them away.[30]

Typical local handloom, early 19th century

25

Pay-day in a cotton mill

The factory workers were comparatively well paid, but suffered from extremely long hours of work. Around about 1830, local manufacturers were paying ordinary two-loom power weavers 8s a week; weavers on the larger sheeting looms, 12s a week; and tacklers about 18s or £1 a week. The standard hours of work were the maximum permitted since Hobhouse's Factory Act of 1825 - i.e., 12 hours a day from Monday to Friday, and 9 hours on Saturday, making a total working week of 69 hours.[31] The overworking of the factory operatives and the semi-starvation of the handloom weavers were two sides of the same coin. The cotton manufacturers had invested heavily in their new machinery. Naturally enough, they wanted to get as much use out of it as possible, and ran it for the maximum hours that the law permitted (and sometimes longer). So the handloom weavers became a reserve army of labour, used only when the manufacturer's orders in hand exceeded the capacity of his machines, and competition between the handloom weavers for what little work was available drove their wages ever downwards.

The remedy favoured by the Radicals was to limit the hours of labour in the factories. This would not only protect the factory workers, including the children, from the excessive hours that they were forced to work, but would also ensure more work for the handloom weavers. If they had been further protected by a legal minimum wage, this would have done much to improve the living conditions of the people in the industrial areas. But the Government was unsympathetic to remedies of this kind. Its perceived indifference to the troubles of the weavers and the factory workers added yet more fuel to the demand for Reform.

26

Chapter 3

The Reform Agitation

In 1830, as the handloom weavers of the North tried to keep body and soul together on 3d a day, and the pauperised agricultural labourers of the South and East rioted and set fire to hay-ricks, the accession of a new King brought renewed hope of Parliamentary Reform and of a Government more sympathetic to the sufferings of the people. The Manchester Political Union, formed in July 1830, was one of the first of a new upspringing of committees formed to agitate for Reform. Its members were mostly shopkeepers and small masters, with a smattering of radicals. Only three of its members were men of wealth or status. They included John Fielden of Todmorden and his brother Thomas.[1]

When in November the Whigs returned to power for the first time since 1806, hopes were raised yet higher and public meetings were called all over the country.

A very full account of the meeting held in the Todmorden township of Langfield in December 1830 was published in the *Voice of the People* newspaper, with the clear intention of encouraging similar meetings in other towns and villages. It opened by calling the township constable, John Veevers, to the chair. The first resolution approved the pledge of Ministers to reform the representation of the people, and attributed the current distress to the enormous taxes imposed by an unrepresentative Parliament. The meeting then called for John Fielden, who gave an animated speech, which was followed by resolutions in favour of annual Parliaments, the vote for all males over the age of 21, and vote by secret ballot. Attention was drawn to the distressed situation of the labouring classes, and the need to repeal those taxes which pressed most heavily upon them, especially the Corn Law, and finally it was decided to send petitions in support of reform for presentation to both Houses of Parliament.[2]

It is striking that the meeting, although comprising "many responsible inhabitants and gentlemen" called for a very radical reform indeed, to include universal

suffrage, annual elections and the secret ballot: measures that would have made Parliament subject to the democratic will, and which later constituted three of the Chartists' famous "six points". At meetings held in the other two Todmorden townships of Stansfield and Todmorden-cum-Walsden, the proposal had been put forward that Todmorden should form its own Political Union. The Langfield reformers discussed this suggestion after dinner at the Dog and Partridge Inn at Lumbutts (now the Top Brink), and a number of them decided to support the proposal.

The Todmorden Political Union

The Todmorden Political Union was founded at "a very numerous meeting of the inhabitants of Todmorden and its vicinity" held at the White Hart Inn on January 13th, 1831, with John Fielden in the chair. A committee was appointed to draw up rules and regulations, then those who had been at the meeting sallied forth to canvas for members and to meet again in the Bridge Street schoolroom a month later.

Six hundred people attended this second meeting. James Fielden of Waterside, John Fielden's brother, set the tone of the meeting by blaming the current distress of the people on an unrepresentative Government, and calling on the middle and working classes to work together for reform. He then moved that the objects of the Political Union be:

1st - To endeavour to obtain by lawful means, and these only, a radical reform in the Commons House of Parliament. 2nd - To prepare petitions and addresses (and remonstrances if necessary) to the King and to the two Houses of Parliament respecting the preservation and restoration of natural rights; to procure the abolition of all injurious monopolies - the repeal of all taxes which affect the Press, and prevent

The Centre of Todmorden in 1823, showing Todmorden Hall and St. Mary's Chapel

the dissemination of knowledge, - the repeal of bad laws and the enactment of good laws. 3rd - To endeavour to obtain the abolition of every species of slavery throughout His Majesty's Dominions. 4th - To promote peace, union and concord among the members of this Association, and to guide and direct their efforts into uniform, peaceful and lawful operations so that they may not waste their strength in loose and unconnected exertions for the obtainment of partial and impolitic measures. 5th - To take cognisance of all real local abuses, and to prevent as far as practicable all public wrongs and oppressions.

James Fielden's words about uniting the working and middle classes in working for reform were not mere rhetoric. The first of the rules adopted by the new Political Union was that: "The constitution of this Society being essentially popular, it admits as equal members all persons whatever whose names shall be registered in the books of the Union so long as they conform to its Rules and Regulations".

Subscriptions were to be what each member could conveniently afford, but not less than sixpence per annum, payable annually or quarterly. So nobody was excluded by poverty: even a poor handloom weaver could manage to find the equivalent of a ha'penny a month.

The general management of the affairs of the Union was entrusted to a Political Council of 21 members which was to meet at least every month. Its main duties were to watch the political situation, drawing up petitions and remonstrances as it deemed appropriate, and keeping the agitation within legal bounds. The emphasis on order and legality might suggest that there were some local reformers who wanted to to use riot and disorder to try to force the pace of change - just like the "physical force" Chartists of later years. The promoters of the Todmorden Political Union, on the other hand, were concerned to be seen to distance themselves from any such impetuous persons, and constantly emphasised their loyalty to the Constitution and the Throne. To this end, the duties of the rank and file members of the Political Union were listed as loyalty to the King, obedience to the law of the land, attendance at meetings, good and orderly conduct, and "to show the enemies of Reform that they are the determined supporters of social order, and the resolute opponents of those who would excite discord, revolution and anarchy". The Political Council had a corresponding duty to "devise means to preserve the peace and order of the town and neighbourhood during any disturbances arising from political excitement", and enjoyed considerable control over the rank and file, as would-be members of the Political Union had to be proposed by a member of the Political Council, which also had the power to expel any member.[3]

Over the next few months the Todmorden Political Union watched the drama being enacted on the national political stage and encouraged with petitions, applauded with addresses, and booed with remonstrances.

The Reform Bill successfully completed its course through the House of Commons on the 22nd September 1831, only to fail in the Lords two weeks later. The entire nation erupted in fury. Arming and drilling were reported from the North, outbreaks of rick-burning from the South. There were riots in Bristol, Nottingham and Derby, and a popular rising was widely feared. At a hastily-convened meeting the Todmorden Political Council decided to distribute 500 copies of an address to the townspeople, calling on them to "obey the laws, rally round the Throne and support his Majesty's Ministers and so avoid giving ammunition to those in the Lords who oppose the Reform Act and are hoping for riot and outrage".[4] The Political Union was continuing its policy of controlling and channelling the agitation. Shortly afterwards, it cold-shouldered some proposals of the Manchester Political Union, saying that it was of the opinion that "the measures you are pursuing being illegal are more calculated to retard than promote Parliamentary reform".

In December, a third Reform Bill quickly passed all stages in the House of Commons, and went for the consideration of the House of Lords, where there was still much opposition to it. By mid-April, the Bill was facing its second reading in the House of Lords, and the Political Union sent an address to Earl Grey, praising his efforts so far, and pleading against any attempts to water the reform down by raising the qualification for the franchise. This, they warned "would inevitably produce great dissatisfaction in the manufacturing districts, and consequences might follow which it is awful to contemplate". An eloquent passage suggests the privations of the times, the great hopes that were riding on Parliamentary reform, and a scarcely-concealed threat of popular action should the Bill be rejected:

> "We form part of an extensive manufacturing district, the people of which have been long suffering from the pressure of the times, and thousands of families among the operatives are absolutely in a state of starvation, who, though in full employment, cannot obtain 3d a head per day to subsist on; and they have bourne (sic) this in the most patient manner, and have evinced a moral principle beyond all praise. They wish for peaceful relief, they have hoped that the Reform measure would lead to an amelioration of their condition, and they now await in awful silence the result of the proceedings in the House of Lords".

Petitions were sent from the Todmorden townships: one from Todmorden-cum-Walsden containing 1,250 signatures, one from Stansfield with 1,325, and one from Langfield signed by 630 people. On the 7th May the Bill was voted down in the Lords. Again there were riots and mass protests. In Todmorden an angry public meeting held on Saturday 12th May was attended by nearly 5,000 people who deplored "the

The same view in 1994

unparalleled effrontery and injustice of those few interested individuals, who have dared to practice their vile machinations, base subterfuges, and false pretences, to deprive the people of their just rights with a tacit intention of leaving them still a prey to grasping selfishness and arbitrary rule".

The King had refused Earl Grey's request that he create enough Whig peers to pass the Bill, and Grey again resigned. More petitions, including one from Todmorden, were sent to the House of Commons. The King asked the Tory Duke of Wellington - an opponent of Reform - to form a Government, and the reformers, dismayed, did all they could to block Wellington, including starting a run on the banks. This was promoted with the slogan "To stop the Duke, go for gold", and it now appears that it was John Fielden of Todmorden who first suggested this slogan to the reformers Place and Attwood.[5] Wellington failed to form a Government, and Grey returned, supported by a promise from the King to create new Whig peerages if necessary. The Tories dropped their opposition, and on the 4th June, the Bill was passed by the House of Lords. The good news reached Todmorden the very same day, and plans for a grand celebration were made immediately.

Roast Beef and Plum Pudding

Great celebrations followed the passing of the Reform Act. The Todmorden Political Union held an open-air dinner and public procession on Saturday 4th August. At half past two in the afternoon 350 people sat down on the Smith Hill, near the White Hart Inn, and enjoyed roast beef and plum pudding and a quart of ale apiece. The tickets were sold at 1s 2d each, and a subscription had been organised to help the members who could not afford such a sum. John Fielden took the chair, patriotic toasts were drunk, and at about 6 o'clock, the procession moved off. The local trades and friendly societies - the Society of Whitesmiths, the Independent Order of Oddfellows, the Royal Foresters, the Druids, the Mechanics' Trades Society, and the Loyal Free Mechanics - all attended with their bands and their flags. The Political Union had commissioned its own flag for the occasion, bearing the words "The Members of the Todmorden Political Union. Union has conquered and will conquer", and the procession marched for about half a mile up each of the three valleys before returning to Smith Hill. The previous Saturday, there had been an even larger celebration featuring the Fieldens' factory workers, who had been given a holiday for the occasion.

They assembled at Waterside at 8.30 in the morning, and walked up the Walsden valley, where the Lumbutts workers joined the procession at Lumbutts Road bar house, the Smithyholme Mill workers and

the handloom weavers joined at Smithyholme Bridge, and the Stoneswood Mill workers joined at the Freemasons' Arms. On the return leg, the procession numbered 1,500 people walking four abreast.[6] They were led by a band, and then came the standard bearers, bearing the commemorative flag which had been subscribed for by all Fieldens' factory people. John Travis described the flag as "a most unique and grand affair, portraying, as it did, the great battle which had been fought and won, in parliament, for reform", and says that it was "a large red silk flag, with broad gimped border (perhaps yellow), properly mounted, and carried immediately behind the band, by two stalwart men and four out-riggers, with ropes fastened to the top cross-bar to keep it steady and upright". On the front was a picture of a mad bull (representing John Bull) charging men representing the enemies of reform into a fierce burning fire (representing Hell), and a motto - probably "No taxation without representation". On the other side was a picture of a hive with a swarm of bees, surrounded by sunshine and flowers, and the motto "Success to industry"[19] After the band and the flag-bearers walked the mechanics and moulders, the masons, the labourers, the engineers, the gas men, the spinning department, the workers from Causeway, Lumbutts, Stoneswood and Smithyholme Mills, the dressers, the twisters-in and winders-on, the powerloom weavers and the warehousemen, with the workers from Messrs. Buckley's Ridgefoot Mill bringing up the rear. They walked up to the Vicarage and to Maltkiln Bridge, giving three cheers for reform at each place, and then back to Waterside where there was a dinner of beef and puddings, dancing and political speeches. John Travis, again, describes the scene:

> "At the time of the great dinner day, the Waterside Holme was open ground - from the warehouse, upon which the public clock was later erected, up to the new barn, or Wadsworth Mill end of the field - and that day the overlookers, cutlookers and hookers, beamers and twisters (winders-on and twisters-in), were the butlers and waiters. A special marquee or pavilion was erected about the middle, on the side nearest the canal, for the employers and their invited friends; a band stand was also set up in close proximity, and the musicians played at intervals during the dining, and again after the speeches later in the day."[7]

Another, more sombre, procession was organised by some Stansfield men to celebrate the passing of the Reform Bill and illustrate the declining fortunes and sad condition of the handloom weavers. Royston Oliver of Wood Mill lent a cart, John Barker of Lower Ashes, a horse, and Abraham Ashworth of Cross Stone Lane, a loom: and a moving tableau of a handloom weaver was paraded through the town and past the diners at Waterside, who cheered loudly as it passed along the rows of tables. The weaver was a diminutive man named James Varley (nicknamed "Schemer"), and his winder was William Greenwood

("Bill o' Sam's") who was slightly humpbacked. The loom was hung with soft bread and red herrings to represent the poor food of the handloom weaver, and a flag of white calico was inscribed

CALICO WEAVERS WAGES
NINEPENCE PER DAY
OBSERVE
WEAVING - PRICE OF 30 YARDS - NINEPENCE [8]

The people hoped for great things from a reformed House of Commons, and probably most of all that it would afford some relief to the near-destitute handloom weavers. In a community like Todmorden, where handloom weaving had been until very recently the common trade, the handloom weavers were not a separate group, set apart from the rest of the society. They were rather, everybody's grandparents, uncles, aunts, children or neighbours, and the sympathetic feeling which their sufferings aroused in the hearts of their relatives and friends had been a mainspring of the agitation for reform.

Voters and reformers

It is difficult to say, with accuracy, how many Todmorden men had the Parliamentary vote before the 1832 Reform Act. The voters of Todmorden-cum-Walsden helped to elect the two MPs who represented Lancashire; and those of Langfield and Stansfield the four MPs for Yorkshire. The franchise for these County MPs was restricted to the owners of freehold property worth at least 40s a year, and the lists of people liable to pay Land Tax (which was payable on freehold property) were used as a basic electoral roll, but they were often inaccurate and disputes as to who was and who was not entitled to vote were common. In the late 1820s there were some 76 male payers of Land Tax in Todmorden-cum-Walsden township, 128 in Stansfield, and 32 in Langfield, so in the entire Todmorden district there may have been about 240 voters. But some of these were outsiders, who already had the vote in respect of property they owned elsewhere in the county. And some were the owners of very small freehold property, worth less than 40s a year, whose right to vote could have been disputed at an election. But what is certain is that the vote was restricted to substantial property owners, and that many men who were partners in important businesses or who were educated professional men had no Parliamentary vote. Nor did many of those most active in local government.

In the Todmorden area, local government was conducted in a very democratic manner. Each township was entirely independent and each appointed its own officers - Churchwardens, Surveyors of Highways, Constables and Overseers of the Poor - who were elected at annual meetings of the "gentlemen, freeholders and ratepayers". In Todmorden-cum-Walsden in 1837, there were about 500 ratepayers, so approximately 1 in 14 of the total population

The Waterside Mill complex in the 1860's. The field where the Fielden's workers celebrated the Reform Act appears in the foreground

31

TODMORDEN POLITICAL UNION:
Council Members, 1831 and 1832

NAME	RESIDENCE	OCCUPATION	VOTE pre 1832	post 1832
ASHWORTH, George	Lacey House	Worsted sp/mrf	NO	YES
ARMSTEAD, James	Shade	Blacksmith	NO	NO
BARKER, John	Bank	Road surveyor	YES	YES
BARKER, John	Barewise Mill	Cotton sp/mfr	NO	YES
BENTLEY, John	Castle Street		NO	NO
BUTTERWORTH, Gbt.	Toad Carr		NO	NO
CHAMBERS, John	Todmorden	Cotton sp/mfr	NO	YES
CLEGG, John	Stansfield Br.		NO	NO
COCKCROFT, Alfred	Toad Carr		NO	NO
DRAPER, Thomas	Hebden Br.		NO	NO
FIELDEN, James	Waterside	Cotton sp/mfr	NO	YES
FIELDEN, John	Waterside	Cotton sp/mfr	YES	YES
HAIGH, John	Stoneswood	Overseer/manager	NO	NO
HARDMAN, Giles	Foxholes		NO	NO
HARDMAN, James	Roomfield	Surgeon	YES	YES
HILL, John	Millwood		NO	NO
HELLIWELL, Wm.	Frith's Mill	Cotton sp	NO	YES
HOLT, Edmund	Lumbutts	Overseer/manager	NO	NO
HOLT, James	York Street	Joiner	YES	YES
HOLT, John	Todmorden	Timber merchant	NO	YES
HOLT, John	Smithyholme	Overseer/manager	NO	NO
INGHAM, William	Mankinholes	Gentleman farmer	YES	YES
LANCASTER, Henry	Knowlwood	Schoolteacher	NO	NO
MITCHELL, John	Mark Lane		NO	NO
NOWELL, John	Scout		NO	NO
OLIVER, Royston	Woodmill	Corn miller	NO	YES
ORMEROD, William	Gorpley Mill	Cotton sp/mfr	NO	YES
RATCLIFFE, John	Woodfield	Tenant farmer	NO	YES
SCHOLFIELD, Wm	Todmorden	Ironmonger	YES	YES
SIMPSON, Thomas	Carr Hse. Fld		NO	NO
STANSFIELD, James	Ewood	Attorney	NO	YES
STANSFIELD, Wm.	Charlestown		NO	NO
SUTHERS, James	Blind Lane	Beerhouse keeper	NO	NO
TILLOTSON, Sam.	Ibbot House	Card maker	NO	YES
VEEVERS, John	Kilnhurst	Carrier	NO	YES
WHITE, George	Todmorden	Unitarian minister	NO	NO

TOTAL MEMBERS, 36:   **TOTAL VOTERS, pre-1832: 6, post-1832: 18**

Source:
compiled from: *Minutes of the Todmorden Political Union*, 1907
Land Tax Returns. Registers of Electors, 1832.

was entitled, in theory, to attend and vote at these meetings. Each township also elected a "select vestry", whose members assisted the overseers of the poor. The overseers simply carried out the day-to-day administration: all important decisions were taken by the select vestry acting as a township committee or council. The men who served on the vestry were mostly cotton spinners and manufacturers, small landowners, tenant farmers and shopkeepers. Few had the Parliamentary vote. In Langfield, of the eleven men who served most frequently, only six were voters; and in Todmorden-cum-Walsden, it was only three out of fourteen.[9]

The most active and committed reformers in Todmorden were the members of the Council of the Todmorden Political Union. Over the two years of its existence it had 36 members. Sixteen of them were men of substance or position - mainly cotton manufacturers, with the occasional landowner, corn miller, or other business or professional men. The other members included a blacksmith, a joiner, a schoolteacher, a tenant farmer, a beerhouse keeper, and three overseers or managers from the Fielden mills. The occupations of the remaining twelve cannot be traced from the local trade directories, and so their occupations can be assumed to have been humble - factory workers, handloom weavers, or employees of some kind. Of the entire 36 members, only six already had the vote. George Ashworth, who leased the massive worsted mill at Callis, had no vote. Nor did the attorney, James Stansfield. And nor did men such as James Fielden, John Barker, and Royston Oliver, who worked in substantial family-owned enterprises, but did not personally own freehold property.

An extraordinarily high proportion of the leading reformers in Todmorden had connections with the Unitarian Chapel. If the Church of England used sometimes to be called the "Tory party at prayer", the Todmorden Political Union could, without much exaggeration, be called "the Unitarian Chapel at politics". Six of the twenty-one members of the first Political Council - George Ashworth, John Fielden, John Mitchell, Royston Oliver, James Suthers and George White - were Unitarians, as was Giles Hardman who was a Political Council member the following year. John Holt and Thomas Thomas, also, were members of the Unitarian chapel in its early years, and were also active in the Reform Movement. This is a very dense concentration, bearing in mind the chapel's small membership.[10] Unitarianism was a very democratic and rational creed, which took a great interest in social questions, and it was not only in Todmorden that strong links between Unitarianism and radical reform are to be found. But those links were reinforced here by the John Fielden connection. By 1830 Fielden was shouldering most of the expenses of the Unitarian Chapel and school, and he was also the main promoter of the Todmorden Political Union.

After the Reform Act, Stansfield and Langfield were included in the constituency of the West Riding of Yorkshire, which sent two MPs to Parliament, and Todmorden-cum-Walsden was in the Southern division of the county of Lancashire, which also elected two MPs. More people were entitled to vote, as the old electorate of 40 shilling freeholders was joined by the occupiers of copyhold property worth £10 a year, and of leasehold property worth £50 a year. Nationally, the Reform Act increased the number of voters from about 500,000 to about 800,000 - an increase of about 60%. In this area the new electoral rolls showed 137 voters in Todmorden-cum-Walsden, 171 in Stansfield, and 87 in Langfield. The total number of voters in the three townships had risen from about

240 to about 395. The increase seems at first glance to be roughly in line with the national average, but the proportional increase in the number of voters was in fact probably somewhat greater than the average, as the new lists included very few of the non-residents who had made up a considerable proportion of the names on the old lists. The main gainers by the reform were cotton spinners and manufacturers - men such as John and William Barker of Barewise Mill, Thomas Bottomley of Spring Mill at Ramsden Wood, James Fielden of Waterside, Robert Law of Ramsden Clough, William Ormerod of Gorpley Mill and Henry Ramsbottom of Salford steam factory, none of whom had had the vote previously because they were not freeholders. Others who gained the vote were men who rented substantial houses, farms or public houses.

But the increase in the number of voters had fallen far short of local hopes. The full radical programme of universal male suffrage, vote by ballot and annual Parliaments had been adopted at the Langfield meeting in December 1830, where it had been advocated not only by those who were hoping to gain the vote, but also by some enfranchised freeholders, including John Fielden, Dr. Hardman and William Ingham. Fielden, Hardman and Ingham, and three other voters, had subsequently been Council members of the Todmorden Political Union, which also had supported demands for a very broad franchise. In the event, the franchise was widened just enough to admit a few more of the property-owning middle classes. After the Reform Act, only 18 of the 36 members of the Council of the Todmorden Political Union had the vote. The select vestry members had not fared much better. In Todmorden-cum-Walsden township five of the fourteen most active members still had no parliamentary vote, and in Langfield, the figure was four out of eleven. Amongst the rank and file of the Political Union, and the general population of Todmorden, the proportion of those disappointed by the Act was even greater.

An unexpected outcome of the Reform Act was that Todmorden, indirectly, gained its own MP, when John Fielden was elected to the reformed House of Commons by the Radicals of Oldham. Fielden had been gaining prominence in regional politics since 1826, when his plan to secure an agreed minimum rate for handloom weavers had attracted a lot of support. Since that time, he had become a regional leader of the pro-Reform agitation, had lobbied the House of Lords on behalf of a Railway Act, and had published a pamphlet on currency reform. He was also known as a successful businessman, and for his efforts to improve conditions for factory workers. The Borough of Oldham was allotted two seats in the reformed Parliament, and the Radicals of the town invited John Fielden and William Cobbett to stand for election. At the polls in December, Fielden and Cobbett trounced the opposition, and were elected to the House of Commons. But they found few supporters or sympathisers in the House. Fielden had consented to become an MP "not with a view of joining party men or aiding in party movements", as he later said, "but in order to assist, by my vote, in doing such things as I thought would benefit the labouring people as well on the land as in the factory and at the loom. I have, all my years of manhood been a Radical Reformer, because I thought Reform would give the people a power in the House of Commons that would secure to them that better condition of which they are worthy".[11]

But the reformed House of Commons was to be a great disappointment to him, to his Oldham electors, and to the vast majority of working people who were still without effective representation. It proceeded to enact legislation which made the situation of the labouring people worse rather than better, and which Fielden and Cobbett were powerless to oppose. As Cobbett put it, they had "hardly more power in the House than as if they had been two little robins, or a couple of sparrows".[12]

After the Reform Act

The Todmorden Political Union did not disband after the Reform Act was obtained. For one thing, it did not consider that the reform had gone far enough; and for another, it had from the very first had a wider brief, pledging itself to seek "the redress of local and national grievances". The aims of the Todmorden Political Union, as stated in the rule book, included the abolition of the Corn Law and other monopolies, the repeal of taxes on newspapers, and the abolition of slavery. One of its first acts had been to prepare an address to the King praying for clemency towards the "deluded persons" who had been sentenced to death for their part in riots and rick-burnings in the agricultural counties, and in August 1831, the Union resolved that George White and John Fielden should draw up a petition "against the present taxes on knowledge", and in March 1832, it supported moves to extinguish the tithe system. A "local abuse" that came under the scrutiny of the Political Union was the alleged harsh treatment of a pauper at Ashes in Stansfield. A committee was appointed to investigate the matter, and reported progress at the next meeting.

After the Reform Act, the Todmorden Political Union seems to have become a sort of local Radical Association, organising support for, amongst other things, a restriction of the hours of work in factories. When George Crabtree was touring the Calder Valley in 1833, raising support for a Ten Hours Bill, he stopped at the White Hart Inn and sent for James Suthers, the Secretary of the Political Union, who told him that he was in weekly correspondence with John Fielden, and they were planning to hold a public meeting during the Easter recess, when, amongst other things, the Ten Hours Bill would be discussed.[13]

By this time the factory workers were able to earn

Holebottom Mill

considerably more than the impoverished handloom weavers. Typical local wages for adults were from 13s to 16s a week for men, and from 6s 6d to about 7s a week for women. But factory work, especially for adults, was still very much the exception rather than the rule. In 1833, Firth and Haworth, cotton spinners of Causeway Mill, employed only fifty-four people; and Thomas Sutcliffe, cotton spinner of Stoodley Bridge, employed only one hundred and fourteen. Most of these workers were very young people. Thirty-seven of Firth and Haworth's fifty-four employees were under 21 years of age.[14]

The complaint of the factory workers was that they were forced to work excessively long hours. The standard working week of 69 hours was made up of twelve hours work on weekdays, and nine on Saturday. The half an hour break for breakfast and hour for lunch did not count as working time, and so the employees (often including children as young as seven or eight) were on the mill premises from six in the morning until seven-thirty or eight at night. Such long hours left no time for children to play, and little for adults to attend to their household duties, or to enjoy leisure, education or recreation.

The more unscrupulous millowners at this time sometimes employed two sets of hands, one of them working a nightshift, so that the machinery could be run continuously. Some Todmorden manufacturers roundly condemned this practice. The Inghams of Haugh Mill wrote to the 1833 Factory Commission that: "We consider night-work unnatural, and a thing which ought on no occasion to be allowed to any manufactory: and we consider its effect on trade is to glut the market, and that evil and cruelty attend it in all ways.", and even Thomas Sutcliffe of Stoodley Bridge, who maintained that very young children actually benefited from factory employment, would not consider employing them in shifts, "because we consider night-work both demoralising and injurious to their health". But at least one Todmorden millowner did try to run his mill at night, until he was publicly shamed into giving up the practice. Abraham Stansfield, universally known as "Th' Old Buck", was the owner of Holebottom Mill. In March 1832, he was exposed in *The Poor Man's Advocate* newspaper as a "Midnight Robber of the Repose of the Poor", by working his factory in the night. No doubt popular pressure was brought to bear on Stansfield, and five weeks later the paper reported that he had given up the practice of working his mill by night.

The popular campaign for a Ten Hours Act was not successful in 1833. The Government, instead, brought in its own Factory Act which restricted children aged between nine and thirteen to 48 hours of factory labour a week. It did not make any new restrictions on workers over 13, and in fact threatened to worsen their position, as employers would almost certainly employ children in two shifts, and could therefore actually lengthen the hours of work for older workers.

The Fieldens were far from satisfied with the 1833 Act. John Fielden's view was that "our factory system will not be what it ought to be, until the time of all be reduced to eight hours per day".[15] He became acquainted with Robert Owen, the well-known philanthropist, who had demonstrated at his own cotton mills at New Lanark that it was possible to drastically reduce the hours of labour, and still make a handsome profit. In 1833, Owen was touring the north, promoting his scheme for co-operative societies and labour exchanges, and in November he stayed a few days with John Fielden at Dawson Weir in Todmorden. Here they dreamed up their plan for National Regeneration - on the 1st March, 1834, the day when the 8-hour day for children in cotton factories was due to come into force, the adults should insist on working the same hours as the children, and for their present rate of pay. Fielden saw the plan as a chance for employers and workers to co-operate to improve the moral and physical condition of the working class. He hoped that the manufacturers would agree voluntarily to support National Regeneration, seeing it as a way to put an end to the over-production and undercutting that were endemic in the industry. Fielden promoted the new scheme in Lancashire, where he secured the backing of John Doherty, the spinners' leader; and Robert Owen converted some of the Ten Hours committees of West Yorkshire. Todmorden had its own National Regeneration branch,[16] and by early March was reporting some progress in interesting local trades societies in the scheme. But in the spring of 1834, the anger which followed the sentencing of the "Tolpuddle Martyrs" to transportation for joining a trades union, put an end to any possibility of co-operation between employers and workers. The plan was postponed, and the collapse of the Owenite trade unions later in the year meant that it was never put into operation.

John Fielden's home at Dawson Weir, opposite Waterside Mill

Part of Stansfield Township, 1834-5

Chapter 4

Revolt Against the New Poor Law

Todmorden owed its Radical reputation above all to the strenuous, and at times, violent, opposition which the town mounted against the Poor Law Amendment Act of 1834 - or the New Poor Law, as it came to be known. The local opposition was so fierce that the Act was never fully implemented, and Todmorden for many years enjoyed the distinction of being the only English Poor Law Union without a Union workhouse.

The New Poor Law was one of the first pieces of legislation brought in by the reformed Parliament, and it was introduced hurriedly to alleviate a crisis in the agricultural counties of the South, where poor rates were rocketing upward, whilst more and more labourers were being sucked into the downward spiral of pauperisation. But the Act, and the report on which it was based, showed little familiarity with the very different conditions of the industrial areas. In these areas the Old Poor Law was generally agreed to work reasonably well. It came under pressure - especially in places which were heavily dependent upon a single industry - mostly when a trade depression put nearly an entire community out of work at one time.

Under the Old Poor Law, each parish or township was separately and independently responsible for its own poor. In the Todmorden area, as previously mentioned, each township elected an overseer and a select vestry to collect the poor rates and dispense relief. Todmorden-cum-Walsden employed in addition a paid overseer, but in the other two townships the more substantial citizens took it in turn to serve without payment. Some of the paupers received a regular pension. These were mostly aged widows, the long-term sick, and others who could not support themselves by their earnings alone, and they were given an allowance, according to need, up to a maximum of about 2s a week. People who found themselves in sudden difficulties could also apply for assistance, and the Todmorden-cum-Walsden overseer explained as follows some of the circumstances under which he granted relief in 1837/8: "come from America and poorley", "in fever", "wife laying in", "funeral expenses", and "Mother in prison and he (Father) run off and left them".[1] Nearly all assistance was "out-relief" given in cash to people living in their own homes; and although there were small workhouses, relief was not conditional upon people entering the workhouse.

The Poor Law Amendment Act made few specific provisions, but gave wide powers to the three Commissioners based at Somerset House in London to reorganise poor law administration in line with their own notions - which were known to have as a central policy that out-relief should cease, and all paupers should be sent to a workhouse, where conditions should deliberately be made more unpleasant than those endured by the poorest independent labourers. This policy was widely perceived as entirely inappropriate for northern industrial towns, where no workhouse could ever accommodate all those who needed temporary help during a trade depression. The New Poor Law was hated and feared by the working classes, who foresaw that people would accept work on any terms at all rather than submit to entering the workhouse, and so, inevitably, it would have the effect of lowering wages. But despite some opposition and sporadic outbursts of violence the Act was soon put into operation in the south of England.

In October 1836, Assistant Poor Law Commissioner Alfred Power arrived to put the Act into operation in the North. His efforts were resisted in many towns, notably Huddersfield, Dewsbury, Oldham, Burnley, and Ashton-under-Lyne, but nowhere more so than in Todmorden.

The Todmorden Poor Law Union [2]

Power's first task was to group townships together into Poor Law Unions. Usually centred on a market town, they varied considerably in size. The Todmorden Union was one of the smallest, comprising just six townships - Todmorden-cum-Walsden, Stansfield, Langfield, Heptonstall, Erringden and Wadsworth.

Each Union was to be governed by a Board of Guardians. This was a new local authority that would take over the administration of poor relief from the township overseers and select vestries, although the overseers were to remain responsible for collecting the poor-rates. The Boards of Guardians did not enjoy the degree of independence that their predecessors had commanded: they were subject to orders from the Poor Law Commissioners in London. The Guardians were to be elected by the local ratepayers. This allowed plenty of scope for the opposition. In Todmorden, John Fielden immediately called for a total boycott of the proceedings. The elections for the first Todmorden Board of Guardians were to be held on 15th February, 1837, and a big public meeting of the ratepayers and other inhabitants of the township of Todmorden-cum-Walsden was arranged for the day of the elections, to whip up public feeling and enforce the boycott.

The public meeting was unanimous in its opposition to the New Poor Law. It deplored the Commissioners intention to "place those poor, whom we love and respect, and who have been guilty of no crime, in a Workhouse, and under a discipline and restraint more intolerable than is allotted to Felons in a Gaol". The Todmorden ratepayers found the new arrangements "destructive of that self-government, which we have had handed down to us by our forefathers, and which we feel it is our duty, as well as our interest to maintain", and declared themselves "well satisfied with the management of our own affairs in this township" and pledged themselves, "individually and collectively, to resist any foreign interference with the management thereof".[3] The ratepayers of Todmorden had, as we saw in the last chapter, recently been disappointed in the Reform Act of 1832, which had

failed to give many of them, however active they might be in local government, any say in the election of the national Parliament. They did not now intend to meekly hand over control of their local affairs to a non-elected body of Commissioners appointed by a Parliament which had not been of their choosing. They vowed uncompromisingly that "we will make no return of Guardians...we will pay no rates to any overseer acting for any Union, if one should, in opposition to our wishes, be formed; and that we will indemnify our Churchwardens and overseers for any penalties inflicted on them, for acting in obedience to our instructions, in opposing the introduction of the Poor Law Amendment Act into this township".

The total boycott of the elections for Guardians that John Fielden demanded was successful in the townships of Todmorden-cum-Walsden and Langfield. It was here that the Fieldens' extensive factories were located, and where personal contacts and loyalties, patronage and the threat of its withdrawal, and the mobilisation of the Fieldens' huge workforce could all play their part in encouraging compliance. It seems that the threat of closing the works was a particularly potent one,[4] and would presumably operate as much on local traders as on the operatives themselves. (The possibility of 3,000 wages being lost to the local economy would no doubt concentrate the minds of local shopkeepers). In Stansfield, the opponents of the Act, not daring to try for a boycott, put up anti-Poor Law candidates. The other three townships, at the Hebden Bridge end of the valley, lay outside the Fieldens' sphere of influence. They all elected Guardians. The result was an incomplete board, made up of just eleven Guardians instead of eighteen, and James Taylor of Todmorden Hall, who as a magistrate was appointed ex-officio. The first meeting of the Board of Guardians was held at the Golden Lion Inn, Todmorden, on February 15th.

It seems that this first Board had a slender majority of anti-Poor Law Guardians. The first step in implementing the law was to elect a clerk to the Board. Some of the anti-Poor Law Guardians tried unsuccessfully to block the election; they failed in this, but did manage to get their own man, the attorney James Stansfield, elected by a majority of two, in preference to the solicitor Mr. J. Sutcliffe, who was the choice of the pro-Poor Law faction. The new clerk had reputedly been largely responsible for drawing up the set of anti-Poor Law resolutions which had been adopted at the public meeting in Todmorden[5], and his appointment put an opponent of the new law in a key position to hinder its implementation locally.

The Board of Guardians now began to be concerned whether, lacking as it did representatives from two of the six townships, it was in fact a legally constituted body; and if it was not, whether its members could be held legally responsible as individuals for its actions. The Clerk was instructed to ask the Poor Law Commission to request an opinion from the Attorney

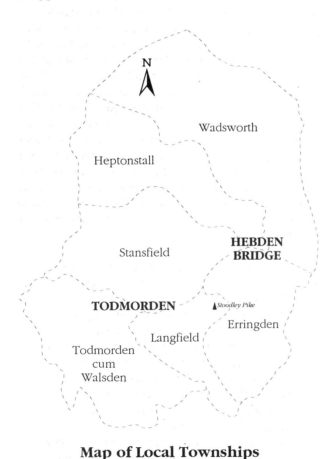

Map of Local Townships

Todmorden Hall, home of James Taylor

General, but before an answer arrived, the parochial year came to an end, and with it the term of office of the first Todmorden Board of Guardians. The necessity for another round of elections meant that battle would be joined once more.

March 1837 - March 1838

The next parochial year passed off quietly enough in Todmorden.

At the elections of March 1837 the townships of Langfield and Todmorden-cum-Walsden maintained their boycotts. Guardians were elected for the other four townships, but like their predecessors, they were uncertain about their legal competence to act. By June, the Poor Law Commission had managed to reassure them on this point, and they proceeded to make arrangements to take over the registration of births, marriages and deaths. On the 23rd June, these arrangements were completed, and the Board adjourned until the order came for it to take over the administration of poor relief.

Meanwhile, the Poor Law Commission was continually writing to the Clerk to the Board of Guardians with requests for information: for details of workhouses, of paid officials, of expenditure for the last three years, and so forth. This gave the Clerk and the township overseers an obvious opportunity to frustrate the Poor Law Commission and its officials. On 3rd June the Clerk wrote to Power saying that he was gathering the required information regarding poor rates and expenditure, etc., but not until the 9th

February of the following year was it actually sent, and then only "as far as present information enables me".[6] The Clerk may have deliberately dallied. As we have seen, he was against the New Poor Law in 1837, and it is impossible to tell from his letter book whether he had changed his colours, or was using his position to delay and frustrate. The ratepayers and the township overseers were well aware that refusal to supply statistics was a fairly safe way to harass the Poor Law Commissioners. Langfield simply refused to co-operate, and supplied no information at all. In Stansfield the overseers called a meeting of freeholders and ratepayers who unanimously resolved "that the Questions, sent by A. Power, Assistant Poor Law Commissioner, be not answered".[7] But a few weeks later, they climbed down a little and decided to make the township books available to the Commission or its officers, but not to explain them, thereby avoiding outright confrontation, but still making it very difficult for the Commissioners to work out the averages they required.

The same meeting went on to give a very clear statement of the Stansfield ratepayers' opinion of the New Poor Law:

"That it is the opinion of this meeting that although some parts of the New Poor Law might be introduced into this township with advantage, yet that taking it as a whole, its introduction would be highly detrimental both to the Ratepayers and the Poor and this meeting most especially objects to the unlimited powers of the Poor Law Commissioners given them by the New Poor Law and is of the opinion that to carry out the orders of the said Commissioners received and produced this day into full execution would next year cost a sum of Money equal or exceeding what has lately been annually levied for the relief of the poor and would be attended with no consequent advantage whatever".[8]

Less implacably hostile to the Act than their counterparts in Todmorden-cum-Walsden, the ratepayers of Stansfield were nonetheless also reluctant to yield power to mere Commissioners, and totally opposed to proposals which they believed would cost them more, without any benefit accruing to the poor. After carrying this resolution the meeting agreed to petition for the reform of the New Poor Law, the organisation of the petition being entrusted to a group of seven respectable citizens.

The autumn saw a massive petitioning campaign getting under way in the North. In Bury in October, John Fielden urged the people to petition for universal suffrage and for the repeal of the New Poor Law, saying - "if I am not supported by the petitions of the people, I can make very little impression upon the House. Without petitions, I cannot be heard".[9] The campaign was forwarded by the formation of the South Lancashire Anti-Poor Law Association in November. It was claimed that 107 places in Lancashire produced petitions signed by a total of 122,847 people, and on 20 February 1838, supported by those petitions, John Fielden in the House of Commons, and Lord Stanhope in the House of Lords, moved the repeal of the Poor Law Amendment Act. When Fielden's motion received only a derisory seventeen votes, the news was received with disbelief and dismay in the North.

So, on the eve of a new round of Guardians' elections, Todmorden had had a quiet year. The Guardians had not met for months, having no business to transact until they were ordered to take over the relief of the poor. The opposition had been quietly uncooperative about supplying statistical information, and had otherwise concentrated on petitioning. Some excitement had no doubt been generated by the lecture given in the Unitarian chapel on January 10th by J. R. Richardson, the fiery speaker who was the rising star of the South Lancashire Anti-Poor Law Association, but then had followed the disappointment of the crushing defeat of hopes for a repeal of the Poor Law. Evidently, if the law was to be set aside, this would not be achieved by constitutional means.

March - June 1838

For the elections of March 1838, the stakes were raised. The New Poor Law had by now been successfully implemented in several of the quieter Northern towns, and it was to be expected that the Board of Guardians now elected would be called upon to actually introduce the law in Todmorden. A

Working Men's Association was formed at a meeting in the Unitarian chapel on 28th March. Its aims were to resist the introduction of the Poor Law Amendment Act into this district, and to try to secure its repeal, and the main weapon was to be a campaign of exclusive dealing. The president of the association was Joseph Hirst, who, like many of the other members, was an employee of the Fieldens.[10]

Under John Fielden's encouragement, the opposition stuck to its previous election tactic of the boycott. Langfield township completely boycotted the elections and returned no Guardians at all. In Todmorden-cum-Walsden, out of four pro-Poor Law candidates whose names had been put forward, three withdrew under popular pressure; but William Helliwell refused to do so, and was considered to be duly elected.[11] In the other four townships, anti-Poor Law men refused to stand. The Board of Guardians which was returned, although incomplete, was predominantly composed of wealthy gentlemen and manufacturers who intended to introduce the New Poor Law in the Todmorden Union.

A scandal broke over the conduct of the election in Todmorden-cum-Walsden township. The Todmorden overseer, William Stansfield of Bridge End, was accused of illegal practice: seemingly, a list of four (presumably) anti-Poor Law candidates, pushed under his door at night, had simply disappeared. It was claimed that he had handed it over to Joshua Fielden. The Poor Law Commissioners were furious about the incident of the disappearing list, and intended applying to the Government to start proceedings against the Todmorden township officers for "conspiracy or such other indictable offence".[12] The Todmorden overseers called a meeting of ratepayers in the Old Church on 2nd April. William Robinson of Stones took the chair, and the ratepayers approved the overseers' obstruction of the elections for Guardians, and promised to support them if proceedings were taken against them. Alfred Power wanted to go further, and indict not only the officers, but "certain other parties... particularly the Messrs. Fielden".[13] It seems that the Government advised restraint for the time being, but John Fielden was about to give Power even more cause for annoyance.

In March, Fielden had called on James Taylor, the doctor and magistrate who had accepted the post of Chairman of the Board of Guardians, and threatened that if there was any attempt to introduce the law in Todmorden, he and his brothers would shut their works and throw their 3,000 hands out of employment. This threat was reported by Power to the Poor Law Commission in a letter dated the 9th May. Power's own opinion was that Fielden's investment was so vast that he would only close his works for a few days, if at all: even now, he said, the firm was preparing premises for another 1,000 powerlooms. He advised calling Fielden's bluff and putting the Todmorden Union into operation soon. Criminal proceedings against Fielden and others could be held as an option in reserve.[14]

The Fielden Mills Close

The Poor Law Commission took Power's advice and Fielden's bluff was called. On June 23rd the order came for the Guardians to meet on the 6th July, and every week thereafter, and to take over the relief of the poor of Todmorden Union from the township overseers on 12th August.

John Fielden, who was in London at the time, wrote an open letter to the Todmorden Guardians on July 2nd, threatening to close his mills indefinitely unless the Guardians all resigned.

His letter pointed out that the vast majority of ratepayers and inhabitants of the Todmorden Union were hostile to the New Poor Law, and that it was generally believed in the four townships that had elected Guardians that they would only put the Registration Act into effect. He argued that the New Poor Law would depress wages, because a workman would accept less money rather than break up his home and family and go into a workhouse. And he threatened, "in the name of my brothers, as well as on my own part, I now inform you that if you are willing to be made the instruments of the Poor Law Commissioners in reducing your neighbours to slavery, we will not become your instruments by employing the slaves of your making... We have resolved to avoid the scandal of participation with you by closing our works, and ceasing to employ the people until such time as a sense of shame or of justice shall induce you to abandon your cruel and humiliating functions". Unless the Guardians resigned, the Fielden mills would close on the 6th July - the day appointed for the Guardian's first meeting.[15]

A group of Stansfield ratepayers asked the township constable to call a public meeting on the 6th July. He refused to do so, but nonetheless, seventeen ratepayers called on the people to assemble in Todmorden at 8 am, and march to the Kilnfield at Eastwood, above the inn where the Guardians held their meetings. It was to be a massive demonstration of popular feeling, and the placards advertising the event left the populace in no doubt as to its duty: "It is expected, that every man will so act on this important occasion as if the Salvation of his Country depended entirely on his own Individual Exertion".[16] The workers from the Fieldens' mills, and from some of the other workplaces in the town were given a holiday for the occasion, assembling in Todmorden and marching down the Halifax Road with the customary band playing and banners waving. The Waterside banner showed a hive of bees with the motto "Justice, fidelity and good feeling. Free trade and well paid", and some of the other flags carried that day bore the inscriptions "Bastille, the Poor Man's Hell", "Oastler for Ever", and "Pluck not the fatherless from their mother's Breast".

By mid-afternoon between three and five thousand people had assembled in the field and business began in earnest. A Hebden Bridge shoemaker

The canal and railway viaduct at Gauxholme, early 1840's

named Abraham Marshall was elected to the chair, and motions against the Poor Law carried. After the speeches were done, a seven man deputation was formed to go and put their case to the Guardians, and call on them to resign.[17] But the Guardians were not at the inn as expected. Seriously alarmed by the proposed public meeting, they had met secretly a day earlier than planned, and had rushed off a set of resolutions to the Poor Law Commission in London, and to the Home Secretary, saying that the Guardians could not bring in the law unless the influence and opposition of Fielden could be overcome by the Government.[18] The Kilnfield meeting agreed to reconvene on Monday to hear the reports of the deputation to the Guardians, and the next day, Saturday 7th July, the Fieldens' mills were pronounced closed.

When the people reassembled outside the White Hart Inn on the Monday to hear the reports of the delegations to the Guardians, the authorities were prepared for trouble. The magistrates - John Crossley, James Taylor and another from Pontefract - were inside the inn, ready to read the Riot Act if need be. Forty-two townsmen had been sworn in as special constables, and troops from the 10th Hussars had been positioned a mile up the Burnley Road.[19] The Government had given the Guardians the protection they had asked for.

A hustings had been set up in the market place outside the inn. By 1 o'clock in the afternoon about 1,000 people had gathered. By 2 o'clock, the crowd had swollen to about 4,000. John Ratcliffe of Woodfield, farmer, was called to the chair, and business began. Canvassers had been out, asking ratepayers to sign a memorial to the Guardians praying them not to act to bring in the new law. They reported that nearly all those applied to had signed, and they had met with only 9 refusals out of 804 in Todmorden-cum-Walsden, 6 out of 315 in Langfield, and only 16 out of 683 in Stansfield. Next came the report of the deputation which had met three of the Guardians on Saturday and asked them to resign. The Guardians replies were reported back to the meeting. Royston Oliver had replied that he would consider resigning, but he had heard that if the Todmorden Guardians resigned, the Union would be split by the Commissioners and divided between Rochdale and Halifax, and the poor would then be worse off. William Sutcliffe agreed the Act could be improved, but thought this should be done by petitioning; he would resign once he had broken the law or harmed the poor. William Helliwell replied that his opinion was given on the placard he had published in Todmorden that morning. On the placard Helliwell had announced his opposition to all Commissioners, Factory and Poor Law alike; accused John Fielden of seeking popularity and his own self-interest; of agitating the hand-loom weavers, spinners and factory infants on the subject of wages whilst simultaneously installing more and more power looms and self-acting mules to do away with their labour; and of arbitrarily shutting his doors to those whose labours had enriched him, under the pretence of the Poor Law, but really out of self-interest and of being tyrannical and dictatorial.[20]

John Fielden then addressed the meeting. Conscious of the military presence, his criticism of the Poor Law was deliberately non-inflamatory. He briefly defended himself against Helliwell's aspersions, saying that the people knew the record of his brothers and himself for wages and constant work, and ended by calling on the people to go peaceably to their homes and not have recourse to any violence. The only call to action was his exhortation that they should "let those who were turning them upon their own resources also be turned upon *their* resources"; by which phrase he signalled his support for the Radical Association's exclusive dealing campaign, and echoed the call for a rate strike made by the radical shoemaker Marshall earlier in the meeting. Marshall had announced his intention to "button up his breeches pockets, and when they came for the rates, let them sell by auction". Other working men who addressed the meeting included Joseph Hirst, a Waterside factory worker, and George Davies, a watchmaker of Salford in Todmorden.

The threatened use of military force had effectively countered Fielden's tactic of closing his mills. He attended the Guardians' meeting on 13th July with a deputation, but they were not afraid of him now, and after he had left proceeded to make the necessary arrangements for taking over the administration of poor relief. Fielden was left with no option but to climb down, and re-open his mills, which he did on July 16th. But if he could not pressure the Guardians into stepping down, he could starve them of funds. The next tactic would be the rate-strike. A printed placard was posted in and about Todmorden, signed by John Fielden and addressed to the Board of Guardians. It read:

> "To oppose force to force we are not yet prepared; but if the people of this and the surrounding districts are to be driven to the alternative of either doing so, or surrendering their local government into the hands of an unconstitutional board of lawmakers, the time may not be far distant when the experiment may be tried... ...your real difficulties may only commence when the period arrives for the relief of the poor being administered by your board...You have heard that tithes could not be collected in Ireland; and if you persevere you may have the satisfaction of knowing that rates cannot be collected in England.[21]

Rate Strike

From 20th July, the Guardians began to meet weekly, and make their arrangements for taking over the administration of poor relief on 12th August. The Union was divided into two districts - one centred on Todmorden, and one on Hebden Bridge. An Assistant

Overseer (to collect the poor rates), and a Relieving Officer (to dispense them) was appointed for each district. The overseers of the six townships were billed for their share of the costs of setting up the Union, and the overseers of Langfield and of Todmorden-cum-Walsden refused to pay. In this they were acting in accordance with the wishes of the ratepayers, who had assembled in township meetings, directed the overseers not to comply with the demands of the Guardians, and promised to indemnify the overseers for any personal loss.

The overseers, having refused to pay the demands of the Guardians, were taken before the magistrates; the Langfield overseers at Halifax, and the Todmorden ones at Rochdale. The Halifax magistrates were reluctant to convict, because as the Todmorden Board of Guardians was incomplete, there was some doubt in their minds as to whether its orders were legal. Matters were delayed whilst they sought a higher opinion. Proceedings were held up at Rochdale too, because although the magistrates found the case against the overseers proved, some confusion arose as to which section of the Act they had been convicted under,[22] and further delay was caused when the overseers entered an appeal. But by the beginning of October, the Halifax magistrates, with the backing of the Poor Law Commission, convicted the Langfield overseers. The Rochdale business quite independently reached a conclusion at approximately the same time, and so both sets of overseers had fines imposed upon them for disobedience to the call of the Guardians. Since they refused to pay the fines, distress warrants were issued, allowing their goods to be taken and sold.

Some calicos were taken in this way from the Todmorden-cum-Walsden overseers, William Robinson and William Crossley, and in the late afternoon of Saturday the 21st October an attempt was made to sell the distrained cloth by auction in front of the White Hart Inn.

The auctioneer was Abraham Stansfield - otherwise known as "Th' Old Buck" - whom we have already met as a "Midnight Robber of the Repose of the Poor". One of Todmorden's most distinctive figures, he was later described by Travis as follows:
> "A tall, gaunt fellow he was, dark-grisly, and with thick shaggy brows beetling over eyes that "winked" incessantly. A snuffling of the nose accompanied the winking, and a general sympathetic movement of all the facial nerves and muscles gave him the appearance of always making grimaces; insomuch that the writer, when a child, could never look upon him but with a sort of subdued terror. Another peculiarity of the man was that he stammered frightfully;
> ...Over his tall, lean, six-feet figure, winter and summer alike (for we do not remember ever to have seen him without it) was thrown a brown woollen cloak of antique pattern, with lamb's-wool-lined collar, and

fastened by some peculiar brass chain arrangement".[23]

Many comical anecdotes circulated in the district, telling of his courting days, of his sea-voyage to Belgium (he was convinced that only his fervent praying had saved them all from shipwreck), and of the way he had tricked a creditor by paying him off in notes of the Stoodley Bridge Bank (which was headed by Thomas Sutcliffe - the "Old Buck's" brother-in-law), the very evening before the bank collapsed.[24]

When the "Old Buck" stood up to auction the distrained cloth in the town market place a large crowd of men and women soon assembled and proceeded to jeer and jostle him, to tear off his clothes, and eventually chased him home to Holebottom. A few days later he tried once more to auction the cloth. On this occasion he had to be taken home under the protection of a posse of constables, but they could not prevent the crowd again tearing off his clothing, and pelting him freely with mud and cow-dung. He was heard to swear repeatedly that never again would he attempt to sell Poor Law calicos.[25]

These scenes were merely a prelude to the much more serious disturbances that were soon to take place at Mankinholes.

The Mankinholes Riot: Friday, 16th November 1838 [26]

On Thursday November 8th, William Ingham of Mankinholes, who was the overseer for the township of Langfield and a much respected gentleman-farmer, was visited by two police officers who had come from Halifax to mark the goods that would be taken from him and sold if the fine remained unpaid. He offered them one of his cows, but this was refused, and instead they marked goods worth £15, including, as he said, "a French cupboard, which had been taken from the French in the late war, and on which I set great store".

Eight days later, they returned with a horse and cart. William King, the Sergeant of the Watch, and James Feather, the Under-deputy, were not anticipating trouble and were unarmed. They must have had a moment's uneasiness when a young man they met on the road, not knowing who they were, told them how "Th' Old Buck", attempting to auction distrained calico in Todmorden a few days previously, had been nearly stripped, and the calico twisted round his neck. Nevertheless, the officers proceeded to Mr. Ingham's, arriving there at about 2 o'clock in the afternoon.

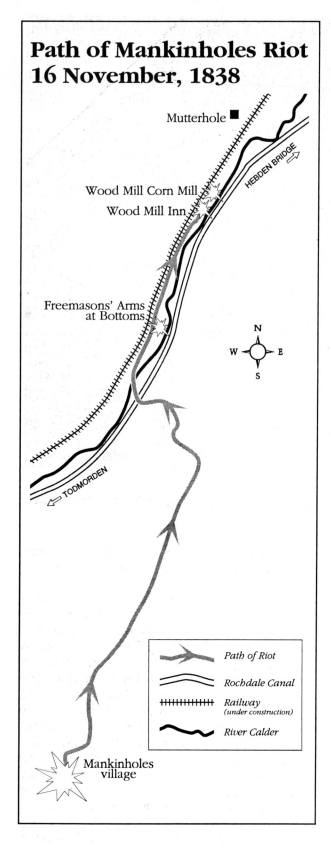

Path of Mankinholes Riot 16 November, 1838

Mutterhole ■

HEBDEN BRIDGE →

Wood Mill Corn Mill
Wood Mill Inn

Freemasons' Arms at Bottoms

N
W ● E
S

← TODMORDEN

	Path of Riot
	Rochdale Canal
+++++++++++	Railway (under construction)
	River Calder

Mankinholes village

At this signal, hundreds of workpeople employed in and around Lumbutts and Mankinholes rushed to the scene. There came outworkers from farms, operatives from mills, and quarrymen, masons and other workers from the railway under construction. It was estimated that the crowd now numbered one or two thousand people, or even more.

The younger police-officer, Feather, tried to take their horse and cart to Todmorden for safety, but got only two hundred yards before he was set upon by a gang of men, rolled in the mud and forced to turn back. Outside the house, the horse and cart were thrown over, Feather was thrown on top of the horse, and with cries of "Kill him, kill him", the crowd began to stone both horse and man. Under the torrent of stones Feather crawled to the house and regained safety, temporarily. Now the crowd's fury was turned on the horse and cart, but some of them observing that "the horse had done nothing amiss", it was turned adrift. Meanwhile, some of the railway navvies, who had brought their mattocks with them, made short work of the cart, which was then set on fire.

Now the crowd began to cry for the officers to be delivered up to them, threatening to burn the house down if this demand was not met. Ingham appeared, and begged the crowd to spare the lives of the officers, and the reply came back that "we'll spare your lives if you will take an oath before Mr. Ingham, that you will never come on such an errand again, either here or elsewhere, and also go on your bare knees and beg us pardon". The oath was hurriedly sworn - the Methodist Mr. Ingham "accidentally" providing a dictionary instead of the Bible - which subterfuge passed unnoticed by the cheering crowd. But neither of the officers would submit to the humiliation of kneeling and apologising. The three men stepped outside the house. The crowd pushed Ingham back in, threw the officers down, beat and half-stripped them, then hounded and pelted them down the road.

The lucky chance of a cart blocking a bridge enabled King to gain the Freemasons' Inn at Bottoms, where Mrs. Hollinrake, the landlady, forced the pursuing crowd out of her house. Feather was stabbed in the leg whilst he tried to get into the inn but he managed to struggle on to Wood Mill where a man thrust him into the house of Samuel Oliver, who was a corn-miller and brother to the Guardian Royston Oliver. The crowd broke some of Samuel Oliver's windows, and surrounded the Wood Mill Inn, where the Guardians had just finished the business of the day.[27] A few of the windows of the inn were broken, and then the rioters began to disperse, and the remainder were driven off. When all was quiet King was brought over to join his fellow-policeman at Oliver's house. As little remained of their own clothing, each was disguised as a miller before being put on board the stagecoach "Perseverance" which took them back to Halifax.

Once more Mr. Ingham refused to pay his fine, and so the officers began to remove the marked goods. By now, word was getting around that the policemen had arrived (they had been expected, though it had not been known when they would come), and a crowd was gathering. A woman who was standing on a grassy knoll called out "Ring th' 'larum bell! Ring th' 'larum bell!", and straightaway a nearby bell began to ring violently, followed almost instantaneously by several others, including that of the Fieldens' Lumbutts factory, which rang incessantly for ten or fifteen minutes.

Mankinholes Hall, reputedly the home of the Langfield overseer, William Ingham

The Second Todmorden Riot: Wednesday, 21st November [28]

The first riot was as nothing compared with the destruction of the following Wednesday. The atmosphere in Todmorden was very tense, as arrangements were made to swear in most of the tradespeople and substantial householders as special constables on the following day; but for what purpose, no one could imagine.

The rioting was apparently sparked off by a rumour that the Halifax police, accompanied by soldiers, had arrived at Wood Mill and were on their way to Mankinholes to make one more attempt to take William Ingham's furniture. A thousand people quickly gathered, arming themselves with clubs and staves. They streamed down from Mankinholes to Wood Mill and, finding the rumour false, visited in turn the houses of the Guardians and other known supporters of the New Poor Law.

First they broke the newly-repaired windows at Samuel Oliver's house, where Feather had eventually found sanctuary, and again shattered the windows of the Wood Mill Inn where the Guardians held their meetings. Next, all the windows and doors were broken at the house of Royston Oliver of Mutterhole, a Guardian who had so far refused to resign, and

whom Power had described as "one of the most active Guardians in favour of the law".[29]

The rioters then went through Todmorden to Dulesgate (the area around present-day Bacup Road), where they destroyed windows, doors and furniture at the houses and mills belonging to Messrs. Ormerod at Stoneswood, William Helliwell of Frith's Mill, and William Greenwood of Watty Place. William Helliwell, a master cotton spinner, had defied public pressure and refused to resign his post as the sole Guardian for Todmorden-cum-Walsden township, and Messrs. Greenwood and Ormerod, corn millers and cotton spinners respectively, were reported to be "strenuous supporters of the obnoxious law". In the centre of Todmorden they broke the windows of the draper's shop belonging to Miss Ann Holt, who had spoken across the counter of her support for the new Law. The surgery at Bank Buildings belonging to Jeremiah Oliver, who was also the Registrar for Births, Marriages and Deaths, was next to be visited, and its contents smashed.

The greatest damage of all, estimated at about £1,000, was done at Todmorden Hall, the residence of James Taylor, Esq., surgeon, magistrate, and chairman of the Board of Guardians. Here, windows, doors, furniture and carriages were smashed, and wines, spirits and preserves were carried away from the cellar. James Suthers, beershop keeper and Assistant Overseer under the New Poor Law for the Todmorden district,

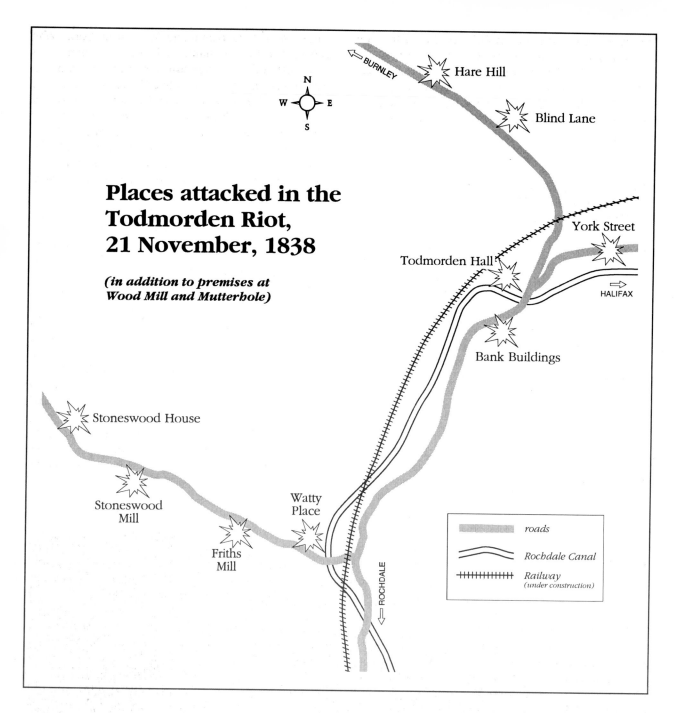

Places attacked in the Todmorden Riot, 21 November, 1838

(in addition to premises at Wood Mill and Mutterhole)

Hare Hill

Blind Lane

York Street

Todmorden Hall

HALIFAX

Bank Buildings

Stoneswood House

Stoneswood Mill

Watty Place

Friths Mill

BURNLEY

ROCHDALE

roads

Rochdale Canal

Railway
(under construction)

was in his house in Blind Lane, writing out a fresh poor rate when he was warned that the rioters were coming. It was about a quarter to six in the evening. He sent his wife and children to take refuge in the house next door, and Suthers went out, taking the township books with him for safety. His eldest son, John, was in bed, ill with typhus fever, and had to be left alone in the house. The crowd broke all the lower floor windows, tearing away the frames and curtains, and smashed pots and glasses from the beershop, before moving on to James Greenwood's house at nearby Hare Hill.[30] James Greenwood was a corn miller and Poor Law Guardian, and brother to William, whose house at Watty Place had already been attacked. Again, doors and windows were broken, and the riot began to take a very serious turn when the crowd set fire to the kitchen, breakfast-room and staircase.[31] The fire was speedily put out by one of the fire engines from Waterside Mill.

The crowd, meanwhile had returned to York Street in

Todmorden, where windows were broken in the office of James Stansfield, clerk to the Board of Guardians, and at the shop belonging to Henry Atkinson, shoemaker, who was another pro-Poor Law tradesman. The crowd was moving on towards Lowerlaithe and Millwood, where lived the Guardians William Sutcliffe and John Hill, when a person stepped amongst them, spoke to them of the illegality and folly of their actions, and persuaded them to disperse. This person was later identified as William Robinson of Stones, the Todmorden overseer and himself a strong opponent of the New Poor Law.[32] The rioters dispersed just in time. A squadron of cavalry arrived from Burnley about an hour after the rioting ceased, and they were later joined by over a hundred infantry soldiers from the same place.

On the day after the riot, a hundred and twenty special constables were sworn in, and on the following day, a virtual Council of War was held in Todmorden. It was attended by Colonel Wemyss who was the Commander-in-Chief of the District, by the commanding officers of the various regiments stationed in the district, and by the local magistrates, and not until about 10 o'clock that evening were their plans finalised, and the constables sent to summon the specials to attend at 7.30 the next morning.[33]

The Apprehension and Trial of the Rioters

On the morning of Saturday 24th November, a large force assembled in Todmorden. There was a company of Dragoons, just arrived from Manchester, more than a hundred infantry soldiers, and a hundred and twenty newly sworn-in special constables. Accompanied by the policemen who had been so brutally assaulted in the first riot, they made their way up the hill to the village of Mankinholes, and surrounded the houses and mills. The specials and other officers then entered the Fieldens' Lumbutts mill, and after arresting every male they found there, ordered the manager to stop the machinery and marched him and his men off to the White Hart Inn to be examined before the magistrates. Not a few people who had been prominent in the riot had already fled the village, but King and Feather managed to identify several participants, fourteen of

whom were then committed for trial at York. John Fielden's offer to stand bail for the men was refused,[34] and that afternoon they were put into two omnibuses and taken to York Castle. According to the *Halifax* Guardian, the crowd which turned out to see them go was dispirited and could only produce a faint "three cheers" for the prisoners. Some of the prisoners were little more than boys, and the newspaper reported that "many of them appeared completely bewildered and terrified at their situation. One poor fellow swooned away".

The prisoners named by the *Halifax Guardian* were: Joseph Taylor (25), Jeremiah Sutcliffe (18), John Walton (28), Joseph Gaukroger (27), Thomas Greenwood (22), Gibson Lord (17), John Fielden (22), William Crabtree (17), John Crabtree (19), Enoch Thomas (32), John Uttley (24), James Kershaw (25), James Kershaw (52) and Abraham Crabtree (25). They were all single men, except for John Walton, who was married with three children; Abraham Crabtree, who was married with two children; and the elder James Kershaw, who was married, and had been eleven years a soldier.[35] The records of the trial name in addition William Barrett, Arthur Lowden, and John Helliwell.[36] Richard Weatherhill, who was the first rioter named in both policemen's depositions managed, somehow, to elude trial. He later became infamous in Todmorden for a thousand pranks and escapades.[37]

Bacup Road ("Dulesgate"), the scene of the anti-Poor Law riots in 1838

Later that same day, five people were apprehended in Todmorden. Two of them, George Turner and William Lord, were identified as having been involved in the attack on Mr. Helliwell's house during the second riot and were sent for trial at Liverpool.

In January, 1839, Fielden's efforts to have the accused released on bail were at last successful, and the men held at York and Liverpool returned temporarily to Todmorden.[38] George Turner and William Lord appeared at Liverpool before Baron Parke, on Friday 5th April, 1839, on the charge of having "on the 21st November last, at Todmorden, with divers other persons, riotously assembled, and begun to pull down the house of William Helliwell and also a certain mill of the said William Helliwell". One of William Cobbett's barrister sons defended Turner, at Fielden's expense.

William Helliwell gave evidence that during the riot several hundred persons had assembled at his house, smashed his windows, broken the iron rails in front of his house and the panels out his front door, and there had been a great deal of shouting and throwing of sticks and stones, which had alarmed his wife and children greatly.

Several witnesses were called to say that they had seen the two accused men in the crowd. Turner seemed to have been more in the thick of it than Lord, who produced witnesses to give evidence that his presence had been involuntary, and that he had gone home as soon as he could. Turner was found guilty, but the jury recommended him to mercy on the grounds that he had been influenced by others, and he was sentenced to nine months hard labour in Lancaster Castle.[39]

The Mankinholes rioters were tried at York on March 21st before Mr. Baron Alderson. Their trial immediately followed that of six men charged with riot and assault during an anti-Poor Law riot in Dewsbury the previous August. The Dewsbury men were each sentenced to six months in York Castle. The seventeen Todmorden prisoners were also found guilty; but they only received what was, in effect, a suspended sentence. Each was bound over in his own recognisance in the sum of £50, on condition that he returned for sentencing when called upon to do so.[40]

Why were the Todmorden prisoners treated so leniently? The judge gave it as his opinion that: "there were parties far more deserving of punishment in reference to these transactions, than the misguided men who then stood before him for sentence".[41] The parties the authorities saw as "far more deserving of punishment", were, above all, John Fielden and his brothers, and the part Fielden had played in instigating the riots had already been the subject of an official investigation. This had come to nothing, because no reliable witnesses could be found to give evidence against Fielden. The authorities may have had in mind that the convicted Todmorden rioters (with deferred and potentially severe punishments hanging over them) might, if the need arose, be pressured into supplying the evidence needed to convict Fielden.

The Fieldens Under Investigation

Following the riots, the Government had been quick to send investigators to Todmorden to see whether there was any basis for a prosecution of John Fielden, whom, it was alleged, had virtually incited the rioting and allowed - or even encouraged - his workpeople to leave their work to join in. According to the *Halifax Guardian,* it was said in the village that prior to the first riot he had personally arranged for the bell of his Lumbutts factory to signal the arrival of the police officers, and that horsemen had been set to watch for the arrival of policemen and to report back to Waterside Mill when they came. One of the newspaper's informants said that once the news reached Waterside, the mechanics and others had made a bee-line for Mankinholes over the fields - (although another informant said that no more than forty workers had gone from Waterside, and they by stealth). Another suggestion of Fielden's involvement came from Feather and King, who reported to the

Friths Mill, attacked in 1838, but still standing in 1994

Lumbutts Mill, 1994

newspaper that men in the crowd had said they would not kill them, saying, "We will spare your lives - Mr. Fielden has told us to spare your lives".[42]

Assistant Poor Law Commissioner Alfred Power was in no doubt about John Fielden's guilt. "What has taken place has been with his connivance, and perhaps by his suggestion", he wrote to the Poor Law Commission the day after the second riot, although admitting that Fielden's responsibility would be difficult to prove. The Todmorden Board of Guardians was pressing for an example to be made of Fielden, and the Commission drew up the case against him for the consideration of the Home Secretary, Lord John Russell. The main points were: that he had said in speeches that he intended to resist the law by all means in his power; that such speeches were of a nature to encourage violent resistance; that he had declared recently that he would still resist if he lost his life for it; that he had advised a Guardian to resign with regard to his personal safety; that he had use threats and intimidation to Guardians; that it was arranged that persons with whom he was in communication should watch for the constables and give a signal, and that whilst he was in the management of his factory the bell was rung by one of his servants, and the great body of his servants went out and riotously assaulted officers of the law; that on this occasion he violated his duty as a magistrate, nor did he use any of his power as an employer to restrain his people, but rode out of the

town leaving his previous acts to operate to their natural and therefore intended effect; and that he had held out promises of payment - if not actually paid - workmen who left their work to join the riot.[43]

All of these charges related to the first riot. With regard to the second, Power believed that although John Fielden, his brothers, and one of his sons might be implicated as instigators of the riot, more probably it had been incited by the Todmorden Working Men's Association; and when it transpired that John Fielden had not been in Todmorden at all on the day of the riot, but had left for Manchester the previous day, there seemed little chance of proving any complicity.[44]

The best chance for prosecuting Fielden for his part in the riots, the authorities believed, was in connection with the use of the Lumbutts factory bell as a signal, and Colonel Wemyss was dispatched to Todmorden with the special brief of finding out who had authorised the ringing of the factory bell. Following the second riot, yet more special investigators - Sir Frederick Roe, the Chief Magistrate of Bow Street, Mr. George Maule, the Treasury Solicitor, and Mr. Goddard, a metropolitan policeman - descended on the town to assist the magistrates with their inquiries into the authorship of the riots.

Colonel Wemyss reported that it was said that it was William Robinson, one of the overseers for Todmorden-cum-Walsden, who had arranged for the Lumbutts factory bell to be rung.[45] Robinson was described by Wemyss as a steward of Joshua Fielden, which seems to suggest that Robinson was probably acting under Fielden orders; but William Robinson was far from being the vassal of the Fieldens that Wemyss's description might suggest. He was an educated man - a surveyor, who was employed to map the township on more than one occasion. He was a land steward to his kinsman and fellow-Quaker, William Greenwood; and a very substantial tenant farmer who later became a timber-dealer and builder. He was also a radical reformer who, two months before the riots took place, had chaired the inaugural meeting of the Todmorden Chartist Association (see Chapter 5). The use of the Lumbutts factory bell as a signal could easily have been arranged between Robinson and the mill-manager, Edmund Holt - who was himself deeply involved in radical politics. Holt had been a member of more than one deputation sent to "reason" with the Guardians; and most significantly, was one of the committee members of the Working Men's Association formed to make the New Poor Law unworkable in the Todmorden district.

Edmund Holt's connection with the Working Men's Association is suggestive. Alfred Power came to the conclusion, that whilst the Fieldens had almost certainly instigated the first riot, the second had probably been provoked by the Working Men's Association. This organisation numbered about five or six hundred men, and had already successfully initiated an exclusive dealing campaign, which, by withdrawing trade from Guardians and other supporters of the New Poor Law, soon had two of the Guardians, who were corn dealers by trade, complaining that they had suffered a considerable loss of custom.[46]

The Government investigators found it impossible to gather any convincing evidence against John Fielden. The town closed ranks against the outsiders. Only six people were prepared to sign depositions concerning the riots: Feather and King, the two policemen from Halifax; William Helliwell, (the sole Guardian for Todmorden-cum-Walsden), and his servant Eli Crossley; and Samuel Oliver and the widow Anne Taylor of Todmorden Hall, whose houses had been attacked by the crowd. The depositions made by Oliver and Mrs. Taylor could not have been more brief. They simply gave a short factual account of the damage done, and refused to name names. Oliver declared that "It was dark and I could not recognise any of the rioters" and Mrs. Taylor stated "I do not know the names of any of the rioters". Even the offer of a reward of £100 for information leading to the conviction of the instigator or instigators of the riots, produced no useful information.

The Guardians Backslide

After the riots, all attempts to put the New Poor Law into operation in the Todmorden Union ceased. The Guardians were paralysed by fear. Several of them resigned immediately, whilst a few continued to attend meetings, but dared not act. By December only five Guardians were still attending meetings. They reported threats, intimidation, and violence from opponents of the Poor Law in Hebden Bridge, and requested Halifax magistrates to station a military force there, in addition to the soldiers at Todmorden. A large anti-Poor-Law meeting at Hebden Bridge was being planned for Christmastime, and the Guardians feared a further outbreak of violence.[47]

A further problem was the uncertain legal status of the Todmorden Board of Guardians. The Fieldens were contesting its legality in the courts, on the grounds that, being incomplete, it was not legally competent to act; and it was not until early in 1843 that the Court of the Queen's Bench at last decided that the Board was legally constituted. Once this was decided, the Poor Law Commission made a rather belated attempt to put the Todmorden Union back on the rails, but in the meantime, the Commission took a conciliatory attitude, whilst the Guardians did everything in their power to undermine the Commission and its officers, ignore the Poor Law Amendment Act, and return as much as possible to the old ways of doing things.

The March 1839 election of Guardians produced the most incomplete and most virulently anti-Poor Law Board of Guardians yet seen in Todmorden. Neither Todmorden-cum-Walsden nor Langfield returned any Guardians at all; Erringden elected only one; three of the four Stansfield Guardians sent in their resignations before the election even took place (though they attended the meetings nonetheless); and Heptonstall elected two anti-Poor Law Chartists. So instead of the eighteen Guardians there should have been, there were only eight. Four of the eight refused to sign any orders, and so, as the chairman, Joseph Ingham of Haugh, complained to the Commissioners, "we four have all the responsibility of the Union upon us".[48] The Todmorden Board of Guardians then began to implement a scheme to dissolve the Todmorden Poor Law Union, and return to the old system of poor relief. On the 2nd July, the Guardians sent a memorial to the Poor Law Commissioners, praying them to dissolve the Todmorden Union, and informing them that the Guardians' wish was to employ one officer for each township, to be responsible for both collecting the rates and relieving the poor. Suitable officers had already been elected in vestry meetings for all the townships except Heptonstall.[49] This was a return, in all but name, to the old system of poor relief, and would make the Board of Guardians virtually redundant. It is probable that the Board intended to resign, once the scheme was in operation.[50]

Rather surprisingly, the Poor Law Commission did not immediately crack down on this blatant attempt to undermine its authority, but even appeared to sanction the new arrangements by confirming the appointment of John Barker as Assistant Overseer/ Relieving Officer for the township of Stansfield. Alfred Power had noted that Barker was a good officer,[51] and for the time being, getting competent men in post seems to have been the priority; re-arranging their areas, and separating the responsibilities of rates collectors and relieving officers could be done later. Power still had more than enough problems in Todmorden. The legal situation was still unclear; there were only four Guardians upon whose support he could rely; and Stansfield township was now threatening to join Todmorden-cum-Walsden and Langfield in refusing to supply the Guardians with funds.[52] Then in March, as their term of office drew to an end, the Board of Guardians decided to send a memorial to the Poor Law Commissioners, with a further request for them to dissolve the Union, this time on the grounds that the Union had only led to increased expenditure, and that it was impracticable to carry out the provisions of the New Poor Law in the manufacturing districts. They were angry that the poor rates in Todmorden-cum-Walsden and Langfield, which were outside the Union and managed their own affairs, were only 1s in the pound; but in the Union townships the rate ranged from 2s to 3s in the pound; and this in spite of the fact, as they said, that it was utterly impossible to economise more than they had done, and Langfield township was "notorious for behaving well to the poor".[53]

The new Board, elected in March 1840, was in Power's opinion, an improvement on the old, and he saw some prospect of progress if the legal situation

Spinks Hill Farm. In 1844, part of the building was the workhouse for Wadsworth township

could be resolved.[54] He was soon disappointed. The new Board was soon following the same course as its predecessor, resolving on the 14th August that at the end of the present quarter, it would employ only officers chosen by the ratepayers, and would dispense with the services of the auditor.[55] Power was disposed to interfere as little as possible. The neighbouring troublesome Union of Rochdale was about to be brought into operation, and so it would have been a very imprudent time to provoke trouble in Todmorden. Besides, the plan to install one officer to each township had broken down the previous year, because some of the men chosen by the ratepayers were not thought competent to fill the offices, and it might break down again.[56] But this year, some able men were elected, and Power advised sanctioning their appointments.

The Poor Law Commissioners, who had first been presented with this plan more than a year previously, and who had so far declined to either approve or condemn it, finally saw that this was a plan for virtually dissolving the Union and returning to the former township government. This, they said, they could not sanction, and would send Assistant Commissioner Charles Mott to Todmorden as soon as his other duties permitted. Mott wrote to the Commissioners from Todmorden in March 1841, promising that he would "lose no opportunity of endeavouring to get the Guardians to act more in conformity with the law",[57] but in this he had no more success than the unfortunate Power. By the previous October, the Guardians had succeeded in implementing their scheme of one officer to each township, and had followed this by deciding to meet only fortnightly. It

was still undecided whether the Todmorden Board of Guardians was legal or not, the appointments of officers made by the Guardians had neither been approved nor disallowed by the Poor Law Commission, and with these appointments still uncertain, the accounts could not be audited.

It is hardly surprising that when Charles Mott eventually made his report to the Poor Law Commission on the state of the Todmorden Union, he told them that "the whole of the proceedings of the Guardians are irregular and at variance with the law and the directives of the Commissioners". Each township had its own separate officer, and its own small workhouse. The Guardians made no regular calls for funds on the townships, merely dividing expenses such as the clerk's salary amongst the townships at the end of each quarter. Todmorden-cum-Walsden and Langfield paid nothing. He advised issuing fresh orders to Todmorden.[58]

"A Blind Resistance, against all Reason or Argument"

Almost as soon as it was decided that the Todmorden Board of Guardians, though incomplete, *was* legally constituted, the Poor Law Commissioners tried to bring Todmorden into line with the law. Assistant Commissioner Charles Clements was requested to "take an early opportunity of attending the Board of Guardians tampering with that Union", which he did at the end of April 1843. Here he found that "the whole business of the Union is at present conducted in the most unsatisfactory manner". He wanted the Union divided into proper districts for relief, with a full-time relieving officer for each. And he wanted the Guardians to meet weekly in Todmorden, in a "proper place", instead of, as they were doing, meeting once a fortnight, in a public house at Eastwood, with the clerk bringing along only such papers as he thought would be needed, and where there could be "no regularity or system in their proceedings". He attended a Guardians' meeting and persuaded them, as he thought, to redeploy their officers, appointing three of them as relieving officers, and three as assistant overseers. The Guardians seemed amenable, then, after he left, threw the motion out. "Such a transaction needs no comment", complained Clements, finding in this duplicity an example of the attitude he discovered throughout the district, "that of a blind resistance, against all reason or argument, to any proposition for the more efficient working of the Law".[59]

The Guardians were eventually persuaded to adopt a plan more to the liking of the Commissioners, and agreed to divide the Union into three districts, each formed by the union of two townships; Todmorden-cum-Walsden with Langfield, Stansfield with Heptonstall, and Wadsworth with Erringden. Each district was to have two officers, one to collect the rates, and one to give relief.[60] But if the Commissioners thought that the Todmorden Guardians had capitulated, their triumph was short-lived, for the very next day the Guardians fired a broadside on another front. They mounted their attack on the subject of workhouses.

The Workhouses of the Todmorden Union

Todmorden Union still had six small workhouses, one in each township. All of these institutions were run along similar lines. The township provided the building, equipped it with beds, bedding and other necessities, and paid for fuel. The inmates had clothing provided and were given a cash allowance with which to feed themselves. There was little, if any, supervision of the inmates, nor were they subjected to any rules or regulations. Men and women, the sick and the insane, old people and mere children, were all crammed together in the workhouse - which was often no more than a cottage - and left to get along as best they could. The conditions in these poorhouses must have been appalling, but probably no more so than in many of the cottages of the independent poor. Although these parish poorhouses were often called workhouses, they were seldom equipped for any serious work to be carried on in them, and were mostly receptacles for the aged, sick or homeless poor. The Poor Law Commissioners had a very different idea of what a workhouse should be, believing that all recipients of relief should, ideally, be housed in one large workhouse, serving the whole Union, which would be clean and well-regulated but deliberately comfortless, and whose inmates would be subject to strict rules and regulations.

In January 1844 Assistant Commissioner Clements made a report on all the workhouses in the Todmorden Union.[61] The workhouse for Todmorden-cum-Walsden township at Gauxholme, he said, occupied the middle floor of a three storey building which was built against a hill, and the paupers' accommodation was entered by way of an external staircase. There were three rooms and a windowless closet. The first room was occupied by an old woman; the second by a man, his wife and child, and two other women and a girl; the third by six men, two women and a child; and two more women slept in the closet. Some of the poor received an allowance from the overseers, whilst others went out to work. One of the paupers was supposed to be in charge of the others, and an old women was given tickets which she could take to any shop in town to get food for the children without parents.

The Stansfield workhouse occupied part of a three-storey building at Mount Pleasant, near Cockden Mill. Another part of the building was occupied by the township's Relieving Officer - although the two parts did not directly connect. The workhouse was not crowded, but, according to Clements, was filthy, littered with rags and lumber, and altogether "as disgusting a place as can well be imagined". It comprised two double rooms on the ground floor,

The old workhouse at Gauxholme, still standing in 1994

one of which was occupied by a sick old woman. On the first floor, one room was occupied by a man and his wife and another woman and child, and the other by three women and three children. In the garret, one room housed three men, another contained three men, a woman and a child, and in the third - to Clements' horror - there was a lunatic chained to a bed.

This unfortunate man was called James Ogden, and he had become of unsound mind the previous summer whilst living with his wife and family at Ovenden near Halifax. He was brought back to Stansfield (where he had his settlement), where he had attacked the Relieving Officer and hit one of the other paupers over the head with a poker. He was then boarded for four or five weeks with a farmer called Ely Stansfield, who had frequently treated lunatic paupers. Ogden improved and returned to Ovenden, but had a relapse and, as he appeared to be violent again, the Guardians directed the Relieving Officer to chain him up whilst he was in the workhouse - though he was led out to work almost every day by one of the paupers. Clement's opinion was that Ogden should have been sent to an asylum, where he would have been given appropriate treatment, but the Guardians disagreed. They usually preferred to lodge the lunatic poor locally, and in this had the support of some local doctors, who thought that the mentally disturbed would be unlikely to get "soothing and kind treatment" in an asylum.

The Langfield workhouse was a cottage at Croft Carr which belonged to the township and had room for about twenty occupants. At the time of Clement's survey it was occupied by an old woman, a woman with four illegitimate children, and two sisters, one of whom also had an illegitimate child. One of the sisters worked in the mill and supported herself, her sister and the child. The woman and her four children all slept together in one bed, the bedding of which was described as actually black with filth, and the children as dirty as could be. Conditions in the workhouses at Erringden, Wadsworth and Heptonstall were similar.

Clements' report was very critical about the workhouses, which were described in general as "one confused mess of squalid filth and wretchedness", and the Poor Law Commission wrote to the Todmorden Guardians demanding that reforms be made. Unexpectedly, the Todmorden Guardians went on the offensive, replying that they did "not think it expedient to use the workhouses in the several Townships for Union purposes... and that if the Poor Law Commissioners should consider it incumbent on them not to allow the workhouses to be used as heretofore, then the board will abandon them altogether with a view to dispense with any workhouse system whatsoever".[62]

Rather to everybody's surprise, the Poor Law Commissioners replied by authorising the Guardians to close the workhouses. They reasoned that the present arrangements being illegal, as well as totally inadequate, little would be lost by closing them down. Besides, they were intending in a short time to impose the Outdoor Labour Test Order on the Todmorden Union, thereby requiring the Guardians to set to work all the able-bodied male paupers to whom they granted relief.[63] The Labour Test had by now come to be seen by the Commissioners as a suitable alternative to workhouses for the industrial areas. Even they had by now accepted that it was not feasible in these areas to lodge all paupers in a workhouse: when there was a trade depression, no workhouse ever built could accommodate all those who required temporary help. But a similar deterrent to pauperism could be achieved by requiring that all paupers worked - often at stone breaking, or road repair - in return for relief. But only a few weeks later, the imposition of the Labour Test in Todmorden was postponed until such time as it was running smoothly in those Unions where it had already been imposed,[64] and that time never came.

The Todmorden Union continued to be a thorn in the side of the Poor Law Commissioners. The Guardians continued doggedly to relieve the poor in the customary way, and if pressure brought by the Commission occasionally succeeded in bringing their practices more into accordance with the law in one respect, the Guardians could be relied upon to find another way in which they could frustrate the Commissioners and the law. In 1853, there was a downturn in trade, and the Guardians granted relief to men who were in employment, but whose earnings were insufficient to keep their families because they were working short-time, or the mill had been stopped for a few days. The Poor Law Board pointed out that this was not permitted, and sent an inspector to give the Guardians "every advice and assistance". It was to no avail: the practice continued.

Todmorden Poor Law Union continued to run its small cottage poorhouses, in defiance of the law and the Poor Law Commissioners, well into the second half of the 19th century. By now every other Poor Law Union in the land had been brought into conformity with the law, and each, to the terror of its poor, had built its "Bastille". The Todmorden Guardians resolved in February 1852 "that a workhouse should not be built",[65] and kept to this resolve until the Poor Law Board threatened to divide Todmorden Union between Rochdale and Halifax. Thus outmanoeuvred, the Guardians procured land for a workhouse (at a place coincidentally called Beggarington) in 1873, and the first paupers were moved from the cottage poorhouses at Gauxholme, Blackshawhead and Erringden to their new home in February 1879. The building later became known as Stansfield View.

So in the end, Todmorden had to give in and build a workhouse. But by that time, the worst excesses of the mid-Victorian workhouses were a thing of the past, and attitudes towards the poor had become slightly more humane. For more than forty years, Todmorden had held out - against the Law, the Government, the Poor Law Commission and all its officers.

The Todmorden Anti-Poor Law Movement

In the view of Alfred Power and of the judges who passed sentence at the trials of the Todmorden rioters, responsibility for the violence and intransigence of Todmorden's revolt against the New Poor Law lay squarely with the Fielden family, and with John Fielden in particular.

John Fielden himself appears to have been dismayed by the destruction which took place and the possibility that he had in part incited it. Like most popular radical leaders of the time, Fielden sometimes appeared to encourage violence. On one occasion, at an anti-Poor Law meeting at Oldham, when the crowd shouted "We'll take our clogs to them" (meaning the Poor Law Commissioners), Fielden replied "That is right, take your clogs to them". On another occasion, it was alleged, he had openly declared in Todmorden that he would "fight up to the knees in blood" in resistance to the law.[66] In part he was responding to the expectations of his audience, which was composed, in the main, of the powerless and frustrated. In part it was a bluff.

John Crossley of Scaitcliffe Hall

Violent language and the threat of popular action had appeared to work at the time of the Reform agitation, and might work again. But even before the Todmorden riots, Fielden had already begun to distance himself from the more headstrong elements of the popular radical movement, especially when violence to persons seemed to be advocated. At a dinner given to Fielden by the Manchester radicals on June 4th 1838, J. R. Stephens observed that within three miles of his home there were 5,000 firearms in the hands of the people, and he only wished there were fifty times as many. But Fielden had replied that he "could not recommend the use of firearms, nor could he identify himself with any gentleman or any cause which recommended the people to provide themselves with arms for the purpose of overturning the Poor Law Amendment Act".[67]

But in Todmorden the Act *was* overturned with violence, though directed mostly at property rather than persons. After the riots, Fielden distanced himself yet further from the more extreme radicals. His support for Chartism, for example, extended to petitioning, but not much farther. But whilst the part played by John Fielden and his brothers in Todmorden's revolt against the Poor Law was a very important one, their influence can be overstated. The most noticeable aspect of the local campaign against the New Poor Law is that it involved almost the whole community and many different strands of opposition.

People who actually supported the Act were few indeed in Todmorden. The most conspicuous amongst them were John Crossley and James Taylor. John Crossley was the son of the John Crossley of Scaitcliffe who had been John Fielden's opponent in the "new church" dispute. John Crossley senior, who had died in 1830, had been the only magistrate for many miles around, and although his son was only in his early twenties when his father died, he was very soon appointed in his place and was himself the sole Todmorden magistrate until his kinsman James Taylor joined him on the bench. James Taylor was the son of Anne Crossley of Todmorden Hall, (the niece of John Crossley senior), who had married a surgeon and educated her four sons to follow in their father's profession. Taylor began to practice as a surgeon at Todmorden Hall in about 1828. The people whose property was attacked in the riots can also be counted amongst the local supporters of the New Poor Law. These included (apart from Taylor himself), the Poor Law Guardians Royston Oliver, William Helliwell and James Greenwood. Others were some of the holders of offices under the new law - James Stansfield, James Suthers and Jeremiah Oliver; and a number of tradespeople who had spoken out in favour of the Act - the Messrs. Ormerod, William Greenwood, Ann Holt and Henry Atkinson.

Some of these same people were to be found, in Dec. 1838, appealing against the poor rate set by the township of Todmorden-cum-Walsden. The appeal was partly on the grounds that they had been assessed at too great a sum and others too little, or not at all; but partly because they claimed the rate was illegal and "for purposes other than the relief of the poor". These "other purposes" were to fund the township's fight against the New Poor Law, and the objectors were John Crossley of Scaitcliffe, William Greenwood of Watty Place, John Buckley of Ridge Foot, William Helliwell of Friths House, Abraham Ormerod of Stoneswood House and John Barker of Barewise.[68] These were all very substantial men - a landowner and magistrate, two corn millers and three cotton spinners or manufactures - and it was they who formed the nucleus of the pro-Poor Law (or perhaps anti-Fielden?) faction in Todmorden. Several of them were later prominent in the anti-Corn Law agitation.

But this pro-Poor Law faction could not even rely on the support of the majority of the Guardians, many of whom were ambivalent about the Act. Joseph Ingham, who was Chairman of the Board of Guardians in 1839/40, claimed that when he came into office he was "unshackled and free from prejudice as it regards the New Poor Law...free from any feeling against the measure and unpledged as to what course he should take",[69] but within the year he was asking the Poor Law Commission to dissolve the Todmorden Union. The resolve of even the most pro-Poor Law of the Guardians was undermined by the riots; and probably the final blow came when it was revealed that the poor-rates were higher in the Union

James Taylor of Todmorden Hall

townships than in those operating illegally outside the Act. In general, the successive Boards of Guardians were prepared to put up a show of compliance with the new law, but were in fact very reluctant to depart from the old ways of doing things, particularly if this meant risking their persons, homes or businesses, or increasing expenditure without any gain to the poor.

A pivotal position in the fight against the New Poor Law was occupied by the township overseers. They were still responsible for setting and collecting the poor rates, and were therefore in a position to starve the Guardians of funds. The townships of Langfield and Todmorden-cum-Walsden had no difficulty in finding men who were of sufficient standing to act as overseers, but who were prepared to defy the New Poor Law and refuse to hand money over to the Board of Guardians. At the height of the agitation the Langfield overseer was William Ingham of Mankinholes, who was a substantial landowner. He was about 31 years of age at the time of the Mankinholes riots and had already been involved in the Reform agitation. He had at the Langfield Reform meeting in December 1830 moved a resolution in favour of vote by ballot, which he called "the only effectual preventative to bribery and undue influence at elections".[70] Subsequently he was a member of the Council of the Todmorden Political Union. He also had radical religious views, and was one of the founders of the "Black Dyke Red Barn", or Wesleyan Association Chapel at Lumbutts after the secession from the main Wesleyan body in 1835. The Todmorden-cum-Walsden overseers were William Robinson of Stones, and William Crossley of Knowlwood Mill. Robinson was another well-to-do democrat. He was a tenant farmer on a scale unusually large for Todmorden, and in 1851 farmed 132 acres and employed 18 labourers. He was a Quaker, a frequent member of the select vestry for Todmorden-cum-Walsden between 1831 and 1843, and, as already mentioned, had chaired the meeting at which Todmorden's Chartist Association was formed in October 1838.

The ratepayers of Todmorden Union demonstrated their opposition to the New Poor Law by refusing to supply statistics to the Poor Law Commissioners, promising to indemnify any overseers who were taken to court, and petitioning against the new Act. This strand of the opposition involved people from all social classes. Over 1,000 ratepayers agreed to support the Todmorden-cum-Walsden overseers in their refusal to obey the Guardians' first call for funds, and they included, as well as weavers, tradesmen and artisans, 4 gentlemen, 77 farmers, 3 ministers, and about a dozen manufacturers.[71] This, and the other petitions that were organised against the New Poor Law, were signed by such a high proportion of ratepayers, and refusals to sign were so few that, even making allowance for a degree of pressure and intimidation, there must have been an overwhelming degree of popular hostility to the New Poor Law in the Todmorden area.

The general populace kept up an atmosphere of fear and intimidation directed at anyone suspected of cooperating with the Board of Guardians or its agents. A Guardian's servant had "Bastille" or "skilly" shouted at him as he went about his master's business in the town. William Ingham, the Langfield overseer, was threatened that if he paid over to the Guardians "either money or fine (he) would be trod into the earth and (his) body cut up to make garter bands with". And Poor Law officers were threatened with assassination, and had their windows repeatedly broken.[72]

A very important part in the agitation was played by the Working Men's Association, which was formed at the end of March 1838 with the declared aim of preventing the New Poor Law from being introduced in the Todmorden Union. Colonel Wemyss reported that it was "a numerous body, holding frequent meetings, but whose proceedings are so secret that even their secretaries are known only to themselves". At the time of its formation, its chairman was Joseph Hirst, who was employed at Waterside as a power-loom overlooker, and members tickets could be obtained from John Lord of Clough Hole, Thomas Greenlees of Maltkiln, John Butterworth of Hallroyd, Edmund Holt of Lumbutts, and Abel Marland of Bottoms in Walsden. Of these men, only Edmund Holt, who was the overlooker of the Fielden's Lumbutts mill, can be identified with certainty; but it does appear that the Working Men's Association was made up chiefly of workers in the Fielden mills, and organised by the overlookers from those mills. The committee met in the schoolroom at Waterside factory, and Alfred Power later reported that the Working Men's Association had between 500 and 600 members and was chiefly composed of the Fieldens' mechanics and workmen.[73]

Others who are known to have been prominently involved in the agitation include the proposers and seconders of motions at local anti-Poor Law meetings, and the people who formed deputations to try and persuade the Guardians to bow to the popular will. A meeting held on the Kilnfield on July 6th 1838 was addressed by Mr Hudson of Eastwood; John Barker; John Holt of Waterside; John Newall; Mr. Davies, watchmaker, of Todmorden; John Lord; Jeremiah Howarth of Walsden; John Helliwell; Joseph Hirst and Charles Liddel. And at another held in May 1842 to consider petitioning for abolition of New Poor Law, Joseph Hirst was in the chair and the speakers were John Haigh, James Gibson, William Scholfield, James Lord, John Clegg, Gibson Cockcroft, William Fielden, E. Gibson, Robert Brook, Barker Greenwood and Henry Shepherd.[74] The deputation which was appointed at Kilnfield included, from the Todmorden end of the valley, "Edward" Holt of Lumbutts, and John Holt of Todmorden. And the men who, having met the Guardians, reported back to the Market place meeting a few days later, were Thomas Halliwell, William Scholfield, Thomas Thomas, Martin Mitchell, John Fielden, John Sutcliffe and Edmund Holt.[75]

Some of these people can be identified. Most of the delegates who reported back to the Market Place meeting were experienced local politicians and well-known men in the community. John Fielden himself was amongst them. Another was Thomas Thomas, a grocer and draper of North Street who served as a member of the Todmorden-cum-Walsden select vestry, as constable or as overseer on many occasions between 1821 and 1842. Martin Mitchell was the landlord of the Greyhound Inn at Wadsworth Mill. William Scholfield, ironmonger, was a frequent select vestry member and Churchwarden, who had been actively involved in the Reform agitation. Edmund Holt, who took a prominent part in every local radical agitation, was the overlooker of the Fieldens' Lumbutts Mill. Other Fielden employees, besides Holt, were active in the anti-Poor Law agitation. John Holt of Waterside was one of the speakers at the Kilnfield meeting, and also a member of the deputation appointed to speak to the Guardians. In 1831, whilst a manager or overlooker at the Fieldens' Smithyholme mill, he had been a member of the Todmorden Political Council. By 1841 he was the cotton manager at Waterside, and when he died in 1857 he was the general manager of the Waterside factory, and lived in John Fielden's old house at Dawson Weir. Joseph Hirst, the powerloom overlooker who was president of the Working Men's Association, addressed the Kilnfield meeting and chaired the 1842 one. And John Haigh may have been the John Haigh of Stoneswood who was a member of the Political Council in 1831, and an overlooker at the Fieldens' Stoneswood factory in 1851.

Not all of the anti-Poor Law activists were Fielden employees or otherwise influenced by the Fieldens. One of the men who spoke at the Kilnfield meeting was George Davies, a watch and clock-maker who lived and worked at Salford in Todmorden in the late 1830s and early 1840s. He must have spoken for many like himself when he said:

"He knew that there were individuals who had exerted themselves to introduce the law here, and who said that the feeling against it was caused by Mr. Fielden's influence. But he (Mr. Davies) would tell those individuals that three words had never passed between him and Mr. Fielden, and therefore he could not be influenced by that gentleman. It was his own feelings that had led him to do what he had done, and to say what he had said, and many others acted from similar motives".[76]

George Davies was right in so far as hatred of the New Poor Law was so deep and so general in Todmorden, that it cannot simply be attributed to John Fielden. But he and his brothers had encouraged that hatred, and encouraged the people to believe that, no matter what excesses might occur, they would have the protection of the wealthy and influential Fielden family.

Chapter 5

Chartism in Todmorden

The groundwork for a renewed agitation for the working-class vote was laid in the North by Feargus O'Connor who, in December 1835 and January 1836, toured the manufacturing districts of Lancashire and Yorkshire, setting up Radical Associations to campaign for the suffrage. In January 1838 he began to publish the *Northern Star* newspaper. Published in Leeds with a discernable northern emphasis, it was a quality paper that carried news and opinion on just about every topic that was likely to interest its radical working-class readership, including co-operation, emigration, utopian communities, trade unionism, radical poetry and Parliamentary debates, as well as the latest news in the campaigns against the New Poor Law and in favour of factory legislation and universal manhood suffrage. Most importantly, it acted as a noticeboard whereby Radical societies and organisations - even those in tiny villages - could keep abreast of developments in the national movement, and advertise their own meetings and lectures.

At about the same time that O'Connor was opening the campaign in the North, a group of people were coming together in the capital to form the London Working Men's Association. With this group originated the "People's Charter", drafted as a petition in January 1837 and published the following year, which called for the famous six points of electoral reform: universal manhood suffrage, vote by ballot, annual Parliaments, equal electoral districts, payment of members of Parliament, and the abolition of property qualifications for MPs.

In January 1838, when the Halifax Radical Association celebrated its third anniversary, there were twelve Radical Associations in the parish of Halifax.[1] But there was none as yet in Todmorden, which had not been included in Feargus O'Connor's tour of the manufacturing districts. The place of such an association may have been partly filled by the old Todmorden Political Union, which, as we have seen, continued in existence after the passing of the Reform Act to support the radical agenda and John Fielden's Parliamentary efforts - but, if so, it appears to have faded away before the Chartist agitation

began in earnest. The Todmorden Working Men's Association was founded at the end of March 1838, and, although its initial and most pressing concern was with defeating the New Poor Law, it is probable that it was, in fact, a Chartist organisation. Its name suggests a connection with the London Working Men's Association, which had sent missionaries to the North a short time previously, and some of the leading members of the Todmorden W.M.A. were strong supporters of the Chartist movement.

Chartism was a significant force in national politics in the decade 1838-1848, but the progress of the movement was not smooth and continuous, but marked by three great surges of activity - one in 1839, one in 1842, and one in 1848. Each was fuelled by an economic crisis, and each featured a great national petitioning campaign involving the collection of millions of signatures, the presentation of the petition to Parliament, and the rejection of the petition by an overwhelming majority in the House of Commons, followed by angry months in which rumours of arming and drilling were rife, and rebellion or even outright revolution feared.

The First National Petition

The first campaign to draw up a National Petition in support of the Charter was opened in the North with a huge Universal Suffrage meeting on Kersal Moor near Manchester. This was followed by dozens of smaller local meetings in surrounding towns and villages, at which the National Petition was adopted and local delegates elected to attend a National Convention of the Labouring Classes which was to be held in the new year. The first of these local meetings was at Todmorden, held on Springwellfield on September 28th 1838, at which two or three thousand people gathered to hear stirring speeches by Feargus O'Connor, the popular Northern Chartist orators the Rev. J. R. Stephens and Dr. Fletcher, and Todmorden's own John Fielden. This was the first visit to Todmorden for O'Connor, who later became a frequent and popular visitor to the town. He had not been to Todmorden previously, he said, because the working classes of the town "had already constituted as their Parliamentary leader a man whose kindness of heart and disposition had endeared him to the working classes of that happy valley". That man was, of course, John Fielden: who, addressing the meeting as neighbours and friends, gave a long and enthusiastically-received speech in which he advised his hearers to combine together peaceably to demand their political rights, and not to be distracted by any offers of piecemeal reform. He was glad that the people of Todmorden had commenced this movement, he said, and especially glad that they had done it themselves, he having had nothing to do with it, and knowing nothing of it until he had seen the placards on the wall calling the meeting.

The chairman of the meeting was William Robinson of Stones, the anti-Poor Law overseer for Todmorden-cum-Walsden. To loud cheers from the crowd assembled on Springwellfield, he castigated the conduct of the Whig Government, deplored the way in which the people's hopes for reform had been disappointed in 1832, and spoke of "that right of representation in Government to which all men are by nature entitled, and without which they must for ever remain slaves". Resolutions were passed endorsing the right to universal suffrage, adopting the National Petition, and agreeing to send William Greenwood, grocer, as Todmorden's delegate to the National Convention. Joseph Hirst and George Davies, whom we have also already met as anti-Poor Law activists, were amongst the proposers and seconders of the resolutions.[2]

The Chartist cause quickly attracted a mass following locally. Within a few short months of the birth of the Radical Association, the trustees of York Street Methodist Chapel were attributing the difficulty of attracting new members partly to "The Political spirit which almost universally prevails in this part of our Country...Nearly all the inhabitants of this densely populated vale are radicals. Many of them instead of attending the Lord's house (at least on the Lord's day) dispise (sic) all religion...and their Sabbaths are chiefly spent in reading over the *Northern Star*, 270 copies of which come into Todmorden weekly".[3]

By June, the Todmorden Radical Association had collected over seven thousand signatures to the petition calling for the adoption of the Charter. Nationally, more than a million signatures were collected, and the National Convention met to organise the presentation of the petition to Parliament. John Fielden and the Birmingham radical Thomas Attwood agreed to present the petition to the House of Commons. This they did on July 12th, but the House rejected the petition by 235 votes to just 46. The National Convention was unable to agree on what further measures, if any, should be taken and dissolved itself at the beginning of September. It was widely rumoured that a national uprising was planned, with South Wales, the West Riding of Yorkshire and Scotland taking the lead.

Only the Chartists of South Wales attempted a rising, and that was a sorry affair. In the early hours of November 4th, 1839, a body of armed Chartists marched on Newport. The magistrates, forewarned, had concealed soldiers in the Westgate Hotel, and when the Chartists stormed the building a number of them were shot dead and the rest fled to the hills. John Frost, Zephaniah Williams and William Jones, the leaders of the revolt, were quickly arrested, convicted of high treason, and sentenced to death by hanging, drawing and quartering. A few days later the sentence was commuted to transportation for life.

It may be, as often claimed, that the Welsh rising was intended as a signal to spark off a chain of revolts across the country, and that its failure aborted a national rising. In the West Riding rumour was rife, but there was no concerted Chartist rising - only isolated insurrectionary outbursts in Sheffield, Dewsbury and Bradford in January 1840. But there is evidence that Chartists in the village of Midgley - only six miles from Todmorden - were making preparations for armed revolt:

"Midgley men made weapons for themselves out of bars of iron, scythes and the like, and it was related to me long ago that they even experimented with home-made bombs in the form of gunpowder in bottles which they exploded by way of experiment in Well Lane below Lacy Hey".[4]

The Second National Petitioning Campaign

In the spring of 1840, the Chartist movement was disorganised and dispirited. The failure of the isolated revolts of the winter - humiliating enough in itself - had been followed by the arrest and imprisonment of nearly every Chartist leader of note. In July the National Charter Association was formed to coordinate and revitalise the movement. It established a five-member Chartist Executive, based in Manchester, which directed the movement as a whole and the activities of its paid lecturers. The Executive was supported by the contributions of the local Chartist associations, whose members paid 2d for a membership card, and 1d a week thereafter, and were organised, on a plan adopted from the Methodists, into "classes" with about ten members to each.

The new plan was quickly adopted by Chartists in the nearby towns of Halifax, Milnrow, Rochdale, Oldham, Burnley and even little Sowerby, who in the spring of 1841 were all actively promoting the cause; but seemingly all was quiet in Todmorden.

Then in July 1841, amidst the excitement of a general election, Todmorden Chartism was revived. Charles

Towneley, a rich Whig landowner of Towneley Hall near Burnley, was intrepid enough to address a meeting in Todmorden market place. He was heckled by the Chartists, and that evening many new recruits joined the Chartist Society, which began to meet weekly at Samuel Barker's house at Toad Carr. Soon it had attracted so many new members that a new meeting room was opened in Millwood. On Sunday 5th September a camp meeting was held on Langfield Common and about 3,000 people gathered to hear the Chartist lecturer, Dr. McDouall. By September, the Chartist Society was holding its meetings in the large lecture room of the Mechanics' Institute in Bridge Street. Visits from Chartist lecturers were arranged, and at the end of October, the Todmorden Chartists could report:

> "The Chartist cause is getting on bravely here
> - since our last notice in the Star we have got
> 24 new members, and we have formed a
> debating society connected with the society,
> which is likely to do a great amount of
> good".[5]

During the early months of 1842 the Todmorden Chartists threw themselves into the new campaign with such enthusiasm that again and again they earned the praise of the Chartist Executive for their dedication and hard work. It seemed in these months that the whole town was bent upon the single object of getting the People's Charter made law.

As the new petitioning campaign got under way, the Todmorden Chartists systematically canvassed the district and succeeded in collecting 8,400 signatures[6] - even more than the 7,328 that had been collected towards the first petition in 1839. The population of the three Todmorden townships was just over 19,000 in 1841, many of whom were juveniles, or inhabitants of the Blackshawhead district which would have been canvassed by the Colden Association, which was formed in January 1842. So the eight thousand people who signed the Charter would have represented most of the adults living within two or three miles of the town of Todmorden.

This second great Chartist campaign took place against the backdrop of the deepest trade depression that there had been for many years. The first signs of a downturn in trade had become apparent locally in the summer of 1841. Trade was slack, and the mills were soon working short time. A letter published in the *Northern Star* in December 1841 described the impoverished condition of the people as observed by a pedlar, or "travelling Scotchman" as he described himself. For twenty years he had been travelling the country between Todmorden, Saddleworth, Shaw, Lees, Oldham, Middleton, Heywood, Wardle and Rochdale, and had seen his customers becoming gradually poorer. Many houses which he had known well-furnished were now stripped, the furniture having been gradually disposed of to buy food, and

The Centre of Todmorden in the early 1840s

now his customers were mostly ruined and unable to buy the clothing, tea and coffee, and other things they used to buy from him. Six years ago, he reported, Todmorden had been his best district, but it was now very much worse, and the mills there had been working short time for months.

The situation was to get much worse before there was any improvement. The township book for Stansfield - the only surviving local record charting the progress of the distress - shows that in 1840, Stansfield township usually gave poor relief to about 600 persons a quarter, depending upon the season. During the final quarter of 1841, the number needing relief shot up to 876; and in the first quarter of 1842, there was another huge increase to 1550 paupers being relieved by the township, at a cost of £613 10s, or about twice the 1840 average. The population of the township at this time was about 8,500, so nearly 1 in 5 people was in receipt of poor relief. This was a burden that the township could not bear alone, and at the beginning of August a local distress committee was formed to apply to the Manufacturers' Relief Committee for assistance.[7]

In spite of the hardship of the times, Todmorden was extraordinarily successful at raising funds for Chartist causes. The balance-sheet of the Chartist Executive for the period January-April 1842 showed that Todmorden had contributed more than any other locality, and the thanks of the whole Chartist body were offered "to the Halifax district, to Todmorden, London, the Potteries, Nottinghamshire and other places, who have done their duty so well".[8] In July 1842 the General Secretary of the Chartist Executive congratulated the Chartists of Todmorden on raising more money than any other place enrolled in the Association, saying that "If every place acted like Todmorden, the Executive might employ twenty lecturers next week".[9] The money was raised in part from members' contributions. In November 1841, Todmorden had only had an association for four months and had already paid for 150 membership cards, and new members joined the association after each of the Chartist lectures that were becoming a frequent fixture of Todmorden life. Chartist balls and tea-parties were also organised to raise funds. They were very well attended, and raised considerable sums. Money was also raised by selling products whose manufacturers donated a proportion of their profits to the cause. One such product was "Pinder's blacking", which could be obtained from Robert Brook of George Street, James Gibson of Shade, Enoch Horsfall of Millwood and William Cunliffe of Dobroyd.[10] Another was "The Yorkshire Chartist Beverage or Breakfast Powder", which was manufactured by Thompson Brothers, wholesale tea-dealers of Halifax, who donated 10% of the proceeds of sale to the Chartist Council.

The female Chartists of Todmorden made a very large contribution to these fund-raising activities. Their association seems to have been formed early in 1842, just before that of the Hebden Bridge women,[11] of whom the *Northern Star* reported in February 1842 that: "At a meeting of the Chartist Council of Hebden Bridge, on Wednesday evening, the 2nd inst., a number of females attended and came to a resolution to form a Female Chartist Association at the above place". The women then elected a treasurer, secretary and chairman - all of them men. The Todmorden women's first venture was to organise a tea and entertainment at the Chartist meeting on New Year's Day, 1842. Then in February, they put on a tea party and ball which featured country dances, and comic and sentimental songs and recitations, and which was so well-attended that it had to occupy two of the largest rooms in Todmorden at the time - one in the Mechanics' Institute, and one in the York Tavern. This event raised more than five pounds towards the expenses of the National Convention. The women organised another ball in May to raise money for the wives and families of the transported Welsh Chartists, Frost, Williams and Jones. The women did not restrict themselves to fund-raising, either, but took an active part in the political agitation, holding their own meetings and inviting their own lecturers.

The second National Petition claimed over 3 million signatures; but when it was presented to the House of Commons on 1st May, this one also was dismissed contemptuously, by a vote of 287 against to only 49 in favour.

In spite of this set-back, Chartist activity continued unabated throughout the summer. The Todmorden Chartists were busy with meetings, balls and lectures, were still enrolling new members, and at the beginning of June announced that "We now number 700 members, male and female". When summer came, great camp meetings were held on the commons and the moors, and whole families would climb up into the hills to enjoy the fresh air and the company, to listen to the speeches and join in the singing of Chartist hymns. A camp meeting at Heyhead Green in Langfield one June Sunday was attended by 1,500 people, in spite of terrible weather which forced an adjournment to the Oddfellows' Hall. A few weeks later, Feargus O'Connor visited the upper Calder Valley, and was met by 20,000 people at Luddenden Bar - so many that when he addressed them, the hillside appeared "one living mass of living Chartist" (sic)[12] They then formed a great procession to accompany him to Todmorden, but were caught in a downpour and had to quickly secure a large building on the outskirts of the town in which to take refuge. Throughout July, the Chartist lectures continued, and new members continued to enrol - fifty after a lecture by Thomas Cooper of Leicester, "many" following a lecture by Mr. Marsden of Preston, another twenty-one after a talk by Mr. McCartney of Liverpool.

The slump in trade was by now the deepest there had been for many years, and most of the operatives were out of work, or only partially employed. In Stansfield township, average weekly earnings for people in full work had dropped to 9s for men, 5s for women and 2s 6d for children. But the majority of the workpeople were only partially employed, and their average earnings were only 2s 6d for men, 1s for women and 6d for children. Then there were 205 men, 440 women and 1165 children who were unemployed and destitute. Most of these were entitled to relief from the Stansfield overseers, but 267 of them had no settlement in Stansfield and nearly half of these were not being relieved by their own Poor Law Unions, and so were utterly without income from any source.

The Great Strike or "Plug Riots" of 1842 [13]

For a few days in the middle of August 1842, to the great alarm of the respectable and propertied classes, the utmost confusion reigned in the industrial districts of Britain. Hundreds of thousands of operatives had left their work and were refusing to return until wages were restored to 1840 levels. Some of them were further demanding that the Charter be immediately granted. The strikes had begun in the Midlands, and then spread to Yorkshire, Lancashire, Tyneside and parts of Scotland and Wales, bringing manufacturing and coal-mining to a standstill in these districts. The larger towns were thronged with threatening bands of out-of-work operatives. In Preston, Salford, and Halifax, amongst other places, there were clashes between the strikers and the military. Many feared the strike developing into a Chartist uprising, and on August 13th the situation was considered sufficiently grave for the Queen to issue a proclamation commanding the Justices of the Peace to do their utmost to apprehend and bring to justice those persons who had lately "assembled together in a riotous and tumultuous manner", and used threats and intimidation to prevent people following their usual occupation. As a further inducement, a £50 reward was offered for information leading to a conviction.

The authorities perceived the unrest as all the more threatening because the series of strikes appeared to be conducted according to a well-thought-out plan. The strike was carried from town to town by a rolling programme of turn-outs. The strikers from one town, arming themselves with thick bludgeons, marched to the next, immobilising each mill on the way by knocking the plug out of the boiler. The turn-outs usually warned that if the mill was re-started without their permission they would come back and burn it down. Then they left, with the workers from the newly turned-out mill often accompanying them to the next place. There was remarkably little damage done or violence offered. Most of the mill-owners preferred to co-operate with the deputation of determined strikers who requested that they, or the mill-engineer, be permitted to rake out the fire and remove the plug from the boiler rather than have the mill over-run by the angry crowd which stood behind the deputation.

But if the strikes were pre-planned, who lay behind them? Contemporaries were uncertain on this point, and historians still dispute it. Some thought the Chartists responsible. But the national Chartist leaders seemed to be taken genuinely unawares by the strikes, and were divided amongst themselves as to how to respond. On the other hand, local studies are demonstrating overwhelmingly that some of the people who were most conspicuously involved in the 1842 strikes (or at least, those who were prosecuted for their involvement), had a long history of participation in local Radical and Chartist politics. This was the case in Todmorden as elsewhere. Other contemporaries, including Feargus O'Connor, believed that the strikes had been deliberately provoked for political ends by the Anti-Corn Law League, by inducing its members to reduce the wages of their operatives at a time when such reductions would be bound to meet with resistance. In the summer of 1842, after a long depression, trade was beginning to improve and a good harvest was in prospect. Under such circumstances big cuts in wages would be widely perceived as unjust. The reports of the Lancashire and Yorkshire strikes in the *Halifax Guardian* do quite frequently refer to League members welcoming the strikes when they came, but perhaps, like some of the local Chartists, they simply hoped to profit from a situation not of their making.

The Lancashire and Yorkshire strikes started when the masters of Ashton-under-Lyne, whether under the inspiration of the Anti-Corn Law League or from some other motive, attempted to reduce the wages of their workpeople by 25%. The Ashton workers struck, and over the next few days the strike spread to nearby towns and then to Manchester. There the strike was endorsed by a conference of trades' delegates, and on Thursday 11th August processions of strikers marched to Rochdale, Stockport and Oldham, where they stopped the mills by knocking the plugs out of the boilers.

Next morning, Todmorden was visited by the turn-outs. The *Halifax Guardian* reported that:
> "One party came from Rochdale,
> Littleborough and the neighbourhood;
> another came over the hills from Bacup. The
> latter was a most formidable looking force,
> being composed entirely of upgrown
> determined looking men, who were all
> armed with thick hedge stakes. Some idea
> may be formed of the numbers of the mob,
> when it is stated that it took about twenty
> minutes for them to pass a given point".

The Todmorden magistrates had been expecting the turn-outs and had sworn in about two hundred special constables in preparation. They had also sent to Burnley for military assistance and a troop of about thirty Hussars arrived that morning. Messrs. Fielden's works were the first to be visited by the strikers. The commanding officer of the Hussars and the magistrates John Crossley and James Taylor went to John Fielden and offered him their assistance if he would

The Dusty Miller Inn, Mytholmroyd, visited by the plug-drawers

hold out against the mob, but he declined, saying that the people only wanted a fair day's wage for a fair day's work, and this they ought to have. John Crossley viewed the strike in a more political light: it was his understanding, he said, that the people wanted to be the masters and make the laws.[14] But again Fielden turned down his offer of protection, and not the slightest opposition was offered to the turn-outs by any member of the firm, and one of the partners even distributed money amongst them, adding also that the firm was quite willing to agree to the wage rates being demanded.

Each mill in Todmorden was then visited in succession, the boiler fire raked out, the plugs removed, and the workers ordered to quit the premises. Only slight resistance was offered by any of the mill-owners, and no injury or violence was done. The turn-outs also visited many of the provision shops and public houses, where bread and ale were freely given to them, the shopkeepers and innkeepers thinking themselves fortunate to get off so lightly. When all the mills had been stopped a public meeting was held and resolutions passed that there should be no return to work until the wages of 1840 were restored; that females having children, even one, should cease to work where machinery was used; and that the hours of labour should henceforth be ten a day. The speakers - none of them Todmorden men - urged the people to keep the peace and injure no man or property, then they would gain their cause. The turn-outs then left the town, leaving the Todmorden people to meet again that evening, confirm the previous resolutions, and agree to join the Rochdale people the following morning in turning out the mills of Hebden Bridge, Mytholmroyd and Cragg Vale.

At about seven o'clock on the morning of Saturday 13th August, the Todmorden strikers began to gather

near the railway arches in the centre of town under the watchful eye of John Heap, constable. "The meeting on Saturday morning was I should judge", he later deposed "attended by upwards of 2,000 persons - the larger part of the number were armed with sticks and bludgeons some of them very large - about eight o'clock the mob left the ground where they had met and proceeded principally in a body from Todmorden towards Mytholmroyd".[15]

They reached Hebden Bridge at about nine, by which time their numbers had been considerably augmented by the workers from the mills they had turned out along the way. The *Halifax Guardian* commented on the large number of women amongst the turn-outs, and how at Hebden Bridge, forcible entry was made into many houses "and demand made for bread, tea, sugar &c., the latter (they said) they wanted "for th'wimmin" ". The mill-owners of Hebden Bridge offered no resistance and the mills were soon stopped. The procession of turn-outs was now so long that it took nearly two hours to pass through Machpelah Bar on its way to Mytholmroyd. At Mytholmroyd the principal mill, which belonged to Walker and Edmondson, was stopped without any opposition. By now the crowd was hungry and food was demanded and supplied at two gentlemen's houses, and the Dusty Miller public house was beset by thirsty strikers demanding beer.

The turn-outs now proceeded up the Cragg Valley stopping all the mills as they went. An account of the stopping of Joseph Hinchliffe's Highest Mill was later given in evidence by Thomas Marshall who worked there as a cotton rover. He said that at about 11.30 on Saturday 13 August four men, all of whom were armed with thick bludgeons, came into the mill premises and asked for the overlooker. Marshall recognised one of the men as William Smith, a Langfield man whom he had known for at least a dozen years. Mr. Hinchliffe, junior, was on the premises and at first refused to co-operate with the turn-outs, so the four men waited till about a hundred more came up and then they set to work trying to release the water from the dam. They had brought a handle with them, but when they could not get it to fit, they started to talk about tearing the dam bank down. At this point Mr. Hinchliffe sent the handle out of the mill, and the water was run off from the reservoir which was the only large one in the valley and served several mills. The turn-outs then left, but warned that if (as they suspected they might) the workpeople resumed work once they had left, they would come back and burn the place down.[16]

The Halifax magistrates had feared the turn-outs might reach their town on Saturday afternoon. Some did get as far as Sowerby, but large numbers of the Todmorden strikers, after stopping the mills in Cragg Vale, made their way back home over the hills by way of Stoodley, and Sunday passed quietly. Determined to resist the expected invasion of turn-outs from the Todmorden valley, the Halifax magistrates spent the day formulating their plans. Some tradesmen were even called out from their places of worship to be sworn in as special constables.

On Monday morning there were two companies of infantry, two troops of Hussars, and two or three hundred special constables mustered in Halifax Piece Hall, awaiting the arrival of the Todmorden turn-outs, when the unexpected news came that a large crowd from Bradford was coming to assist the Lancashire strikers, and was about to enter the town. The entire force was dispatched to block the entry of the Bradford contingent. The Riot Act was read and the Bradford turn-outs appeared to withdraw - but only to make a detour through the fields and join with the Todmorden force, which was even now entering Halifax entirely unopposed. The *Halifax Guardian* estimated that the turn-outs from Todmorden formed a procession of about 10,000 people, 4,000 of whom were women marching four abreast in the centre of the procession singing Chartist hymns as they went. Another 10,000 people accompanied them, but not in processional order, and the Bradford turn-outs who joined them numbered between 4,000 and 5,000. Altogether, about 25,000 strikers invaded Halifax that morning.

At the top of Park Street they were met by the military. Again the Riot Act was read, and placards reading "The Riot Act has been read. Disperse immediately" were displayed, but only attracted the jeers of the crowd. Again the militancy of the women was noticeable: "approaching to the very necks of the horses they declared they would die rather than starve, and if the soldiers were determined to charge they might kill them". The soldiers were now ordered to clear the street and they formed a compact line and began to move slowly forward. Voices from the crowd urged resistance, and one man was arrested. He was William Southwell, of Mytholmroyd, and was, or had been, an overlooker at Messrs. Fielden's mill. Throughout the morning the soldiers harried the crowd. They opened fire on them more than once, and there were several skirmishes between the rioters and the military. Nonetheless, the turn-outs, by waiting until the soldiers were engaged elsewhere, and then going into the mills and knocking out the plugs, succeeded in stopping nearly all the mills in Halifax. Seventeen more men were arrested. Some were Halifax men, most came from the surrounding towns and villages. One of them, James Sutcliffe, was from Todmorden.

The next day, Tuesday 16th August, there were two serious riots in Halifax - the first in the vicinity of Salterhebble, and the second on Haley Hill. Very early in the morning the magistrates, fearing that an attempt would be made to liberate the prisoners, arranged to have them taken to a place of safety and they were put into two omnibuses and taken under military escort to Elland Station. As they passed through Elland Wood the large crowd gathered there hurled a volley of stones at the soldiers, but they passed without serious incident, and the prisoners were put on the train on their way to the House of Correction at Wakefield. The soldiers, fearing an ambush on their return, took a different route but they were seen as they came down Exley Bank near Salterhebble. An immense crowd had taken up positions on the high ground overlooking the road and armed themselves with stones which they rained down upon the soldiers. None was killed, but Mr.

The Rioters at North Bridge, Halifax

A Chartist meeting at the Basin Stone

Brook, a Halifax magistrate, had his arm broken by the force of an enormous coping stone, and three of the Hussars were unhorsed and badly cut and bruised by the torrent of stones which descended on them. The special constables and the rest of the soldiers were sent to the aid of the Hussars, and the crowd dispersed in the direction of Skircoat Moor where a meeting was convened and a resolution passed that they should next visit Messrs. Akroyd's weaving shed at Haley Hill, - known as "the Shade". Meanwhile the magistrates had determined to clear the Halifax streets of strangers, and had advised the townspeople to keep indoors and ordered the publicans to close the inns and beershops. The Shade and a nearby mill at Bowling Dyke had been thoroughly barricaded against an attack. Armed men had been set to guard both the Shade and Edward Ackroyd's mansion at Bankfield, and a man had been set to watch on Haley Hill and telegraph for the military if they should be required.

At about four o'clock, the turn-outs began to congregate in the vicinity of Haley Hill and the military were sent for. A shot was fired by someone in the crowd which hit one of the officers on the epaulet. Some stones were thrown, and then the soldiers were ordered to fire. A volley was fired at the crowd and several persons were wounded. Then the Hussars dashed up the hill, striking severe blows with their sabres. They were followed by the infantry with bayonets at the ready. "The people" reported the *Halifax Guardian* "appeared terror-stricken". The special constables were shouting to the people to return to their homes, and made thirty-three arrests of apparent ringleaders. It is impossible to say just how many people were injured in Halifax that day. Between them, the *Halifax Guardian* and John Waterhouse, J.P., named ten of the most severely injured.[17] These included a Northowram man who died of his bullet-wound the following day, a Skircoat man who suffered such a severe sabre blow to his head that it split his skull and exposed his brains, and an Ovenden man whose leg, shattered by a bullet, had to be amputated. A further eight or ten people were treated anonymously at a druggist's shop. They had mostly suffered cuts to their hands, which they had raised to defend their heads. Another man had two ribs broken by being trampled by the cavalry, and five or six of the men who were taken prisoner had sabre or bayonet wounds. Others, no doubt, were hurt but were carried away by their friends and their wounds dressed in secret.

There were no Todmorden men amongst the wounded or the prisoners that day, but there were some from the upper Calder Valley. Samuel Bates, a weaver from Cragg, was wounded by a sword cut to the head as well as being taken into custody. An unnamed mill-hand from Hebden Bridge was bruised on the head. Those arrested included Eli Hoyle, a Midgeley weaver, and H. Greenwood, a weaver who had lived at Heptonstall until the previous week.

By seven o'clock that evening, the streets of Halifax were deserted except for the soldiers and constables parading the town. Hundreds, if not thousands, of the turn-outs had taken refuge upon the hills, and when night fell they quietly slipped away. The next day all was quiet in Halifax. Some of the mill-owners met and agreed to re-start their mills the following day, and by Monday 22nd of August it was reported that all the Halifax mills were back at work.

On the morning of Thursday 18th of August, whilst in Halifax the mills were re-opening and the operatives returning to work, the Todmorden strikers were gathering at Basin Stone, high on the moors above Walsden, to hear the report of Robert Brook who had just returned from a meeting of Chartist delegates in Manchester. According to William Heap (the brother of John Heap the constable) Brook spoke of tens of thousands of men ready to back the strikers; and he moved that they never go to work any more till the Charter be got, adding that those who could not do without working must go to the overseers, and if they would not relieve them, "we'll try some means else".[18]

Todmorden continued in a state of excitement for some days more. Dr. Peter McDouall - who was a member of the Chartist Executive and was one of those who was most strongly in favour of turning the strike into an all-out demand for the Charter - was reported to be at the Dog and Partridge Inn at Lumbutts; but made his escape out the back door before the constables could apprehend him. Most of the people were not working, being either on strike, or unemployed. Even before the strike, so many men, women and children had been out of work, or only partially employed and unable to live on their earnings, that the overseers' resources had been nearly exhausted and steps had been taken to set up Relief Committees. On 15th August, as the Todmorden strikers invaded Halifax, the Stansfield Relief Committee resolved to meet weekly and give relief in both money and kind. On the 22nd, with Todmorden still on strike, it placed an order for seven loads of the best oatmeal each week, and ruled that "None of those who have thrown themselves out of employ in the recent Turn-Out receive any assistance from this Fund".[19] But by Friday 26th August most of the mills in Todmorden had returned to work, except for the Fielden's mills which were expected to resume on the Monday.

In some places, the threatened wage reductions were cancelled, or the wage-levels of 1840 were restored, and so the plug-drawing strikes did achieve some of their industrial objectives. But as a political agitation they were a total failure. They brought the achievement of the Charter no nearer, nor could mass protest of this kind ever succeed as long as the Government was prepared to use military force against the strikers. The crowd had on their side the moral and physical authority of their huge numbers: but they had no reply to the guns, sabres and bayonets of the military, and when these were deployed against them they tended to react with astonished terror.

The Trials of the Rioters

It now remained only to try those arrested during the riots. There were four Todmorden men amongst the accused. Three of them had taken a leading part in stopping mills on the 13th August. Thomas Pollard, with another man, had knocked out the plug of the boiler at William Hinchliffe's mill at Scarbottom near Mytholmroyd. William Smith had been one of the men who stopped Joseph Hinchliffe's mill at Cragg Vale. And John Crowther and others had stopped John Titterington's mill at Sowerby.[20] The fourth man was James Sutcliffe, who had been arrested in Halifax two days later. Sutcliffe was described as an active participant in the Halifax riot, who had encouraged the crowd to remain after the Riot Act had been read. He was sentenced to five months imprisonment. Pollard and Smith each got four months, and Crowther got three. All the sentences were for imprisonment with hard labour.

A Todmorden man was arrested in Bradford during the riots. He was Sutcliffe Marshall, a 20 year old tinner, who was committed to the Wakefield House of Correction as a vagrant.[21] The Vagrancy Act was used against rioters in Halifax as well as Bradford, as a committal could be obtained simply by proving that the offender was on private property for an unlawful purpose - it was not necessary to prove any particular act of riot.

The last Todmorden man to be taken into custody in connection with the events of August 1842 was Robert Brook. He was arrested early in September, as were many of the most conspicuous Chartists in the North-West, including Feargus O'Connor, Peter McDouall, Christopher Doyle and George Julian Harney. Fifty-nine Chartists stood trial at Lancaster in March 1843, on a charge of seditious conspiracy, or more specifically, that they "had by large assemblies endeavoured by force, threats and intimidation, to breed such alarm in the country as to produce a change in the Constitution". Some papers found in Brook's possession were produced in evidence showing that he had been at the meeting of Chartist delegates in Manchester on 16th and 17th August. William Heap testified that Brook had, at the Basin Stone meeting on 18th August, encouraged the strikers to stay out until the Charter be obtained. Brook was defended by Mr. Dundas, QC, which shows that he must have had some wealthy friends, as Brook himself was a poor schoolmaster and could not have afforded to hire counsel from his own resources. Most of the other Chartists were undefended. Brook was found guilty of encouraging violence to obtain the Charter, but the convictions were overruled on the grounds that the indictment had been faulty, and all the defendants were set free.[22]

A Harsh Winter

During the autumn of 1842, the Stansfield Distress Committee organised work on road-repair in return for relief. The scheme started at the end of August, and in the first week 50 men were employed in stone-getting, at which they earned about 5s each, and 1630lbs meal were distributed amongst 103 families. The weekly distributions of meal continued until the middle of October, and then the remaining funds were used to employ diminishing numbers of the able-bodied men until the year's end.

As winter approached the Committee began to be concerned about the lack of clothing amongst the poor. They visited 467 families in the township and found great poverty, particularly amongst the hand-loom weavers who, although in "full work" were utterly unable to afford clothing and bedding. It was decided to apply the latest funds received towards clothing and bedding, and a few days before Christmas there was a grand distribution of 230 pairs of cotton blankets, 140 coverlets, 1856 yards of calico and 252 pairs of clogs, which were apportioned amongst 468 families. It is particularly ironical that calico cloth should have been the chief article distributed, as most of these families were calico weavers and their dependants.

The Anti-Corn Law League

In these lean years of the early 1840's, with so many of the working people in need of the most basic necessities of life, Chartism offered a political solution to their predicament. An alternative remedy that was put forward was to abolish the Corn Law of 1815 which made it illegal to import corn until the price of the home-grown product reached 80 shillings a quarter, and which thus kept food prices artificially high. The Anti-Corn Law League was formed to promote this object.

The first we hear of a local branch of the Anti-Corn Law League is in a report from Todmorden printed in

the *Northern Star* of 30th October, 1841, which says that: "Mr. Barker, president of the Corn Law League, has repeatedly attempted to reduce his workpeople's wages, but has often been compelled to give up the attempt. About three weeks since he reduced the weavers as follows: those that were getting 1s 2d to 1s, and those that got 1s per cut to 10d, and of course a turn-out was the consequence. The mill has been standing a fortnight." John and William Barker were cotton spinners and manufacturers at Barewise Mill, between Robinwood and Cornholme in the Burnley valley. Actual or attempted wage cuts were very common in late 1841, as the trade recession deepened; but painting the League supporters as merciless wage-cutters was a tactic which the Chartists used with great effect against their political rivals.

About two months later the local Chartists successfully routed an attempt to form a branch of the Anti-Corn Law League when they swamped a meeting held in the Baptist Chapel at Millwood. According to the *Northern Star*, their object was only to promote a fair and calm discussion, but not surprisingly, discussion turned to rowdy argument and the meeting concluded with three cheers for the Charter and three dismal groans for the League Clique, and only three people could be persuaded to come forward and be signed up as members of the Anti-Corn Law League.[23]

Another brush between the Chartists and the League supporters occurred during one of Feargus O'Connor's visits to Todmorden. He was harangued at his hotel by "two most obtrusive, and ignorant, and impertinent slave-drivers" - supporters of the League - whom, he complained, kept him up until 3 o'clock arguing and vilifying Chartism in general, and John Fielden in particular. He gave their names as Stansfield and Chambers. "Stansfield" was John Stansfield, cotton spinner and manufacturer of Ewood Mill, and his friend "Chambers" was Charles Chambers, who with his brother William was in business at Salford as a gingham manufacturer and cotton dyer. Feargus O'Connor represents these two men as supporters of Joseph Sturge and "the new and improved Corn Law Repeal Confederacy", a faction

The Baptist Chapel at Millwood

Officers and Committee Members of Todmorden Anti-Corn Law Association

NAME	ADDRESS	OCCUPATION
Wm. Helliwell	Friths	Cotton spinner and manufacturer
John Barker	Barewise Mill	Cotton spinner and manufacturer
Wm. Hauworth	Bankfield	
Peter Ormerod	Stoneswood Hse.	Cotton spinner and manufacturer
John Veevers	Kilnhurst	Carrier
Charles Chambers	Todmorden	Cotton manufacturer
William Fielden	Clough	Cotton spinner and manufacturer
Thos. Bottomley, Jr	Spring Mill	Cotton spinner and manufacturer
John Law	Ramsden Wood	Cotton spinner and manufacturer
James Fielden	Clough	Cotton spinner and manufacturer
Jeremiah Oliver	Todmorden	Surgeon
Edward King	Todmorden	Clog maker
William Taylor	Cheapside	
Henry Atkinson	Todmorden	Boot and Shoe maker
Robert Mills	Patmos	Temperence Hotel Keeper
Joshua B. Fielden	Old Shop	Shopkeeper/Landowner
John Stansfield	Ewood	Cotton spinner and manufacturer
William Brook	Pavement	Shopkeeper
John Taylor	Pexwood	
Wm. Sutcliffe	Causeywood	Overlooker
Thomas Wild	Roomfield Lane	

Source: compiled from the Resolution Book of the Todmorden Anti-Corn Law Association

which, he claimed, numbered not more than seven in Todmorden, but "which gave the people much trouble".[24]

The ex-Baptist Chapel, Millwood, in early 1994

In November 1842, with still much distress amongst the working people and no sign yet of an improvement in trade, a Todmorden Anti-Corn Law Association was formed to meet weekly at the White Hart Inn and to try and obtain a repeal of the Corn and Provision Laws. As we have seen, there had previously been at least a loose grouping of Free Traders in the town, and one or more attempts to gather a more formal group together, but now a determined effort was to be made to solicit subscriptions and promote the cause.[25] Officers were elected, a committee appointed, and a roll book begun. The roll book shows that subscriptions were collected from December 1842 to October 1843. Two hundred and forty-seven people subscribed to the Association over the term of its life, many of them being manufacturers, innkeepers or traders. All the major cotton manufacturers of the district supported the League, with the exception only of the Fieldens of Waterside and the Inghams of Cinderhill Mill. The officers and committee members of the Association were drawn mainly from the ranks of the cotton masters, with a sprinkling of shopkeepers and tradesmen, and their Whiggish political colour can be deduced from the fact that three of the twenty-one had been amongst the small number of local supporters of the New Poor Law who had suffered the destruction of their property in the riots of November 1838. Amongst its most enthusiastic supporters were William Helliwell,

Joshua Barnes Fielden, the Messrs. Ormerod Brothers, and the firm of Firth and Haworth, all of whom made large donations to League funds.[26]

A visit to the town by the anti-Corn Law lecturer Mr. Acland in December 1842 almost developed into a physical fight between the Chartists and the Repealers. It was announced that he would deliver his lecture in the Oddfellows' Hall, and an hour before the appointed time, both factions began to assemble outside the hall - each with the intention of monopolising the room and excluding the other party. By eight o'clock the crowd was so large and so tumultuous that the shopkeepers, fearing a riot, put up their shutters. And when the doors were opened there was such a rush to get in that bonnets, caps and shawls were trampled underfoot. Some people used a ladder which some workmen had left nearby to get in to the hall through the windows, and one of these was the *Halifax Guardian's* correspondent, who found a scene inside which he compared to "a bull baiting, or a promiscuous brawling rabble of men, women and boys quarrelling with each other under the influence of gin". The utmost noise and confusion prevailed until the parties at length agreed that Mr. Acland, for the Repealers, and Mr. Leach, for the Chartists, should take it in turns to speak for half an hour at a time, which they did alternately, until a late hour.[27]

The Todmorden Anti-Corn Law Association's own records finish in December 1843, and it was probably not active thereafter. The Chartists, though, kept up their tactic of publicising cases of mistreatment of their workpeople by the local Free Traders. It was reported that Peter Ormerod of Stoneswood Mill, who had just given £100 to League funds, had without any notice suddenly reduced the wages of his spinners by 7s a week, and a fortnight later, that one of the spinners (having presumably complained) "was discharged and told to go to the Chartists and desire them to keep him".[28]

Shortly after this incident, the *Northern Star* pronounced that "Free traders are all but dead here: the leading men by reducing the wages of their operatives have disgusted the people".[29] This was quite probably the case, because when in May 1844 there was an electioneering visit to Todmorden by Richard Cobden and Mr. Brown, the Free Trade candidate for South Lancashire, the Free Trade party was unable to prevent Enoch Horsfall and Robert Brook from subjecting the professional politicians to a searching cross-examination on behalf of the Todmorden Chartists. At the close of the meeting, the audience refused to cheer the Free Trade candidates, and gave three cheers for O'Connor and the Charter instead. The result of the contest between the Todmorden Chartists and the Todmorden Anti-Corn Law Association had been an overwhelming victory to the Chartists.

In spite of the apparent reasonableness of its aims, and the fact that one of the League's leaders was a Rochdale man, the League had difficulty attracting support in Todmorden, especially amongst the working people, who tended to view the League in the same light as Feargus O'Connor. He saw it as a ruse got up by the manufacturers to distract popular support from Chartism, and to enable them, once the price of food was lower, to reduce wages also. The rivalry and partisanship between the Todmorden supporters of the Charter and supporters of the League was intense - and very reminiscent of the heated factionalism that existed between the different religious groups in the town.

Local Chartism, 1842-1848

The Todmorden Chartists were probably never again as numerous as they were in the heady summer of 1842, when there were at least seven hundred fully paid-up members of the Chartist Society. In January 1844, they numbered only two hundred and three. But the Association was very active, and the yearly round of Chartist lectures, tea parties, balls and camp meetings was an integral part of Todmorden life throughout the 1840s.

Each winter brought its series of Chartist lectures, with the new Oddfellows' Hall, opened in 1842, providing a suitably large lecture room. Amongst the lecturers who visited Todmorden most often were Feargus O'Connor, James Leech, Dr. McDouall, Thomas Clarke, Christopher Doyle, Philip McGrath, and Thomas Tattersall of Burnley. The female Chartists regularly organised tea-parties and balls to take place at Christmas, New Year or Todmorden Fair, which generally featured such entertainments as the North Lancashire Glee Singers, or a dramatic performance of "The Trial of Robert Emmett".

Every summer there were outdoor lectures and camp meetings which drew huge crowds from all the surrounding towns. The Chartists often assembled at Heyhead Green near Lumbutts, and Stoodley Pike was chosen as the venue for a camp meeting in May 1843 but the event was ruined by heavy rain - which was especially dismal in such an isolated and shelterless spot. But, undaunted, the Chartists met there again the following month and again in 1846. At least once, a camp meeting was held at Slate Pit Hills, between Todmorden and Bacup (in June 1843), and at Foster Clough Delph, near Midgley (in May 1848). But the biggest gatherings of all assembled near the White House Inn at Blackstone Edge, where there was a natural amphitheatre on the moorland. Isolated though this place was, it was surrounded on all sides by industrial towns, and the Chartists of Todmorden, Hebden Bridge, Luddenden, Halifax, Ripponden, Soyland, Oldham, Royton, Heywood, Rochdale, Bacup, Littleborough, and other nearby places all climbed up to this remote spot for the annual camp meeting. The first gathering there was in 1842, and was said by the *Northern Star* to have attracted 15,000 people, with twice as many attending in 1846.[30]

Big Chartist camp meetings like those at Blackstone Edge were organised by conferences of delegates from all the surrounding towns. In 1842/3, formal links between the Chartist Societies of different towns were greatly strengthened, and Todmorden, situated as it was on a major trans-Pennine route between Yorkshire and Lancashire, was well-placed to link the Chartists of the woollen-producing areas with those of the cotton country. The Todmorden Chartists sent representatives to the annual meeting of predominantly Lancashire delegates at Blackstone Edge, and were also integrated into the network of West Riding Chartist groups through their contributions towards the support of John West, the Chartist lecturer for the West Riding, and through sending representatives to meetings of West Riding delegates. Soon after John West's appointment he made a tour of the Chartist Societies in his area and published his findings in a very interesting series of reports in the *Northern Star.* He toured the upper Calder Valley in January 1844, visiting first Sowerby and then Hebden Bridge, "the oldest Association in England", where he "found Chartism of the right sort, in nowise affected by the ebbs and flows of popular excitement". The next day he proceeded to "Todmorden, the border citadel of Chartism" where his lecture attracted a full audience, with the women in particular attending in great numbers. At the end of the lecture, 20s was subscribed and 43 cards of membership taken up, and he observed that the town "is soon likely to resume its former position of being, for its size, the first Chartist town in England".[31]

It is interesting that John West should have observed that there were a great many women in the audience when he came to Todmorden. It has already been mentioned that the Chartist women of Todmorden were both numerous and energetic: that they arranged their own meetings and invited their own lecturers; that their balls and tea-parties raised large sums of money for Chartist causes; and that they had marched with the men to turn-out the Hebden Bridge and Halifax mills in 1842.

These women were acting in accordance with a long-standing tradition of female participation in popular politics. Whilst women were virtually excluded from the formal processes of politics and local government, the kinds of popular action which were used by the people to pressurise their political masters had always relied upon the support and involvement of the women. They had been prominent in late-eighteenth century food riots, and more recently, in the anti-Poor Law disturbances. But social attitudes were beginning to change. Increasingly, such active participation in popular politics was viewed as unseemly for women, and a more domestic role was urged upon them. A few months

The White House Inn, Blackstone Edge

after the plug-drawing disturbances, the *Halifax Guardian* published an extraordinary diatribe against the female Chartists of Todmorden. The writer noted with satisfaction that fewer women than usual attended a Chartist lecture in the Oddfellows' Hall - which he took to be an encouraging sign of "their return to a proper sense of their duty". It was his opinion that the women

> "have certainly been misled by a set of fellows who, regardless themselves of the decencies of civilised life, would lead unsuspecting woman into scenes of action utterly unsuited to her character and constitution. The presence of females at such scenes of political strife is bad enough; but when they are found mingling their voices in the arena of politics on the Sabbath Day, their position becomes intolerably disgusting, and they degrade themselves even in the eyes of those in whose cause they are engaged; for they may depend upon it that no man would seek a partner for life among women who 'neither fear God nor regard man' after the fashion of these petticoated politicians; and the man who suffers his wife to figure in such places, especially on the Sunday, proves how little he cares for her or her character...We trust that the female chartists of Todmorden and its district will have the honour of leading the way to retirement at home, and if they will have 'conversations on politics', let them be on subjects relating to family 'imports and exports', the 'duties' imposed on each and all; and instead of moving amendments at political meetings, let them move and carry them into execution with the darning-needle at home".[32]

It appears that these "petticoated politicians" were unimpressed by the writer's arguments because in April 1846 we find the female Chartists - on their own initiative, and quite independently of the men - calling a public meeting to petition Parliament against the Irish Curfew Bill. A petition was organised, and within two weeks between three and four thousand signatures had been collected, with the women themselves defraying all the costs of organising the petition.[33]

In February 1843 the Chartists successfully commandeered the post of Township Constable for Langfield. The office of constable was a key one in the Chartist period, not least because the constable had powers to call - or refuse to call - public meetings. At one time the local ratepayers had simply appointed a constable, but now the magistrates were insisting that the proper procedure be followed, and that they be supplied with a list of twenty candidates from which to make their selection. So when the annual meeting of freeholders and ratepayers assembled at the Golden Lion to nominate twenty suitable persons, the Chartists attended in sufficient numbers to elect their leader Robert Brook as chairman, and then success-

fully out-voted the proposed list of twenty candidates with another of their own, leaving the magistrates with no option but to appoint a Chartist as constable for Langfield for 1843/4. This gave them the opportunity to hold as many outdoor meetings in the township as they wished over the following year, of which they took full advantage.[34]

In Stansfield, a bitter battle for the occupancy of township offices was joined annually between the Chartists and the conservatives or "Church party". This is first noted in the *Halifax Guardian* in February 1844, when "after much disputation... a list, comprising principally of Chartists was prepared". But in March 1848, at a very turbulent ratepayers' meeting "the Church party succeeded most triumphantly in nominating their men" as overseers of the poor and collectors of assessed taxes. And at the following year's meeting to nominate persons to serve as township officers, it was nearly two hours before any business could be done because the two parties were fully occupied with abusing each other with their respective misdeeds when in power.

Not surprisingly, Stansfield became particularly notorious for the party spirit in which its township affairs were conducted. It was often complained that township officers were elected purely by their party label, without any regard to their suitability or ability to do the job. Allegations of incompetence and misconduct were frequent - and not infrequently deserved. One Sunday in July 1844, two of the Stansfield constables, John Ormerod and John Lord, got drunk whilst doing their rounds to see that the beer-shops were shut during divine service, and then set about some men who showed amusement at their pickled state. They were taken before John Crossley, JP, on a charge of being drunk and disorderly, and he observed that some very unsuitable people had been selected as constables in some townships, most of them being "men more anxious to create than suppress disturbances...who had no other recommendation than that of always being the first in a fray". Another such was Thomas Simpson, better known as "Tom Tite", who was frequently in trouble during his time as constable for Stansfield, and on one occasion got into a fist fight with William Sutcliffe of Lower Laithe, the treasurer to the Todmorden Board of Guardians.[35]

An allegation of misconduct was also made against John Butterworth, a constable for Todmorden-cum-Walsden township in 1843. He was accused of neglect of duty, and the charge was upheld by the magistrates Crossley and Taylor who fined him 40 shillings. The magistrates' action was perceived as "unjust and tyrannical" and a petition to Parliament was intended to be drawn up, although its organisers (who included the prominent local Chartists Joseph Hirst and Henry Shepherd) said that they "had little hope of mending such a reptile as Mr. Crossley".[36] But not all Chartist constables were incompetent. Both political camps agreed that Enoch Horsfall, who served as a constable for Stansfield for many years, was, although an ardent Chartist, a very able and effective officer who brought many wrongdoers to justice during his term of office.

The Chartist movement, although its direct aim might have been a specific and political one, did a great deal towards the general education of its followers. The *Northern Star* newspaper, and the Chartist lectures, reading rooms, and debating societies all promoted popular education. When Robert Brook was released on bail in October 1842, a letter from him to the people of Todmorden was published in the *Northern Star* in which he noted that "Since the commencement of the Evening Star you have opened five news rooms, or rather reading rooms, for I perceive that other than political education is being attended to. This is cheering". One of the reading rooms was at Walsden, one at Salford and one at Millwood. The Salford room was presumably the nucleus around which grew the "Democratic Chapel" which is first mentioned in August 1843, and which on 3rd September welcomed Ben Rushton of Ovenden as preacher on the day when the Sunday school was opened. The school took both boys and girls, instructing them in reading, writing, English grammar and mathematics, and aimed "to render that instruction which will not only prepare the scholars to become good members of society, but give them the means of judging for themselves which party or sect is best fitted for their adhesion". The *Halifax Guardian* took a less than rosy view of the Chartist Sunday school, describing its premises as "a small dirty garret in Foundry Street", where it educated about thirty pupils.

The Hudsonites

Chartist attitudes to religion covered a very broad spectrum. The Chartist chapels, Chartist Sunday schools and Chartist hymn-books promoted a politicised version of Christianity. Yet other Chartists were actively hostile to all organised religion. According to an item in the *Todmorden Almanac:*

> "...a lot of foolish men who resided at Shade, Gauxholme and Knowlwood held meetings for the purpose of mocking religion. James Hudson was their leader, and his followers were called "Hudsonites". They held meetings at their own houses and they had an annual meeting at Basin Stone. They were distinguished by their peculiar dress, all of them wearing green coats...At their weddings they almost all attended, and rode on donkeys decked with ribbons".[37]

The followers of James Hudson, or "Pope Hudson" as they called him, met at the Basin Stone on the first Sunday in May, from about 1840 to 1848, at least. At these annual camp meetings, a hymn might be given out, but nobody would attempt to sing; or Hudson would pretend to preach, but end it in foolery or a doggerel verse. But behind the foolery are suggestions of something more serious. On one occasion James Hudson gave out his creed as "He believed that Jesus Christ was the Saviour of mankind; that every person had a right to express his opinions; that all the land in the world belonged to all the people in it; and that if he altered his opinions to-morrow he should not be answerable for those he held the day previous!". Another speaker at the same meeting said that no man had a right to live on another man's labour; and on another occasion, James Hudson alluded to his heart receiving a wound to see so much barren and uncultured ground surrounding the Basin Stone. 38 Put all these together - the pro-Jesus but anti-Church stance, the concern with cultivating the barren places, the belief in free-thought and free-speech, and the anti-Capitalist sentiments, and the Hudsonites appear not so much as just a group of foolish young people, and more as anarchist-radicals in the classic Digger tradition.

The Chartist Land Company

Like most early English radical movements, Chartism was suffused by a romantic attachment to the land and its cultivation. The Chartist Land Company, a plan to settle Chartists in independent occupation of smallholdings, was started early in 1845 with the personal backing of Feargus O'Connor. Its object was "to enable Working Men, for a trifling sum, to obtain possession of Land and Dwellings, upon such terms

The Basin Stone

that, by honourable and independent labour, they may maintain themselves and their families in comfort and respectability".[39] This was to be achieved by the working men taking out shares which could be paid for by instalments from as little as 3d. a week. Once sufficient capital had been raised, land would be purchased, divided up into plots, and a house erected on each. The occupants would be selected by ballot and would be the permanent leaseholders of their plots. The rent they

paid would finance the settlement of yet more Chartists on the land, and so on....

The Todmorden branch of the Land Company held its meetings at Robert Brook's house, and Samuel Whitham was the subscriptions secretary. Nearly a hundred Todmorden people, including Brook and Whitham, took out shares in the National Land Company, but the scheme was not supported as enthusiastically in Todmorden as might have been

Todmorden Subscribers to the National Land Company

NAME	OCCUPATION	ADDRESS	NAME	OCCUPATION	ADDRESS
Astin, James	carder	Croft Carr, Lang.	Hawarth, James	grocer	Lobb Mill
Astin, John	spinner	Lee, Lang.	Hawarth, Mary Ann	weft packer	Lobb Mill
Barker, Abraham	weaver	Toad Carr	Haworth, John	carter	Causeway Mill
Barker, James	shoemaker	Lobb Mill	Heyworth, William	weaver	Hanging Ditch
Barker, James	weaver	Ewood Mill	Holt, Thomas	overlooker	Blind Lane
Barker, John	shoemaker	Hanging Ditch	Jackson, Mary	servant	Lobb Mill
Barker, Joshua	stripper	Castle Street	Kershaw, James	labourer	Lumbutts
Barker, Samuel	weaver	Hedge Nook	Lee, William	weaver	Todmorden
Barker, William	carder	Shade	Lord, James	spinner	Shade
Bentley, William	whitelimer	Roomfield Lane	Marshall, Abraham	bookkeeper	Meadow Bottom
Berry, Peter	labourer	Hanging Ditch	Midgley, Luke	manager	Knowlwood
Binns, William	stripper	Castle Street	Mitchell, Samuel	mechanic	Blind Lane
Brooks, Robert	clerk	Brook Street	Moorhey, James	hatter	Millwood
Butterworth, Elias	factory operative	Roomfield Lane	Newell, Amos	weaver	Millwood
Butterworth, John Snr.	labourer	Blind Lane	Ogden, John	mule piecer	Black Dyke
Butterworth, John Jnr.	labourer	Blind Lane	Ogden, John	weaver	Toad Carr
Clayton, John	spinner	Jack Lee Gate	Partington, Lancelot	sizer	Salford
Clegg, Henry	weaver	Brook Street	Pickup, James	sizer	Mount Pleasant
Clegg, James	weaver	Meadow Bottom	Roberts, William	tailor	Oddfellows' Hall
Close, Richard	weaver	Oddfellows' Hall	Robinson, John	shoemaker	Hanging Ditch
Cockcroft, George	spinner	Meadow Bottom	Sampson, Jeremiah	grinder	George Street
Crabtree, Betty	warper	Mankinholes	Schofield, John	labourer	Roomfield Lane
Crabtree, Hannah	dressmaker	Mankinholes	Simpson, Thomas	shoemaker	Hanging Ditch
Crabtree, James	spinner	Meadow Bottom	Stansfield, George	joiner	Hanging Ditch
Crabtree, John	throstle overlooker	Mankinholes	Stansfield, James	whitesmith	Millwood
Crowther, John	weaver	Blind Lane	Stell, William	labourer	Hough Stone
Crowther, Joshua	weaver	Blind Lane	Stott, Samuel	weaver	Brook Street
Cunliffe, William	sizer	Dobroyd	Sutcliffe, Barnes	mechanic	Causey Wood
Dawson, Abraham	carder	Knowlwood	Sutcliffe, George	clogger	Butcher Hill
Dearden, Richard	carter	Millwood	Sutcliffe, Jno. Wm.	minor	George Street
Dearden, William	carter	Millwood	Sutcliffe, Robert	mule piecer	Meadow Bottom
Dewhurst, Charles	labourer	Oddfellows' Hall	Suthers, Enoch	weaver	Honey Hill
Dewhurst, Richard	weaver	Millwood	Suthers, John	iron moulder	Hanging Ditch
Fielden, William	weaver	Oddfellows' Hall	Thomas, Sutcliffe	plasterer	Roomfield Lane
Gaukroger, Andrew	cotton spinner	Lumbutts	Townend, John	warper	Salford
Gaukroger, Thomas	labourer	Lumbutts	Varley, James	cotton twister	Blind Lane
Gibson, James	overlooker	Woodhouse	Whitham, Emma	weaver	Castle Grove
Greenwood, Abraham	weaver	Roomfield Lane	Whitham, James	gardener	Castle Grove
Greenwood, James	weaver	Lobb Mill	Whitham, Samuel	gardener	Castle Grove
Greenwood, John	coal dealer	Jacklee Gate	Whitham, Marshall J.	shoemaker	Castle Grove
Greenwood, Joseph	labourer	Black Rock	Whittaker, Thomas	joiner	Oddfellows' Hall
Greenwood, Richard	weaver	Lobb Mill	Wilcock, William	packer	Studley Edge
Greenwood, Robert	smith	Meadow Bottom	Wilson, John	gardener	Woodhouse
Greenwood, Thomas	gas maker	Dale Street	Wilson, William	iron moulder	George Street
Hauworth, Jonathan	schoolmaster	Lobb Mill	Woodhead, John	blacksmith	Knowlwood
Hauworth, Ormerod	gardener	Lobb Mill			

Source: compiled from Names of the Subscribers to the
National Land Company, (PRO BT 41/474/2659).

expected, given the great strength of the local Chartist movement. The subscriptions sent in from neighbouring places always dwarfed those from Todmorden - not just those from the squalid tenements of the large towns, but also from the smaller places such as Hebden Bridge and Bacup. Hebden Bridge was particularly enthusiastic in its support, and James Greenwood and James Helliwell of Hebden Bridge were amongst the Chartists successful in the ballots for plots at the Chartist colony of O'Connorville in 1846. According to Edwin Ashworth, some Todmorden people went off to the second Chartist settlement at Lowbands, near Tewkesbury in Gloucestershire.[40] The Chartist colonies were short-lived. Within a couple of years the scheme had been wound up, brought down by a combination of financial mismanagement, hostility from the Government and from the parishes where the colonies were located, and the inability of many of the settlers to make a living from the land.

"The Charter and No Surrender"

The Todmorden Chartists did not allow the excitement over the new Land Scheme to distract them from political activity. In the autumn of 1846 the agitation for the Charter was renewed under the slogan "The Charter and no Surrender", and a public meeting in Todmorden adopted the new National Petition and pledged itself to collecting as many bona fide signatures as possible. Within a few months, the all-too-familiar signs of an imminent trade depression became noticeable. By November it was reported that in Todmorden:

> "The streets are thronged with individuals out of employment. Their emaciated appearance is really pitiable. The works on the branch line of Railway to Burnley are stopped, and hundreds are thrown out of work. The factories, with the exception of one small firm that makes fancy goods, are either stopped, or running short-time. The large firm of Fielden Brothers are only running seven hours per day".[41]

Meanwhile the final arrangements for the presentation to Parliament of the third and the greatest National Chartist Petition were going forward. On April 10th, the long awaited day came when the Chartists planned to form a great procession to deliver to Parliament their monster petition, which was mounted on a specially-made cart, and believed to contain 5,700,000 signatures. But the day ended in great disappointment. The Duke of Wellington had been put in charge of protecting the capital, and had brought in large numbers of troops and special constables to guard every public building and strategic site. The Chartist procession was dispersed, and O'Connor and the Chartist Executive alone permitted to deliver the petition to Parliament in three cabs. Later, when Parliament scrutinised the petition, it dismissed it with contempt, declaring that the signatures numbered less than two million and that many of them were forgeries.

The Chartists of Lancashire and the West Riding, at least, were not prepared to accept defeat so easily. Frequent meetings of delegates from the textile towns were held all through the summer of 1848, and the talk was of forceful action.

At the White House Inn at Blackstone Edge on Sunday 28th May, with John Robinson of Todmorden in the chair, the delegates agreed that when they returned to their constituencies they would sound out opinion on the policy of a cessation of labour, and meet again the following week at Todmorden Oddfellows Hall. They also recommended the formation of a National Guard. The representatives from Manchester, Oldham, Royton, Middleton, Heywood, Bury, Rochdale, Littleborough, Bacup, Todmorden, Hebden Bridge, Midgley, Sowerby, Halifax, Mixenden Stones, Queenshead, Elland and Huddersfield kept in close contact all summer. They held frequent meetings and appointed a corresponding secretary. Hebden Bridge became the regional Chartist centre, and at a meeting there on the 9th July, it was agreed by the delegates that all former agitations for the Charter had failed by being based on moral arguments instead of physical power, and they requested the Chartist Executive to assume the office of National Defence Committee.

But all this fighting talk came to nothing. There was no rising of the North in 1848, and it is rather hard to believe that the delegates were doing more than trying to frighten the Government. After all, they published the address of their corresponding secretary (Elias Hitchin, c/o John Smith, 6 Commercial Street, Hebden Bridge) in the *Northern Star* for all to read - scarcely the action of determined revolutionaries! There was much talk of a rising in Yorkshire and Lancashire, and many rumours of Chartists drilling in the hills, but it all faded away at the end of the summer without any serious disturbances taking place.[42]

Chartism after 1848

After 1848, Chartism declined but did not disappear. The annual camp meetings continued to be held at Blackstone Edge, but fewer and fewer people attended them. Only one or two thousand people went to the 1854 meeting. At the height of the Chartist agitation the Blackstone Edge camp meeting had been a major regional event, attracting ten or twenty times as many people. But special occasions could still attract large crowds. Between fifteen and twenty thousand people assembled on Heyhead Green in Langfield on 24th August 1856,[43] to welcome John Frost, the transported Welsh Chartist, who had finally at the age of 70 been pardoned and allowed to return from exile. He toured the country, lecturing on Chartism and the horrors of the convict system, and was given a hero's welcome. Some local Chartists continued to be politically active into the 1850s and 60s, often allying themselves with the Liberal party, of which they formed an extreme democratic wing.

In 1867 the leaseholders of property worth £12 a year or. more were given the Parliamentary vote. One of the former Chartists of Todmorden who benefited was Edmund Holt, the manager of the Fieldens' spinning mills at Lumbutts, who was finally enfranchised - more than forty years after he had spoken in favour of universal suffrage at a Reform meeting at Lumbutts.[44] It was to be another seventeen years before most of the spinners in the Lumbutts mills received the vote, by which time the few Chartists amongst them who had lived long enough to welcome the reform, were very old men indeed.

Who were the Todmorden Chartists?

Chartism was the dominant ideology in Todmorden in the 1830s and 40s. Nearly all working class political activists in Todmorden called themselves Chartists or Radicals, and many were passionate admirers of Feargus O'Connor. The promoters of alternative ideologies could find it very difficult to recruit in the town. As we have seen, the Anti-Corn Law League was relatively poorly supported in Todmorden, and the Methodists of York Street Chapel also ascribed the weakness of their following in part to the competition offered by the Chartists.

There cannot have been many working people living in Todmorden at this time whose lives were not touched, at some point, by Chartism. We have noted that eight thousand and four hundred Todmorden people signed the second National Petition; that between two and three thousand regularly turned out for local outdoor meetings; that seven hundred people were members of the Chartist society in 1842; and that Chartist lectures, tea-parties and balls were a very popular feature of local life for many years. In short, Chartism was part of the ordinary experience of everyday life. Only for the few did being a Chartist mean secret midnight musterings on the moors. For many more people, it must have meant mutual education; or winter-evening tea-parties and balls; or a procession of families climbing up to a moorland camp meeting, with their dinners in a bag, and the small children riding on their parents' shoulders; or the thrill of hearing the strains of "Britannia's sons, though slaves ye be" soaring over the din of the looms in the weaving shed.

But above and beyond the large numbers of people who were involved with Chartism in a casual or sporadic way, were the committed radicals. Some of these can be identified, either because they were subscribers to the National Land Company; because they were arrested during the plug-drawing riots; or because they were the local Chartist activists whose names appear in the *Northern Star* as the speakers at Chartist meetings, the delegates to conferences, or the nominees for the Chartist General Council.[45]

Todmorden Subscribers to the National Land Company [46]

Ninety-one people from Todmorden took out shares in the National Land Company. What sort of people were they? Did they have trades or skills that might have enabled them to make a reasonable living from a two or four acre plot of land? Were they factory workers, hoping to escape from the new industrial world - or aged hand-loom weavers, looking to re-create the weaver-peasant community they had once known?

The lists of subscribers to the Land Company in the Public Record office gives their names, addresses and occupations, so we can tell quite a lot about them.

It is immediately noticeable that the Land Company members were overwhelmingly male. Of the ninety-one subscribers from Todmorden, only five were women. They were Betty Crabtree, a warper of Mankinholes; Hannah Crabtree, a dressmaker from the same place; Mary Ann Haworth, a weft packer of Lobb Mill; Emma Whitham, a weaver of Castle Grove; and Mary Jackson, a servant of Lobb Mill. All of these women, it turns out, were members of Chartist families. Betty and Hannah Crabtree were the unmarried daughters of Grace Crabtree, a widow who farmed 20 acres with the aid of her son, William. Their other brother, John, was a throstle overlooker and also a subscriber to the Land Company. Emma Whitham's father James and brothers James Marshall and Samuel had also taken out shares in the Land Company, probably under the inspiration of Samuel who became the Secretary of the Todmorden branch of the Chartist Land Society. Mary Jackson was an elderly woman employed as a bread-baker by her brother-in-law James Haworth, who had a grocer's shop at Lobb Mill. James Haworth and his son Ormerod were also Land Company subscribers, and it is very probable that Mary Ann Haworth - the final female subscriber - was his daughter. The Land Company was a lottery, with the right to lease a smallholding in a distant place as the prize. It is hard to imagine a woman being independently in a position to take up the offer of a cottage and land in O'Connorville or one of the other Chartist settlements and so it is not very surprising to find that the Todmorden women who subscribed to the Land Company all belonged to Chartist families.

The Todmorden men who subscribed to the Land Company had a wide variety of different occupations, but they were not entirely typical of the Todmorden workforce of the day. There were no farmers or farm labourers amongst them. There were no quarrymen. And there were only two iron moulders, although metal-working was by now a considerable industry in the town. Most of them, in fact, were either textile workers, or else had some kind of portable skill or trade. From the first group, there was a factory manager and three overlookers, three carders, a twister, a warper, a sizer, six spinners, two mule piecers, and nineteen weavers. Also probably employed in textile factories were the factory operative, the gas maker, the packer, the bookkeeper, and some at least of the nine labourers and three carters. The men who had skills or trades that they might hope would earn them a living in a new location included a coal dealer and a grocer, three smiths, two mechanics, two joiners, a plasterer and a whitelimer, five shoemakers and a clogger, four gardeners, a tailor, a hatter, a clerk and a schoolmaster. It is not very surprising that gardeners and shoemakers should have been such enthusiastic subscribers to the Land Company, these being the very people who might realistically expect to make a living from a smallholding. The gardeners would have had a very ready market for their produce, and the shoemakers also could easily have combined their trade with producing fruit and vegetables for the table.

It may be that a large proportion of the nineteen weavers who took out subscriptions to the Land Company were handloom weavers who also saw in the Chartist settlements an opportunity to combine handicraft with subsistence agriculture. Unfortunately, it is not stated whether they were hand or factory weavers. Nine of these weavers can be identified in the census taken just four years later. Only one was stated to be a handloom weaver, one was a weaver of gingham (whether by hand or power is not recorded, but probably hand), five were powerloom weavers, and two had become overseers. This suggests that most of the weavers who joined the Land Society were powerloom weavers - and this is supported by the fact that most of them lived in the valley bottoms, not on the tops, where the remaining handloom weavers were by now concentrated. An exception to this general rule might come from the Toad Carr/Blind Lane area, which had been a handloom weavers' colony and a centre of early co-operation. There were ten Land Society members living in the cottages here, at least five of whom were weavers. One of them was Sam Barker of Hedge Nook, who *was* a handloom weaver and an active Chartist. John Travis says that Sam Barker was a master handloom weaver, employing a few weavers in making cloth for Thomas Ramsbottom of Ewood Mill. He describes him as an amateur politician of the Chartist stamp - though a generation in advance of the movement - who was fond of engaging passers-by in political conversation.[47]

The Men Arrested in 1842

The Todmorden men arrested at the time of the plug-drawing disturbances were Robert Brook, John Crowther, William Smith, Thomas Pollard, James Sutcliffe and Sutcliffe Marshall. They have very different records of involvement with the local Chartist movement.

Robert Brook was the acknowledged leader of local Chartism, both before and after his arrest and trial. Crowther, Smith and Pollard were all arrested in connection with the stopping of mills in Hebden Bridge and Mytholmroyd. John Crowther was a weaver who lived at Blind Lane. There is no record of his active participation in the Chartist movement before his arrest, but a great deal afterwards. He was Todmorden's delegate to the Blackstone Edge meeting in August 1843, was nominated to the General Council of the National Charter Association in 1843 (i.e. he was a member of the local Chartist committee), and was elected District Councilman in 1844. William Smith and Thomas Pollard were decidedly for the Charter even though they had not taken a prominent part in local politics. It was stated in court that William Smith and the others who had stopped Joseph Hinchliffe's mill at Cragg, had said at the time that "they wanted higher wages, and the Charter they would have".[48] And Thomas Pollard was reported by John Smith, constable, to have "come down the road armed with a thick bludgeon and go towards the meeting - he threw up his bludgeon when near me and said "Come on Brother Chartists".[49] Only James Sutcliffe who was arrested in Halifax, and Sutcliffe Marshall who was arrested in Bradford, have no known record of other Chartist connections or activity.

Local Chartists named in the *Northern Star*

More than fifty men are named in *Northern Star* as taking an active part in the Chartist movement in Todmorden. Sometimes an address or occupation is given, and occasionally both, so it has been possible to identify many of the men with a fair degree of certainty, and in many cases to find them on the 1841 or 1851 censuses and so discover more information about their ages and occupations. The results have been summarised in the Appendix, which also shows what Chartist and other political activities the men are known to have been involved in, and when. Their records as Chartists include such activities as being elected as a delegate to a Chartist meeting or convention, being nominated for the Chartist General Council, taking an active part in a public meeting, being arrested, sending contributions to Chartist causes, selling "Pinder's Chartist blacking", and holding Chartist meetings at their houses. No women's names are included on the chart because although they were very active in the cause, they are almost never named in the newspaper. Apart from the five female subscribers to the Land Company, the only local female Chartists whose names I have been able to discover are Betty Holt, Sally Stott, Hannah

The Railway Inn, Lydgate

Haworth and Mally Stephenson, all of Knowlwood, who in 1840 sent to the *Northern Star* their donations for the families of Frost, Williams and Jones. The women were all aged between 25 and 35. Two of them were cotton warpers. The other two were not in employment, but one was married to a cotton warper, and one to a cotton winder. Since Luke Midgley, the manager or overlooker of the Fielden's Knowlwood Mill, also sent a donation at the same time, it seems very likely that the women or their husbands worked at Knowlwood Mill.[50]

The occupations of the men who are known to have been active Chartists cover a broad spectrum. At one extreme are the middle-class radicals, such as James and Samuel Fielden, William Robinson and the Unitarian minister, James Taylor. Their recorded involvement in the movement is limited to such matters as chairing meetings, proposing motions, or attending conferences. The only tradesmen who are known to have been active Chartists in Todmorden are William Greenwood, grocer, William Scholfield, ironmonger, and Joseph Tisdale (or Teasdale), the landlord of the Railway Inn at Lydgate. Rather more were skilled artisans of some kind, including a clerk, a watchmaker, a boot and shoe maker, a machine-maker, a shoemaker, a joiner, a whitesmith, a clogger and a gardener. At least thirteen of the men, and possibly as many as sixteen, were labourers or

factory workers, including Richard Wheelwright, a talented Chartist speaker who was an under-carder at Mytholmroyd until he set up as a radical bookseller in the Shade district of Todmorden. No fewer than five of these most active Chartists worked as overlookers in cotton mills.

Todmorden's Leading Chartists

The leading Chartists in Todmorden were Robert Brook, Enoch Horsfall, and Samuel Whitham, and quite substantial biographies can be drawn up for these three men. Some of the men who, whilst not as significant in the local movement as these three, were still amongst the most committed local Chartists were James Stansfield, Henry Helliwell, William Helliwell and Henry Shepherd, but the details of their lives are much more sketchy.

Robert Brook

Robert Brook was the central figure of Todmorden Chartism from its inception until at least 1846. For most of this period he was the local sub-secretary of the National Charter Association, though in 1843 he was acting instead as sub-Treasurer. He was Todmorden's agent for the *Northern Star* newspaper, and was reputedly also their local correspondent.[51] Both the Chartists and the Land Society often held their meetings at his house during 1845 and 1846. He was a frequent chairman of political meetings, and several times Todmorden's delegate to regional meetings, including, as mentioned earlier, the important one at Manchester in August 1842. Soon after this he was arrested and tried on a charge of seditious conspiracy in company with others who had attended the delegate meeting or were otherwise perceived as local Chartist leaders. Unlike some of these men, who were active as regional or even national leaders of the Chartist movement, Brook's activities seem to have been mostly confined to his home town and he does not appear to have spoken at public meetings in other towns in Yorkshire or Lancashire.

At his trial Brook was found guilty (though the conviction was later overturned), of helping to promote a strike through the use of violence, threats and intimidation. It was given in evidence that on the 18th August at Basin Stone he had given a speech before about 1,000 people, at which he had said "He had been at the delegate meeting at Manchester; and while there, there came three letters from a man whose name he would not tell. The first letter said he had 10,000 men to back him; the second said he had got 15,000, and the third said he had got 30,000... And he said they were gone to Leeds and had driven the barracks and were masters of the town at that minute".[52] This evidence, which was not disputed, seems to support the prosecution case that he was a "physical force" Chartist; but other evidence - slight though it is - points towards him being a rather gentler character. The greeting that he sent to the Todmorden Chartists when he was released on bail affirmed that he had used his influence to get the people to keep the peace. He spoke in favour of unity and education, and advised his followers to "make many friends and few enemies, and let ours be union and good feeling towards one another".[53] And in later years, when personal differences and allegations of financial mismanagement threatened the Chartist movement, the Todmorden Chartists on several occasions met at Brook's house and made appeals for solidarity which were published in the *Northern Star.* [54]

At the time of his arrest in 1842, Robert Brook was aged about 28. He lived on George Street, Todmorden, with his wife Martha, and his principal occupation was that of a schoolmaster. He had held a night-school since 1834 or 1835, and in 1837 had an academy on York Street. He may have turned to teaching because a sedentary occupation suited him, being somewhat lame. At Brook's trial, William Heap of Ingbottom was examined as to the extent of Brook's lameness. Heap was unwilling to either confirm or deny that Brook was lame, but reluctantly admitted that he had seen people that walked better, whether he was lame or not; that Brook sometimes used a crutch when he went out; and that both of his legs seemed equally bad.[55]

By 1845 Brook had become a bookseller with a shop on Brook Street. By 1853, the bookselling business had been taken over by Thomas Barker and Brook had become the proprietor of a temperance hotel at the Oddfellows Hall. Later he was bookkeeper to the firm of W. and R. Robinson, timber merchants and builders, which was owned by the middle class Radical, William Robinson. In 1859 the Robinsons moved to Rochdale and the firm was bought out by a number of their workers, including Brook, who then became a timber merchant in the firm of Dobson, Trenholme and Co., whilst his wife took over the running of the temperance hotel.[56] Brook also actively promoted co-operative principles in Todmorden, being one of the main movers of the Flour Society in 1847, and of the Todmorden Flour Mill Company in 1861.

Enoch Horsfall

Enoch Horsfall - universally known in Todmorden as "Tonic" - was born in Millwood, in or about the year 1810, and lived there all his life, earning his living as a boot and shoe maker.

His name first appeared in the *Northern Star* in 1841, when he was selling "Pinder's Chartist blacking"; the following year he gave a lecture at the Chartist reading room at Bottoms in Walsden; and in 1844, as previously noted, it was Horsfall and Brook who heckled Cobden and Brown. Horsfall is said to have been a very powerful and effective speaker who might easily, if he chose, have earned his living as a paid Chartist lecturer. He certainly came to the notice of Feargus O'Connor, who in one of his *Northern Star* editorials tells of spending a few hours with some Todmorden friends, mostly in "climbing up mountain ladders" to see some allotments which "Enoch Horsfall, with his long legs" had assured O'Connor were only a mile and a half from Todmorden, and which turned out to be more than two.[57] John Travis records that on one occasion, after addressing a Chartist gathering at Sourhall, Horsfall candidly confessed in the beerhouse there, that although when speaking before an audience he always advocated moral force or persuasion for obtaining privileges or maintaining rights, in reality he was a physical force man, and would, if he might have his own way, "hammer them out of the Bigwigs".

Horsfall became one of the best-known local politicians in Todmorden. When he died in 1884 it was said of him that he had played a prominent part in the Chartist movement and in every agitation since that time. He himself had no vote, but was always prominent at election time in all parts of the Todmorden Union, when he would heckle candidates and try to extract pledges from them. He later allied himself to the Liberals, was always ready to act as a canvasser or a speaker, and was a potent force with a large body of the ratepayers - though mainstream Liberals found his views extreme, and his character impulsive.

Horsfall was active in local government. He ran a long campaign in the Stansfield vestry for the restoration of the old system of township officers being directly elected by the ratepayers, instead of being appointed by the magistrates from a list of suitable persons; he was connected with the Board of Surveyors for the township; and, as previously mentioned, served for many years as constable.[58]

Samuel Whitham

Samuel Whitham was a young man of 24 when his name first appeared in the *Northern Star* as a prominent Todmorden Chartist. Thereafter, he was always in the forefront of the movement locally, proposing motions at meetings, presiding at the adoption of the National Petition in 1846, and acting as Todmorden's delegate to one of the Blackstone Edge meetings in 1847. He was a gardener by trade and, as previously mentioned, a very active supporter of the Chartist Land Scheme. Whitham was later a founding member of the Todmorden Industrial and Co-operative Society, and a promoter of the society's education fund.[59] Together with Brook, Whitham was a leading member of the Todmorden Floral and Horticultural Society in the late 1840s. This society had a very varied membership, including gentlemen, professional gardeners, cottage gardeners and working men; but the presence of such men as Brook and Whitham suggests that the society was at least in part, directed at improving the quality of life of working men. Joining a horticultural society, just like joining a co-operative society, could help them supply good cheap food for their families. The Whitham family were Unitarians, and several of their graves - including Samuel's - can be seen in the burial ground of Todmorden Unitarian chapel.

James Stansfield

James Stansfield of Millwood was elected a member of the Chartist General Council in 1841. The census for that year shows two James Stansfields of Millwood; one was a whitesmith (aged 20-24), and one a cotton weaver (aged 15-19). The whitesmith seems the more likely candidate, and was a subscriber to the Chartist National Land Company some years later.

Henry Helliwell

Henry Helliwell, a silk spinner employed by the Fieldens, was also a general Council member in 1841. At the time of the 1851 census, he was 35 years old, unmarried and living at Hanging Ditch. He was also actively engaged in the Ten Hours agitation and the co-operative movement.

William Helliwell

William Helliwell was another nominee to the General Council in 1841, and treasurer of Todmorden National Charter Association in 1844. The *Northern Star* gives his address as George Street. The 1841 census has no William Helliwell at George Street - but does show two men of that name at nearby York Street. One was a 50 year-old cotton spinner, and one a 45 year-old auctioneer. The auctioneer was the same William Helliwell who had at one time been an agent of the Todmorden spinners' and weavers' union, and is probably - though not certainly - the Chartist.

Henry Shepherd

Henry Shepherd, a young powerloom overlooker, was one of Todmorden's delegates to the Chartist conference at Birmingham in December 1842, the other being James Fielden of Waterside. He was also involved in the anti-Poor Law movement and the agitation for a Ten Hours Act.

Local Chartists and the Middle Class

The Chartist activists in Todmorden were drawn almost entirely from the ranks of working men and women, with factory workers and artisans being represented (at least amongst the men) in roughly equal proportions. At its beginning, the movement had some assistance from middle-class democrats, such as John Fielden and William Robinson, but by 1842, most of Todmorden's manufacturers and shopkeepers were supporting the rival anti-Corn Law League. Some of the radical middle-class, including the Fieldens, declined to support the League; but others - including William Ingham of Mankinholes, who had been (and perhaps still was) a radical reformer - were contributors to League funds. The last significant involvement of any member of the middle-class in the local Chartist movement, was the selection at a public meeting of James Fielden as one of Todmorden's representatives to attend a conference in December 1842, which was to debate whether to join Joseph Sturge's middle-and-working class alliance and agitate for "complete suffrage", or to continue to press for the Charter. James Fielden's opinion isn't known; but his co-delegate, Henry Shepherd, pledged himself to support the Charter and Feargus O'Connor.[60]

There is some slight evidence that there was a change of personnel amongst the local Chartist activists after 1846, and the new men were perhaps, more inclined to "physical force" arguments than the old guard. The earlier leaders, such as Brook, Whitham and Horsfall, had not given up their object of improving the condition of the working people; but were now trying to accomplish this through other means, such as education, teetotalism, friendly societies, co-operation and participation in local government.

Chapter 6

Masters and Men

In the years between 1840 and 1850, Todmorden was moving rapidly towards full industrialisation and a factory-based economy. These were years of sudden and severe economic fluctuations, with deep depressions in 1842 and 1848. They were also years of increasing hostility between masters and men. The Chartist agitation peaked early in the decade, but was followed by years of strikes, incendiarism, battles to control local government - and a further surge in Chartist activity in 1848. Against this rising tide of class hostility, the Fieldens of Todmorden and some of their workpeople were working together to persuade the Government to bring in a Ten Hours Act to reduce the permitted hours of labour in factories.

One indication of the harshness of the "Hungry Forties" is that the local population, which had been increasing rapidly since the end of the 18th century, failed to rise between 1841 and 1851. It remained stable at just over 19,000.[1] We can presume - although no figures are available - that many people moved away, either to the larger towns and cities of Yorkshire and Lancashire, or to a new life in America. But those who stayed were adopting a new way of life, too. No longer did the hilltop farmsteads echo to the sound of the handloom weavers' shuttles. People were moving down into the valley, into the town and its environs, and were increasingly to be found working in the cotton and worsted mills, the iron foundries and engineering sheds, the wood-turning, bobbin-making and picker-making factories, and the dyeing and printing and chemical-manufacturing establishments that now crowded the narrow valleys. By the mid-point of the century, nearly two thirds of the local population were living in the town of Todmorden and its suburbs, and the dwellers in the old upland settlements were a diminishing minority.[2] Rapid and uncontrolled urbanisation brought with it the usual problems of overcrowding, poor sanitation and disease. These were less severe than in the large industrial cities, but nevertheless, it was reported in 1849 that the main drains on York Street (now Halifax Road) stood in up to eighteen inches of stagnant water and sink-dirt, even in dry weather, and that Todmorden was rarely without

typhus fever "in its worst and most putrid forms". In spite of the fact that people were dying of typhus and other fevers, it was not until the Todmorden Local Board was set up in 1860 that there was a single body with responsibility for all parts of the developing town, and sufficient powers to compel people to make improvements in drainage and sanitation.[3]

Local Manufacturers

Fielden Brothers was expanding, purchasing Jumb Mill at Lumbutts in 1847, and putting Robinwood Mill in the Burnley valley into operation at about the same time. By mid-century, the Fieldens were employing about 1,700 factory hands in their eleven Todmorden mills, about another 200 at Mytholmroyd, and were, as ever, by far the biggest local employers. Next in size was Ormerod Brothers, owned by Abraham, William and Peter Ormerod, who employed nearly 500 operatives at their Ridgefoot and Gorpley Mills. About 250 people worked for John and Ashton Stansfield at their Lineholme Mill, and there was a cluster of firms with about 120-140 operatives, including Firth and Haworth of Causeway and Oldroyd Mills, Charles Chambers of Salford, William Helliwell of Friths Mill, and Thomas Bottomley of Spring Mill. There were also numerous smaller cotton mills, and several factories where machinery, bobbins and pickers were made. Of these, only Lawrence Wilson's bobbin works at Cornholme was a sizeable enterprise.

Wilson was a first-generation industrialist who had set up in business as a bobbin turner at a small mill at Hough Stone near Todmorden in 1823. A few months later he moved to Pudsey Mill where he remained for seven years before building a new steam-powered bobbin works at Cornholme in the Burnley valley. Here the business expanded until it became the major employer in that part of Todmorden, and formed the nucleus around which the village of Cornholme grew. Mr. Wilson stopped the machinery at the Bobbin Mill for fifteen minutes every morning for communal prayers, built a Methodist chapel and schoolroom next to the factory, and did all he could to persuade the village children to attend chapel and school. Mrs. Wilson was an active partner in the business who, as well as looking after the household generally, attended to the firm's correspondence and accounts, took a part in planning the extension and development of the business, and personally brewed up the varnish that was used in the works. She was also well known for the powders which she made for the local mothers to give their ailing children.[4] The markedly paternalist style of the Wilsons was untypical, but there were nevertheless sometimes conflicts between the firm and the local community. Sam Banks, who worked at the Wilsons' from the age of eight, later recorded that the local mothers quite often threatened to take their boys away from the Bobbin Mill unless Wilson increased their wages.[5]

Strikes and Incediarism

The wage reductions of 1841/2, that were commonplace throughout Lancashire, provoked at least one local strike: at Barkers' Barewise Mill, towards the end of 1841. But the following year, some Todmorden industrial disputes took an unusual and particularly threatening form, when they resulted in at least two deliberate attempts to burn down the factory. (Perhaps this strategy had been suggested by the threats made during the plug-drawing strikes, to set fire to any mills that returned to work before the strikers' demands had been met).

The first incident of this kind took place at Messrs.

Uttleys' Jumb Mill at Lumbutts on 24th September, 1842. Uttleys had been coupling their mules so that they could be run by half the number of operatives, and in consequence had dismissed nine or ten of their spinners. So when one of the masters, late at night, discovered a trail of cotton leading to a skip containing greasy waste and other highly combustible material which was just beginning to smoulder, suspicion naturally fell on the recently-dismissed spinners. One of them, Sutcliffe Sutcliffe, was arrested and tried at the next York Assizes, but no very convincing evidence was offered against him and he was found not guilty. A few weeks after the Lumbutts incident, the watchmen at Spring Mill, where Thomas Bottomley had recently reduced the wages of his powerloom weavers, one night observed two men on the roof of the scutching-room with a box of matches. They escaped only by swimming to safety across the mill-dam.[6]

Dissatisfaction at Waterside

Even the Fieldens' radicalism did not make Waterside factory immune from strikes and disaffection. Occasional strikes there included one of the mechanics in 1834 [7], and in 1845, Mr. Clark, a Chartist lecturer who was visiting Todmorden, was very surprised to hear allegations of the mistreatment of the workpeople in the Fielden mills. He said that during his lecture, he:

> "took occasion to speak eulogistically of Mr. John Fielden, MP, pointing him out as an honourable exception to his class; but the

Laurence Wilson's Bobbin Mill at Cornholme in 1835. Showing (from the left), mill, mill-owner's house and chapel/schoolroom (with cottages underneath)

Fielden Mills, 1856

Mill	Business	Machinery	Power (Steam/Water)	Hands
Waterside	silk spinning	mules	S	32
Waterside	cotton spinning & weaving	mules, throstles	S/W	1102
Dobroyd	cop waste breaking up		S/W	3
Smithy Holme	cotton spinning	throstles	S/W	50
Stoneswood	cotton spinning	throstles	S/W	54
Waterstalls	cotton spinning	throstles	S/W	26
Lumbutts	cotton spinning	throstles	S/W	97
Greenwood	cotton spinning	mules, throstles	W	14
Jumb	cotton spinning	mules	W	15
Causeway	cotton spinning	mules	W/S	23
Mytholmroyd	cotton spinning	throstles	S/W	200
Robinwood	cotton spinning	throstles	S/W	309
Total:				**1925**

Source: JRL, Fielden Papers: papers relating to the mill. Simplified from table dated 14/5/1856

expression of this opinion was treated by the meeting as a fraudulent attempt to cheat them, as they universally declared that the hands in his employ are worse treated than those of any other man in the neighbourhood of Todmorden. This I was astonished to hear, as I had always thought that the talented author of the 'factory curse' was too much of a patriot to allow his work-people to be ill-treated: but the people of Todmorden, who ought to know best, declare that it is so, and some of them told me that the conduct pursued in Mr. Fielden's mill has been more than once communicated to the (Northern) Star, but that for some reason, the communications have never appeared". [8]

We are not told the cause of the dissatisfaction amongst the Fieldens' workers on this occasion, but a few years later, their complaint was about short time working. Cotton manufacturing was subject to severe market fluctuations in the 1840s. The Fieldens always resisted responding to a downturn in trade by undercutting their competitors, because in the end it meant lowering wages. They preferred to keep wage-rates as stable as possible and respond to fluctuating demand by running the machinery for fewer hours per day. But this was not always appreciated by the workers, who often preferred to work longer hours at a reduced hourly rate.[9] The Fieldens' mills seemed to be always the first to cut hours, and the last to return to normal working.

The Ten Hours Agitation

It was against the background of this constant fluctuation in working hours and general shortage of work, that John Fielden was able to press Parliament for an Act to limit the hours of labour in cotton factories to ten hours per day for the women and young people who comprised the majority of the workers in cotton mills. The Fielden mills, for example, in 1856 employed nearly 2,000 workers. In round figures, there were 200 boys and 200 girls under 13; 200 boys aged between 13 and 18; and 900 women aged 13 and over. Only 500 of the Fieldens' workers - about a quarter of the workforce - were men aged 18 or over.

The Factory Act of 1833 had made 69 hours a week the maximum that could be worked by persons under 18 years old, and as they formed such a large proportion of the workforce, most manufacturers had adopted this maximum for all their workers. Fielden Brothers did slightly better, and only worked a 67½ hour week. But this still made a very long day. It was exclusive of meal times, so workers were usually in the factory from about 6 am to 7.30 pm, and some unscrupulous employers broke the law, or worked children in relays, so keeping the adult workers for even longer hours. So there was pressure for further legislation, from the operatives themselves and from benevolent and philanthropic employers, including the Fieldens of Waterside.

John Fielden became a national leader of the Ten Hours campaign, which was funded generously from his private fortune. Many of the leading campaigners in the North - Oastler, Doherty, Bull, Hindley - were already his close friends and associates and became frequent visitors to his mansion at Centre Vale. It was Fielden and Todmorden that linked the two parts of the movement - the Yorkshire campaign, led by the Tory-paternalist Richard Oastler, and the Lancashire campaign, conducted principally by John Doherty and the spinners' trade unions.

In the 1840s pressure for a Ten Hours Act became almost continuous. A meeting in the schoolroom at

Waterside in April 1841 resolved to solicit petitions from the local factories and villages in favour of a limitation of the hours of labour for "all persons who work in factories and are above 13 years to 10 hours per day and 8 on Saturdays".[10] This was part of an orchestrated campaign to produce petitions which Fielden was to present to Parliament. The meeting was chaired by Joseph Hirst, who became the secretary of Todmorden Short Time Committee which met at the White Lion Inn at Shade.

By late 1846 there was hope of Parliament agreeing to a new factory act. A recent campaign had very effectively stressed the danger that excessive hours of factory labour posed to the health and morals of women and children, and with over-production and short-time working endemic in the industry, there was little incentive for anyone to oppose shortening factory hours. Unexpectedly, the task of guiding the Ten Hours Bill through Parliament fell to John Fielden. Ashley (later Lord Shaftesbury) had been the Parliamentary leader of the campaign, but a political crisis forced him to resign his seat at this critical moment and Fielden introduced the Ten Hours Bill into the House of Commons in February 1847. It received the Royal Assent in June and the maximum working day for women and young people in textile factories was fixed at 10 hours, or 10½, with a half-holiday on Saturday. It was hoped that this would mean, in practice, a ten hour day for all mill workers.

Support for the Ten Hours Act had been widespread in Todmorden, which sent three petitions in favour of the Act to the House of Lords in April 1847. One was signed by more than 5,400 "factory workers, general inhabitants, ministers and surgeons". The petition from the mill managers and overlookers had been supported "with very few exceptions", and even the one from the master manufacturers and spinners had been "numerously signed".[11] The men most actively involved in the campaign came, not very surprisingly, from the Fielden mills. The named members of the Todmorden Short Time Committee who celebrated victory with a dinner at the White Lion were Henry Shepherd, John Lord, Joseph Hirst, Samuel Fielden, James Pickles and the Rev. Dowty. Henry Shepherd and Joseph Hirst were powerloom overlookers employed at Waterside. John Lord was the manager of the Fieldens' spinning mill at Robinwood. Samuel Fielden was John Fielden's son. The Rev. Dowty was an Anglican minister and the incumbent of Walsden parish. James Pickles cannot be identified with certainty, but was most probably a powerloom weaver who lived on Peel Street.[12] It is noticeable that the Todmorden textile operatives who were active in the campaign all came from the weaving side of the industry - in contrast to Lancashire generally where the spinners and their union dominated the agitation.

The Ten Hours Act became law during a period of slack trade, and so the master spinners and manufac-

Inside a cotton mill

turers were, at first, quite happy to reduce hours gradually in accordance with the new Act. It was reported in July 1847 that the Fieldens had cut their workers' hours to eleven a day, without any reduction in pay, and that several other Todmorden firms had followed suit. By December most local firms were working a ten hour day. But during the early months of 1848 trade picked up again, and some masters started employing women and children in relays so that they could work the adult men for 12 or 13 hours a day.[13] The relay system clearly violated the spirit of the Ten Hours Act, but had not been explicitly forbidden by it, and so a new campaign had to be launched to protect the Act, and urge the Government to outlaw the relay system.

The Death of John Fielden

Fielden did not live to see the relay problem resolved. In 1845 he had moved from Todmorden to Skeynes, near Edenbridge in Kent, in the hope that his health would improve in the milder climate of the South. On the 24 May 1849, although a very sick man, he went with Ashley to present petitions against the relay system to the Home Secretary. Five days later, Fielden was dead.

At noon on the first Monday in July, Todmorden's mills, shops and public houses were closed as a mark of respect whilst the body of John Fielden was conveyed from his mansion at Centre Vale to its final resting place in the burial ground of the little Unitarian chapel at Honeyhole. The road from Centre Vale to the chapel was lined with spectators, and thousands of people had scrambled up the hill-sides, or even onto the tops of the houses, to get a better view of the procession. On arriving at the little chapel, ten men carried the coffin up the steep steps to the tiny graveyard, and laid it in a grave which not even Fielden's Quaker ancestors could have regarded as ostentatious - it was inscribed only with the name of its occupant, and his dates of birth and death.[14]

Fielden was not forgotten by the working people whose welfare had been so close to his heart. A few years after his death a somewhat grander memorial was erected by public subscription: the bronze statue which now stands in the public park which was once his estate at Centre Vale. One rainy Saturday in April 1875, the statue was unveiled in its original position outside Todmorden Town Hall. It shows him addressing Parliament and commemorates the Ten Hours Act of 1847, which was the crowning achievement of his life's work and a landmark in the history of factory legislation. This alone would have been enough to have earned him the friendship of the working classes, but beyond this he had been the tireless advocate of their interests, in and out of Parliament, for over thirty years, supporting all measures that would improve the lot of the working people, and always encouraging them to combine to promote their own causes.

Fielden Brothers - the Old and New Generations

John Fielden's death in 1849, and that of his brother Joshua two years previously, marked the beginning of a transition to a different kind of relationship between the masters and the men at the Fieldens' works. Joshua had always gone amongst the workpeople more than any of the other brothers, and had always been happy to chat and drink a glass of ale with the elder and more intelligent workmen,[15] and John had commanded great personal respect from his workpeople for his determined advocacy of their rights. But after their deaths, the only surviving members of the second generation were James and Thomas Fielden. James lived quietly and unpretentiously near the factory, supervising the day-to-day spinning and weaving. He shared his brother John's opinions, but lacked his energy and breadth of vision. And Thomas had from youth lived in Manchester, acting as the firm's agent and merchant, and was relatively little known in Todmorden.

Unveiling the Fielden Memorial

When James died in 1859, the management of the firm passed effectively to the third generation - John's sons: Samuel, John and Joshua. The third generation of Fieldens had been brought up in a very different manner from their father. "Honest John" and his brothers, it will be remembered, had been educated alongside the other village children, and like them, had started work in the mill when they were still children. For most of their lives they had lived near the factory, alongside their workers. They had known their senior employees as playmates, fellow workers and political allies. Fielden's sons, by contrast, were educated at boarding schools, two of them completing their education in Geneva. They returned to Todmorden to live in pleasant mansions away from the smoke and pollution of the factories; and in time, they adopted Conservative politics. It would be interesting to know what effect the Fieldens' conversion to Conservatism had on their relationships with their employees, especially as we noticed earlier that several of the Fielden's senior employees were conspicuously involved in the Radical political campaigns of the 1830s and 1840s. These included John Haigh of Stoneswood Mill, John Holt of Smithyholme Mill, Edmund Holt of Lumbutts Mill, Joseph Hirst of Waterside, Luke Midgley of Knowlwood Mill, and John Lord of Robinwood Mill. Haigh and John and Edmund Holt were committee members of the Todmorden Political Union. Edmund Holt and Hirst took a leading part in the anti-Poor Law agitation. The leading local Chartists included Hirst, Haigh, Midgley and Edmund Holt. Hirst became the local Secretary of the Ten Hours campaign, and John Lord, the manager of Robinwood Mill, was President of the Todmorden Short Time Committee. This roll-call of politically-active Fielden managers and overlookers almost certainly represents just the tip of the iceberg - for instance, I discovered no newspaper report mentioning Abraham Fielden, although his son recorded that he was a Chartist and a member of Todmorden Short Time Committee, and once sat on a platform in Todmorden with Lord Ashley. Abraham Fielden also was a powerloom overseer at the Fieldens' Waterside factory. [16]

John Fielden's achievement had been to forge a local alliance between the middle and the working classes. By appealing to their shared sense of community loyalty, their common values of independence and democracy, and to their mutual interests as the producers of wealth, Fielden had, for a time, united the two classes in pursuit of shared political goals. But by mid-century, they no longer had common objectives. The ten hours campaign had reached a successful conclusion, the New Poor Law was a dead letter in Todmorden, and militant Chartism had divided the classes. The alliance fragmented. The Fielden family became more politically conservative; many of the other local manufacturers adopted orthodox Liberalism; and some of the local Chartists were hoping that the long-awaited Chartist rising would come at last.

With many of the local mills back on short time, and growing hostility between masters and men, attempted wage reductions brought another round of strikes.

1850: A Year of Industrial Conflict

The long-running Lineholme strike of 1850 was sparked off by an attempted wage reduction. Towards the end of April the weavers employed at Lineholme Mill by John and Ashton Stansfield came out on strike, and were joined three weeks later by the weavers from the nearby Barewise Mill, run by John and William Barker, who had also tried to lower wages. As the strike continued, other grievances of the workpeople emerged. They complained that they had been charged excessive prices for brushes and other items used in their work; and that the Barkers fined weavers who were even a quarter of a minute late to their work one shilling at least, and in many cases sent them home.

Trade was very slack at all the firms in Todmorden at this time and many of the Lineholme people left town to look for work in Leeds or Bradford. Those who remained started supporting themselves by walking in procession through the town, singing and begging alms from the other mill-hands. This practice of strikers walking in procession and begging was viewed with alarm by the authorities. No doubt it

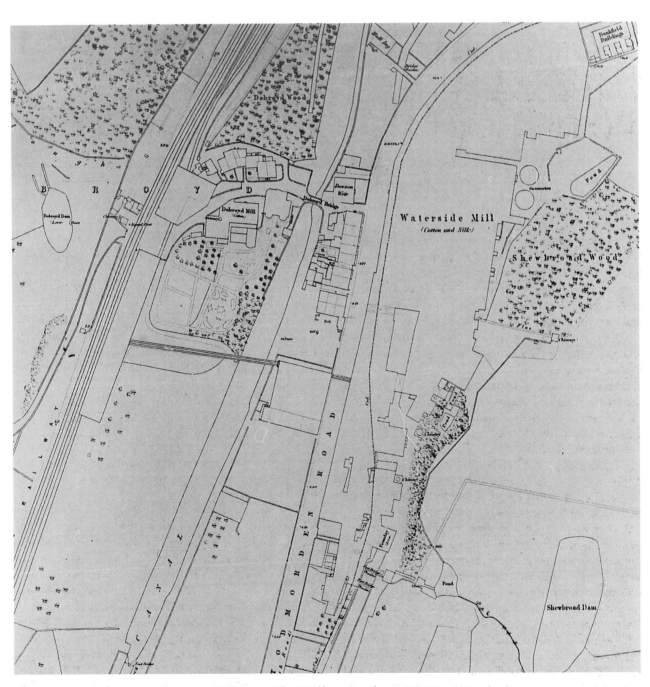

Waterside Mill complex, 1852

85

awoke uncomfortable memories of 1842, and the police were induced to put a stop to it. But the Lineholme strikers continued to perambulate. Some were arrested at Burnley as vagrants, but the weavers engaged the legal services of Mr. Roberts of Manchester, who successfully defended them on the grounds that peaceable walking and the receiving of alms were quite legal, so long as the weavers did not beg but just accepted what was freely given. So the Lineholme weavers continued to walk in procession to Todmorden, Hebden Bridge, Bacup and Burnley, and were supported by the mill-workers in these towns. In August, with the strike in its fifteenth week, they published their eleventh weekly report, showing that they had received £42 6s 7d. in donations that week, and that their expenses had been £41 2s 1d, and they declared that they "still have the determination to stand firm for their rights so long as the public continue to manifest that liberal disposition which they have done formerly". They continued to publish weekly accounts - always showing a slight excess of income over expenditure, with the intention, no doubt, of demonstrating to their erstwhile employers their ability and determination to hold out. [17]

In the summer of 1850, even the factory of the paternalist Lawrence Wilson suffered a strike. It had been Mr. Wilson's custom to increase the wages of his boy-workers by 1s a year - but this year, when the increase came due, he offered just half. The boys refused to take this and walked out, bringing production to a halt. [18]

In August the *Halifax Guardian* reported that the Ten Hours Act had been adopted by most of the Todmorden mills, and that this had mostly been accomplished without any reduction in wages. The more generous masters had raised wage-rates voluntarily and the rest had been compelled to do so by strikes. [19]

A Strike at Gauxholme Mill

A Todmorden strike placard from the 1850s gives the flavour of an industrial dispute of the time. The strike, of Abraham Robertshaw's weavers at Gauxholme mill, is known only through the survival of an undated copy of the strikers' seventh report, listing donations received during the eighth week of the dispute.[20] The strike is evidently being conducted on the same plan as the one at Lineholme in 1850, the strikers perambulating the district and receiving donations. A walk to Bacup yielded £1 19s 6 ½d. Many of the sums listed are small:

a Salt chap with an Ass	8d
Jam a Tum's wife	2d
a man shaving	2d

Some show the strikers stopping at mills or taverns, and a collection being taken there:

Waterside weavers	£2 5s 6d
Causeywood Mill	4s 2d
Ingham's, Castle Street	9s 6d
Mason's Arms	4d
Exhibition Tavern	6d

A surprising donation came from :

L Wilson	5s

This can only be Lawrence Wilson, of Cornholme Bobbin Mill. Why should he support the striking workers of another manufacturer? Wilson, it will be remembered, was a respectable and strongly paternalist employer. It appears that Robertshaw was from another mould. It was rumoured that he had lain the foundations of his fortune by buying "range" or embezzled weft on the black market, and he is known to have demanded that two of his male powerloom weavers pay him rent for a hut in Knowlwood known as the "last shift", and dismissed them when they refused.[21] Perhaps Wilson and Robertshaw fell on opposite sides of a divide between "honourable" and "non-honourable" employers.

Some of the contributors to the fund had suggestions as to what to do with Robertshaw:

Hang th' old chap...	2d
Turn him with wrong end up...	6d
Stand him out, and bury him when you've done...	4d
Cut his tail off, and sew it on again for punishment...	4d

As a postscript to their placard, the weavers appealed for help to return Robertshaw to his village of origin:

> He is a tyrant - that is true!
> But he was once as poor as you.
> He went about a selling print;
> But now his heart is hard as flint.
> Be firm, and then we're not to poor
> To send the tyrant back to SHORE.

Warehouse at Gauxholme Wharf

Chapter 7

Towards a New Co-operative Commonwealth

As hopes of gaining political citizenship for the working class receded, there was a resurgence of interest in building up its own institutions, such as co-operatives and friendly societies, and in schemes for the improvement of the moral and physical condition of the working people through education and temperance. The pendulum was swinging once more, away from direct political action and towards mutual assistance.

Adult Education

Several societies for educating working people were set up in Todmorden in the late 1840s. Many of the local cotton factories were working short time, even before the introduction of the Ten Hours Act made the evenings longer for most factory workers; and at the same time, active participation in the Chartist movement was beginning to decline. Chartism had been a great educating force and had accustomed a large section of the population to attending lectures and meetings in the evenings after work, and so hopes were entertained of attracting people to the various new educational ventures.

Some of these societies, including the Athenaeum, the Church Institute, and the Floral and Horticultural Society, attempted to recruit both from the middle and the working classes. They all complained that the middle classes did not support the societies as they should, and the working classes did not attend. None of them flourished for very long. In January 1848, the Athenaeum had over 100 members, and 612 books in its library, but its fortunes declined rapidly over the next few years. The working-class members attempted to form classes, but these were not successful without the help of the middle-class members.[1] By the time of the Government's Educational Census in 1851, the Athenaeum was in the doldrums, with only 4 proprietary members and 35 ordinary members, and giving only two lectures a year.[2]

A small group of working people made an ambitious attempt to set up a mutual improvement society in the Lineholme area of Todmorden in the autumn of 1847. The "Lydgate People's Institute" met in Lower Nazebottom schoolroom where it set up a library and offered lectures in literature, science and the arts. It was open to both men and women. A large number of people were enrolled at the first meeting, which was chaired by John Lord, the manager of Robinwood mill; and addressed by William Horsfall, an architect, and Abraham Stansfield, a horticulturalist.[3]

Abraham Stansfield did more to promote the cause of working class adult education in Todmorden at this time than any single other person. He was a very talented self-taught botanist, who ran a small business as a plantsman from his house at Vale Cottage in Todmorden. In the summer of 1847, when many local firms were working short-time, he opened his gardens at Vale to the public; and visitors could enjoy the huge stock of garden flowers, wander through the greenhouse, and visit the tea-room. They could also conduct experiments with a large "Cylindrical Electrifying Machine" and an "Electro-Magnetic Machine", or view an exhibition of coins. In January 1851, he and his son Thomas gave a set of lectures in Todmorden on biology, electricity and mesmerism, etc., to the great amusement of a packed hall,[4] and the following year he set up the Todmorden Botanical Society, which met at the White Hart Inn. The Botanical Society was a great success, thanks to the efforts of Abraham Stansfield and his friend John Nowell of Springs, Harley Wood. Nowell was another expert and enthusiastic botanist, and also a working man. He earned his living as a twister-in in a cotton mill.

Temperance and Teetotalism

Alcoholic drink was a normal and even necessary part of everyday life in the early 19th century. Weak beer, often home-made, was a usual beverage, even for children. And people gathered at public houses, not just for fellowship and fire, but often to conduct business. It was in the public houses that friendly societies, Freemasons and trade unions met; that corn-millers attended to do business on their appointed days; that warp and weft were sometimes put out and cloth taken in from the handloom weavers; that meetings of Poor Law Guardians or ratepayers were often held. In the earlier part of the century, even poor relief had sometimes been given out in the public houses. Not surprisingly, excessive drinking was rife. Some pubs never shut their doors. It quite frequently happened that people, making their uncertain way home along unlit streets, fell into the canal and were drowned. Drink also put a tremendous strain on working-class family budgets.

Temperance meetings were held in Todmorden in the late 1830s, and some converts made. One was Ambrose Brook, or "Ould Ambros" as he was known. Brook became one of the best-known local teetotallers, and the anniversary of his conversion to a sober life was celebrated each year on his birthday by the local abstainers.

But it was not until the late 1840s that temperance and teetotalism began to make real headway in the Todmorden area.[5] It seems that, about this time, the desirability of bringing about a moral regeneration of the working classes by turning them away from excessive drinking had become generally accepted, though perhaps for different reasons, by different groups in society. The local teetotal movement was a co-operative effort between magistrates, employers, friendly societies, Chartists, Wesleyans and women.

The magistrates decided to put a stop to the practice of public houses staying open for as long as anybody wished to drink, and gave notice in 1847 that they were to close at 12 o'clock at night, and, according to reports in the local press, this was generally acted upon. One employer who was particularly energetic in promoting the teetotal cause was Lawrence Wilson and it was as a result of his influence that Cornholme village had its Good Samaritan Temperance Society from April 1847, and continued to be a stronghold of temperance for over half a century. It was about this time as well that the Oddfellows began to move away from their old customs of communal feasting and drinking. A tent of Rechabites - a friendly society open only to teetotallers - was established in Todmorden by 1850. The Chartists supported temperance, so long as it was not linked to anti-Chartism or Sabbatarianism. The Wesleyan Association was more than willing to lend its schoolrooms and chapels for temperance meetings. But perhaps the most interesting role of all was that played by the women.

The 1840s saw the extension to the working class of that sanctification of the home and idealisation of the woman's place in it, that was such a dominant theme of Victorian ideology. This was accompanied by a very noticeable abandonment by women of the kinds of political action that they had engaged in during the Chartist times, and a lessened desire to take on paid work outside the home, especially for married women (even if the desire could not always be translated into reality). We have already seen that during the Chartist agitation, the women of Todmorden had been exhorted to get back to their darning and leave politics to the men, and that even a local radical meeting had supported, at the time of the plug-drawing strike of 1842, a resolution demanding: "that females having children, even one, should cease to work where machinery is used". If it had been implemented, this resolution would have excluded virtually all females except adolescents from factory work, and forced any unsupported woman with a child into one of the very ill-paid occupations that were the last resorts of poor women, such as dressmaking, millinery, washing or service. For such women it would have been a disaster. But for married women, after two decades of long hours of factory labour for men, women and children alike, the notion of a home-based wife, taking care of her own children and attending to the welfare and comfort of her family, might have seemed an attractive and even progressive one - for those who could afford it. And affording it depended upon the family having a steady and reliable male wage-earner. Irregularity of employment, illness, and drink - but especially drink - threatened the new domestic idyll.

So it is not very surprising to find women taking an active part in the temperance movement and even travelling around the country lecturing on the subject - an activity which, in almost any other cause, would have drawn severe criticism. Todmorden received lectures on teetotalism by Mrs. Carlisle "the celebrated philanthropist", Mrs. Jackson, and in 1848 by Mrs. Theobald - who addressed the Chartists on the Friday, and the Teetotal Society on the Saturday.[6] By August 1848 Todmorden had its own branch of female teetotallers, and a few weeks later a teetotal meeting in the Wesleyan Association schoolroom at Bridge Street was addressed by Mrs. Law and Mrs. Greenwood, who were both Todmorden women, and who spoke in such "a powerful and forceful manner" that at the end of the meeting eighteen people took the pledge. The Todmorden Female Temperance Society held a tea-party and lecture in the Bridge Street schoolroom the following April, and Mrs. Law took the chair. [7]

It would be interesting to be able to identify these leading local female teetotallers, Mrs. Law and Mrs. Greenwood, and especially to discover whether they were the wives of manufacturers, tradesmen, or labourers - but unfortunately this is quite impossible as neither their first names nor their addresses are given. We might speculate that the female teetotallers were more-or-less direct descendents of the female Chartists, but again, there is no evidence to support this. But it is fascinating to see women taking a major public role - addressing meetings in a powerful manner, taking the chair at social events - at the very time when women in general were supposedly retreating into the home. But the Home was threatened by Drink; and in defence of the one, and opposition to the other, women were permitted and even encouraged to take a public platform.

Friendly Societies

By the 1840s, most of the small local friendly societies had become lodges of one or other of the affiliated orders, such as the Oddfellows or Foresters. The largest order in Todmorden was the Independent Order of Oddfellows, Manchester Unity, which in 1846 had 885 members and nine lodges in its Todmorden district. There were also some lodges that were affiliated to other orders, including a lodge of the Bolton Unity of Oddfellows, and at least two courts of Foresters, two lodges of the Ancient Free Gardeners, and a lodge of Ancient Shepherds.

Friendly societies were now beginning to adopt temperance principles. In 1848 the *Halifax Guardian* commented that the secret societies' dinner-day customs were less pronounced than previously - particularly with the Oddfellows; and the following year Humility lodge followed the usual dinner at the

Men's Friendly Societies
Todmorden Lodges Of Affiliated Orders

Lodge No.	Lodge Name	Place Of Meeting	Membership	
INDEPENDENT ORDER OF ODDFELLOWS, MANCHESTER UNITY				
57	Humility	Spring Gardens Inn Oddfellows' Hall by 1846	215	(1846)
177	Shepherdess	Roebuck Inn Portsmouth	126	(1846)
398	Perseverence	Oddfellows' Hall by 1846	121	(1846)
436	Prudence of the Vale	Shoulder of Mutton	138	(1846)
578	Hope	Shannon and Chesapeake	64	(1846)
680	Mercy	Waggon and Horses, Walsden	114	(1846)
984	Lily of the Valley	Wood Mill Inn (in Hebden Bridge District)	50	(1846)
1338	Queen Victoria	Dog and Partridge, Lumbutts	31	(1846)
1737	Rose of Sharon	Blue Ball Inn, Cloughfoot later, British Queen	59	(1846)
1904	Benevolence	Moorcock, Inchfield	17	(1846)
	Glen View	Shoulder of Mutton, Toad Carr	?	
ANCIENT NOBLE ORDER OF UNITED ODDFELLOWS, BOLTON UNITY				
193	Good Intent	White Hart Inn (1869-73, Golden Lion)	120	(1849)
ANCIENT FORESTERS				
520	Court Goshen	York Tavern	190	(1844)
	Court Alexander	Roebuck Inn	100+	(1847)
ANCIENT FREE GARDENERS				
	Rose of the Valley	Royal George	100+	(1848)
	Lily of the Vale	York Tavern	?	
LOYAL ORDER OF ANCIENT SHEPHERDS				
74	Jacob-at-the-Well	Old Blue Ball, Blackshawhead	130	(1849)
ANCIENT ROMANS				
	Lily of the Valley	White Hart Inn		(1838)

Sources: Ratcliffe, William (compiler), *A list of all the lodges comprising the Manchester Unity of Independent Oddfellows, for 1846-7*
Northern Star 17/11/1838
Halifax Guardian 16/10/1847, 5/1/1844, 8/1/1848 12/8/1848, 21/10/1848, 2/6/1849

Mount Zion Methodist Chapel, Cornholme

Queen's Hotel with a business meeting at the Oddfellows' Hall, during which no intoxicating drinks at all were taken.[8] Over the next few years, several of the Todmorden Oddfellows lodges moved their headquarters from public houses to the Oddfellows' Hall, perhaps partly because many of their members had by now turned teetotal, and when Thomas Greenlees, the operative spinner who was the founder of Oddfellowship in Todmorden, died in 1847 his obituary noted that he had been a teetotaller for ten years. [9]

As we saw, Todmorden had in the early part of the nineteenth century, a great number of women's friendly societies, run by the women themselves and offering benefits similar to those enjoyed by the members of the men's societies. But when the men's societies joined the affiliated orders, women were mostly excluded from this growth and expansion. Some of the orders were actively hostile to female friendly societies, and the Oddfellows of the Bolton Unity agreed at a delegate meeting in February 1832 that if any member became connected with the "Odd Women" or any other Female Secret Societies whatsoever, he should be permanently dismissed from the Order.[10] There was a growing feeling that it was unseemly for women to meet in public houses, and that it was more proper for a woman's insurance needs to be provided for through her husband's membership of a well-regulated friendly society. Nevertheless, at least two local women's societies survived into the 1870s. One was a lodge of female Foresters which met at the York Hotel, and the other was the female friendly society meeting at the Shoulder of Mutton, which became the Rose of Paradise Lodge of Todmorden and District of the Yorkshire Grand United Order of Female Florists.

With married women now mainly dependent on their husbands' friendly society membership, the Todmorden Oddfellows set up a special Widows' and Orphans' Fund in 1845. It was a voluntary scheme, and participating members paid extra contributions which were collected by their lodges and passed on to the district fund. These contributions were to be supplemented by charitable donations and by the profits of a Shrove Tuesday ball. The committee which gave assistance to the widows was as careful with its cash as the most parsimonious Board of Poor Law Guardians. Orphans' school fees were often paid - and the children examined every three months to see what progress they had made. Widow Fielden was allowed half of the cost of a mangle for the support of her family, provided her deceased husband's lodge paid the other half. And widow Law, having "dishonoured herself" was declared "no longer entitled to the benefits of this fund". [11]

There was also around mid-century a great expansion in the numbers of church and chapel sick and funeral clubs. These were set up to provide friendly society benefits for the church members, without subjecting them either to the temptations of the public houses, or to the secret and possibly unchristian rituals of the affiliated orders. York Street Methodists had a funeral society in 1848,[12] and Shore Baptists, who had in 1831 registered disapproval of "secret societies" and had made several early attempts to set up funds to help their members in difficult times, finally established a chapel funeral club in 1850. [13]

Within a few years, each of the three chapels in the Cornholme area had its own sick or funeral club. The Cornholme Methodist Sick and Burial Society was set up in the same year as the Shore Funeral Club, and the Baptist chapel at Vale followed in 1856 with its own Sick Society. 1856 also saw the establishment of the Todmorden Unitarian Church Burial Society, and the Bridge Street Methodist Friendly Society was set up the following year. Many, if not most, of the local chapels followed suit over the next few years, including the parish churches of Todmorden and of Walsden, the Baptist chapels at Wellington Road and Roomfield, and Knowlwood Methodists. [14]

The subscriptions to the chapel sick societies were generally low, and they usually had a high proportion of young working women amongst their members. The affiliated orders, on the other hand, attracted the serious and sober working men, often skilled workers, or small shopkeepers and businessmen, who could afford the rather higher contributions that these friendly societies demanded. There was no reason why a Chartist might not be an Oddfellow, and many were. Richard Wheelwright, the Chartist bookseller, was initiated into Humility lodge in 1845. And in 1862 Samuel Whitham was elected District Grand Master of the Manchester Unity of Oddfellows. [15]

Friendly Societies and Building Societies

Many friendly societies considered bricks and mortar to be a safer investment for their funds than banks, which were notoriously unstable and liable to collapse - as Holgate's Burnley bank did in 1824, and Sutcliffe's Todmorden bank a few years later.

Of the early buildings constructed locally by friendly societies, several took the form of a large open hall on the first floor, with cottages for rent underneath. One was Lanebottom School, Walsden, which was built by a public subscription originated by a friendly society meeting at the Waggon and Horses public house. In this case the upper room was intended as a schoolroom, and the rent from the cottages went to defray the expenses of the school. The "Union Building" put up for the Spinners' and Weavers' Union in the 1820s was built to a similar pattern, with

back-to-back cottages below, and the large room above was let to a local cotton-spinner as a twining room. Even the Oddfellows Hall, opened in 1842, was built to a similar plan, though on a much larger scale, with a large first-floor meeting hall, and a warehouse, a couple of shops and about twenty cottages built underneath and alongside. This was followed in 1850 by Sobriety Hall, built by the Rechabites, which stood on Rose Street in the centre of Todmorden. [16]

The friendly societies also invested in ordinary cottage property. An early example comes from William Greenwood's diary, which notes in 1825 that Portsmouth friendly society had appointed a committee to "take into consideration building a cottage house or two somewhere". The friendly society which met at the Golden Lion, Todmorden, owned a cottage at Honey Hole in 1832. In 1845, an unidentified Oddfellows lodge owned eight cottages at Knotts Nook, which were bought by the

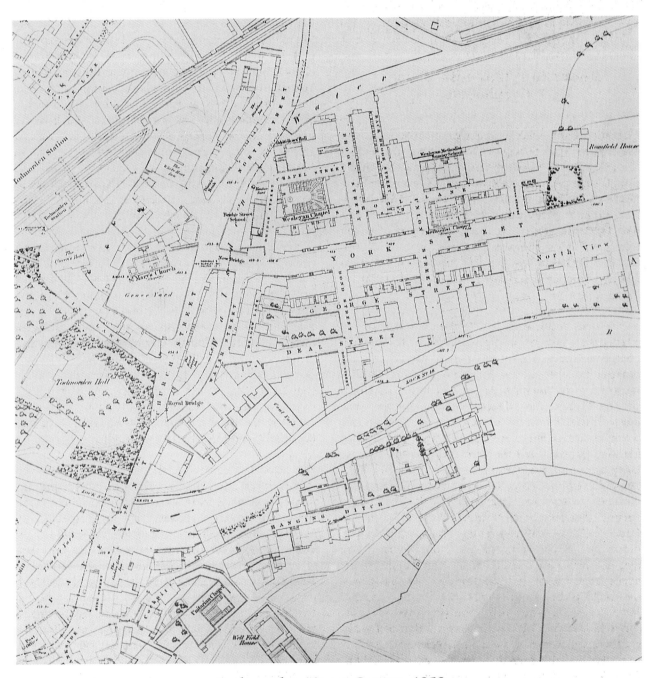

Todmorden Town Centre, 1852

91

Lancashire and Yorkshire Railway Company in about 1852 and demolished soon afterwards. By 1850, the Mechanics' Club was the owner of seven houses at Union Street and Back Union Street, there were six "club" houses at School Lane, and the Foresters' club owned 26 cottages at Goshen Terrace. Humility lodge of Oddfellows, Manchester Unity, also had a house club in the 1840's, and Good Intent lodge of Oddfellows, Bolton Unity, started to build cottages in 1853, the first ones being at East Street and Omega Street in Todmorden, and Hollins Mount at Walsden.[17]

It seems that some of these buildings put up by friendly societies and trade unions were intended simply as an investment for the society's funds, whilst others appear to have been a scheme to allow participating members to become the owners of their own cottages. The second type was similar to a terminating building society, and one local example, I suspect, was the "house club" belonging to Humility lodge of Oddfellows, which in 1845 owed the lodge £480, which was gradually repaid over the next six years. [18]

Todmorden's first building society "open to all classes of the community" was the Todmorden Mutual Benefit Building Society, formed in March 1853. There was an entrance fee of 2s 6d, and a share in the society cost £120, to be paid for at 10s a month, but half or quarter shares could be purchased. When the Directors of the Society had £120 in hand, a share was allocated to one of the members of the society, either by bidding or ballot. The successful member could use the money to build or buy property which was offered as security to the society until his share was paid off. When all the members of the society had had their turn, and all the money owing to the society was repaid, the society terminated.

So by joining the Todmorden Building Society people could become house-owners at a cost of 2s 6d a week. This was a sum which could probably be spared by the better-off sections of the working-class; the tacklers and overlookers, mechanics and skilled men, the sort of people who were the backbone of the friendly societies. It seems that the scheme was a success, for it was followed six years later by the Second Todmorden Benefit Society, which had exactly the same terms as the first society. The secretary to the second society was James Dawson of Wadsworth Mill,[19] who had previously been secretary to the Good Intent lodge of Oddfellows - themselves active and successful builders.

The Co-operative Revival

Following the disappointing rejection of the third Chartist petition in 1848, the formation of co-operative societies became official Chartist policy. At the camp meeting held at Blackstone Edge in July 1850 all the speakers, including Feargus O'Connor himself, urged their listeners to establish co-operative societies as a means towards obtaining the Charter. And at a local Chartist meeting at Carr Green at Lumbutts the following month, William Fielden spoke of how the labourers, who produced all the wealth, had to keep the other two thirds of the community in idleness and luxury. The remedy for this was to join the National Charter Association and encourage the establishment of co-operative stores for the sale of provisions and clothing. The meeting pledged itself to support and encourage such societies. [20]

The Todmorden Chartists had already made a start towards establishing their own co-operative store in August 1847, when a number of factory operatives had come together and decided to try the experiment of forming a co-operative flour society. The price of flour had been very high, but was now beginning to fall, and the operatives wanted to obtain cheaper flour and try to prevent the local flour dealers from forming a ring to keep prices up, as they believed they had done the last time the wholesale price of flour had dropped. There was a crowded public meeting in the Oddfellows' Hall on 17th August, at which it was decided to form a joint-stock company to purchase flour on behalf of its members. The shares were £1 each, payable in instalments of a shilling at the time of joining, and then sixpence per week till the whole was paid. The scheme had originated with the local Chartists - the financial arrangements agreed upon were suggested by Enoch Horsfall, and the chairman of the meeting was Robert Brook. Within three or four weeks £50 had been contributed, and there were already 250 members of the society.[21] Some temporary arrangement had to be made to supply the members with flour until the joint-stock company could be legally constituted: and so at first each member paid in advance for one week's stock of flour, a bulk buy was then made by the society's agent, and when the flour arrived it was weighed out in proportion to each member's contribution. These very early days of co-operative trading were later recalled by John Stott who said:

> "He was at the birth of the society, which took place in a cellar in York Street. (It had been) said that at the beginning they paid as they went along, but they did better than that at the beginning; they took their money one week and got their flour the following week. They carried on in that way for a time; when the time came for dealing out the flour, they took care to have a little to spare after serving all the members, and that was called profit. At that time their flour came from America, and it was not all good flour; sometimes there would come a barrel of sour stuff. They had to take that into serious consideration, and for a while they could not see their way out of the difficulty. Ultimately, they appealed to Mr. Edmund Whittaker, who was a sizer at Sandholme, asking him if, in the event of their getting a barrel of sour flour, he would exchange it for a good one, and he promised to do so. The loss of £5 in those days would have ruined the society, -on

nay, he believed that one barrel of sour flour would have ruined them, if they had not discovered a way out of the dilemma". [22]

There were difficulties and disagreements in the early months of the society's existence. Samuel Whitham later spoke of how "at an early crisis a meeting was called in Sobriety Hall to consider winding up the concern", but he, as chairman of the meeting, had successfully urged that the experiment should continue. Another disagreement amongst the members probably explains why pages containing the names of many of the early subscribers, and nearly all the minutes for 1849, were at some stage torn out of the society's minute book. But by 1850 the society was established in a cellar store on York Street, at or near the corner of George Street. [23]

In August 1850 another store was opened at Shade - a part of the town where many of the members lived. The Shade members ran their store independently of the Todmorden one from the start, and in April 1851 the two societies formally separated. Within a few months, each had registered separate rules with the Registrar of Friendly Societies. The rules for the government of the "Equitable Progressionists' Stores at Bridge End", as the Shade society was now known, were the first to be agreed. Goods were to be supplied to members only, and paid for on delivery, and the stores were to be open from 6.30 to 9.30 on weekday evenings, and 2.30 till 10.30 am Saturday. Shares were £2 each, and each member could hold between one and twenty-five shares, paying 1s to enter the society, and not less than 3d a week, until he or she was the owner of one share. Shares would earn 5% per annum interest, and all remaining profits would be distributed amongst the members quarterly in proportion to their purchases at the stores. A few weeks later, the "Equitable Sincerity Stores" of York Street, registered an almost identical set of rules. [24]

After a while, the Todmorden society needed bigger premises and a shop was bought on Dale Street. The Shade society eventually traded from a shop at Bridge End, which they had asked Fielden Brothers to build for them, but not before it had lain empty for several years. The co-operators refused to pay more than £30 a year for the house and the shop, and so from 1854 until the Fieldens agreed to these terms three years later, the Society occupied some cheaper premises that were later converted to the Woodpecker Inn. [25]

A third co-operative society came into being at Walsden on the 10th December 1849, when a number of factory operatives met at the house of James Howarth of Strines. James Howarth was a powerloom weaver; and the other people present that day were John Wood of Ramsden, a mule spinner; Abraham Jackson of Ramsden Wood, a powerloom weaver; Uriah Brook of Todmorden, a powerloom overlooker; and William Fletcher, a carder. They agreed that each member of the co-op should take out a £1 share, and soon took a house at Bottoms - opposite the road leading to Ramsden Wood - which they opened as a shop in the name of Uriah Brook and Co. Here they began to sell flour and other commodities at cost price to induce people to join the society. This showed the enormous profits being made by the regular traders, and not surprisingly, the co-operators met considerable opposition from these individual traders. By 1851, the society had 58 members, and was worth almost £150. It had also started to pay out dividends, from which we can assume that it had by now adopted the usual co-operative practice of selling the goods at the going price, rather than the cost price, and distributing the surplus amongst the members in the form of periodic dividends.

The Walsden co-op continued to expand, little by little. A better shop, with a warehouse attached was obtained at "The Row" in Ramsden Wood Road and opened in the name of "James Howarth and Co.", and James Howarth became the society's first regular shopman. A second shop was opened at the Hollins in 1854 or 1855, in an old house next to the Hollins Inn, with Samuel Midgley and Edmund Crossley, who were both weavers, as the shopmen. Both shops opened evenings only until 1857, when the Bottoms shop started to open during the day, and rules for the governance of the stores were formally agreed and registered in 1859. [26]

An attempt to establish a co-operative store at Portsmouth in the Burnley valley was less successful. Like the Todmorden and Bridge End societies, it registered its rules in 1851, but it never again appears

The Woodpecker Inn, once the home of the Bridge End Equitible Progressionists

The Dale Street Stores of Todmorden Co-Operative Society, erected in 1882

in the official records. A chance comment by Sam Banks, writing in 1891, reveals why: "The shop where Mrs. Snape lives, was at one time a union shop, but was robbed, it was thought by some of its own members, a large portion of the red flannel was taken. After this, the place was given up". [27]

These early co-operative shops were dependent on the voluntary services of their shopmen. Those who can be traced in the census turn out to be, almost without exception, factory workers - spinners, weavers and card-room hands - and nearly all of them were married men aged between 20 and 40. Their dedication to the ideals of co-operation was such that, after working a full day in the factory, they would go to the co-operative store and serve customers and weigh out and bag groceries, until ten o'clock at night, and then be back at the factory for six the following morning. The men who promoted the co-operative societies, and acted as trustees and the signatories to the societies' rules and regulations, were seldom ordinary cotton spinners or weavers, and quite frequently Chartists. Brook and Horsfall, as we have seen, were the instigators of the flour society from which the Todmorden Co-operative society grew, and amongst the people who signed

documents from the early years of the society, were the Chartists Richard Wheelwright, Samuel Whitham, James Scholfield and Henry Helliwell.

The co-operative societies grew only slowly at first. In 1864, the Todmorden society had 407 members, the Bridge End society 341, and the Walsden society, 232. [28] Only when wages and living standards started to improve over the next two decades, could they begin to attract a mass-membership. By 1887, Todmorden society had 3,010 members. [29] The society celebrated its jubilee in 1897, the same year that Todmorden became a Chartered Borough, and the Co-operative Society marked the occasion by laying the foundation stones of a fine free library which the Society was to donate to the town. The library was equipped with 8,000 books, and is probably the only English municipal library that was the gift of a co-operative society. In its jubilee year, the Todmorden Co-operative Society had a turnover of £130,000 a year. [30]

It had come a very long way since, fifty years earlier, a few people had pooled their meagre resources to buy a barrel of flour, fervently hoping that it would not be sour.

Conclusion

The question that obviously arises from an examination of Todmorden's turbulent history during the second quarter of the 19th century is, to what extent was the town's exceptional militance attributable to the presence and encouragement of John Fielden?

It might be useful, in considering this question, to briefly compare Todmorden with some other Radical northern towns at this time.

Both the anti-Poor Law movement and Chartism attracted enormous popular support in the textile towns of Lancashire and the West Riding of Yorkshire, but this support was not evenly spread across the whole region. Some towns and villages were more militant than others. The districts where the anti-Poor Law movement had its very strongest support - as demonstrated by violent opposition, or by a deep and long drawn out refusal to implement the law - were (besides Todmorden) Huddersfield, Dewsbury, Bradford, Rochdale, Oldham, Bury, and Ashton-under-Lyne.[1] Some of these same places feature in Dorothy Thompson's catalogue of the bastions of the Chartist movement:

> "the districts in which the Chartists were for a time in control, and where traditional authority was most threatened, were in the textile towns of the West Riding - Bradford, Halifax, Dewsbury - of Lancashire and Cheshire - Bolton, Oldham, Ashton, Stockport, Stalybridge - of Nottinghamshire and Leicestershire, the mining and ironworking districts of South Wales and northeast England, and in places like Barnsley or Dundee in which a community of locality, of one or two major industries, and of shared leisure and recreational activities made for speed of communication, common concerns at work and in political action and the kind of mutual knowledge and trust which was essential for the maintenance of organisations which were always on the very frontiers of legality." [2]

Thompson calls attention to the effectiveness of close-knit community in fostering a radical culture. Other historians who have made detailed studies of some of these particularly militant towns during the 1830s and 40s, have identified additional factors which they see as having been instrumental in encouraging radical activism. John Foster, in his classic study of Oldham, refers to the importance of previous radical activity and organisation; of rudimentary policing, or alternatively, policing that could be controlled by the Radicals; and an open, democratic system of local government.[3] Felix Driver, in his recent work on the anti-Poor Law agitation in Huddersfield, makes an explicit comparison with Oldham in emphasising the importance of a previous history of working class organisation and activism:

> "It is clear that the relative effectiveness of anti-Poor Law protest in Huddersfield, as in Oldham, reflected a sophisticated tradition of local radicalism" and "In places like Huddersfield and Oldham, the organisation and strategy of anti-Poor Law protest emerged almost organically from those of other radical movements, such as the factory campaign." [4]

He too, sees Huddersfield's open vestry system of local government as having been crucial.

> "Deprived of a role in other local institutions, radicals saw the open vestry
> as a stronghold of popular democracy. As elsewhere in the industrial
> North, and most notably in Oldham, township meetings and open
> vestries provided "points of access to the local political process" ". [5]

Writing recently about Rochdale in this period, (although in the slightly different context of the origins of co-operation) John Cole also remarks upon the importance of an open vestry style of local government and of previous working-class organisation in the development of a vigorous working-class culture. Additionally, he gives weight to Rochdale's geographical location, which made it the "clearing house for ideas" between Lancashire and Yorkshire; and to the fact that the Rochdale area had many small mills, and consequently many small masters and a weak elite. [6]

All of these factors, considered by these various historians to be conducive to radical political activism, existed to a high degree in Todmorden.

As one of the smaller textile towns (its population was only about 19,000 during the Chartist period), most of whose inhabitants were employed in the single industry of cotton manufacture, Todmorden had in very large measure that quality of community that Thompson sees as having been important for the full development of Chartism. There is plentiful evidence of the existence in Todmorden, from an early date, of independent working-class organisations such as friendly societies and co-operatives; and of working-class involvement in earlier Radical campaigns for universal suffrage, Parliamentary reform and factory legislation. The policing of Todmorden was for most of this period extremely rudimentary, being the responsibility of part-time volunteer constables. They, and other township officers, were elected at township meetings which were open to all ratepayers, and which the Radicals were often able to dominate and use to elect their own men to key positions in local government. Like Rochdale, Todmorden lay on a major trans-Pennine route; but it had the additional advantage of being marginal, split between jurisdictions, and remote from centres of power and control. Also like Rochdale, Todmorden had only a very weak elite. The land was divided into many small farms, the ownership of which was spread amongst a large number of families, and there were many small cotton mills, operated by many small masters. The one firm that was of larger stature was Fielden's - whose owners supported the Radical cause.

As Todmorden displayed so many of the typical features of strongly Radical towns, it is probable that even without John Fielden, it would have been a centre of agitation against the New Poor Law and in favour of the Charter.

Assessing the contribution of Richard Oastler, who was to the Huddersfield anti-Poor Law movement what John Fielden was to the same struggle in Todmorden, Driver writes:

> "Oastler's role in the Huddersfield anti-Poor Law agitation was important;
> but it should not be exaggerated. Indeed, on more than one occasion
> during the struggles of 1837, his ability to control his 'followers' was
> shown to be distinctly fragile." [7]

On first reading this comment, I had a distinct sense of deja vu, having already reached a similar conclusion about John Fielden and the events of 1838. In the world of early 19th century Radical politics, the demarkation between leading and being led was not always clear. As the complex game of bluff and counter-bluff was played out between the local community and the state and its agents, the leader had to conform to the expectations of the crowd, and could find himself out-manoeuvred by his own rhetoric.

Todmorden from the North, early 1840s

APPENDIX:
Todmorden Chartists and their Recorded Activities 1838-1850

The table opposite summarises the recorded activities of 56 Todmorden Chartists.

Source: 1838-50, *Northern Star, Halifax Guardian.*

n.b.   The year 1839 is omitted form the chart - no recorded activities
        * the ages given are for the year 1841

KEY:

a	Arrested
b	selling Chartist Blacking
d	elected Delegate to meeting or conference
h	Chartist meeting held in his House
k	named in *Northern Star*
l	selling Chartist Literature
m	taking active part in Meeting
n	Nominee for Chartist General Council
o	Officeholder
p	Proposed as delegate
s	Sent contribution to Chartist funds
WMA	actively involved in Working Men's Association
NLC	subscriber to National Land Company
TPU	committee member of Todmorden Political Union
SV	member of Select Vestry
APL	active in Anti-Poor Law agitation
TH	active in Ten Hours agitation
CM	actively promoted Co-operative Movement

NAME	Age*	ADDRESS	OCCUPATION	1838	1840	1841	1842	1843	1844	1845	1846	1847	1848	1849	1850	Other Activities
BARK(ER?) Robert							n									
BARKER, Richard		Shade												m		
BARKER, Samuel			Master handloom weaver			h l										
BROOK, Robert	29	George St., Brook St	Agent for *Northern Star*, schoolteacher			d o b	m a	n o	k d o k	h l	m h					NLC, CM
BUTTERWORTH, Jakeh	40	Blind Lane	Powerloom weaver, labourer	m												
BUTTERWORTH, John	35	Back Cheapside	Silk twister			n										NLC
CLEGG, John							m									APL
CLOSE, Richard		Oddfellows Hall	Weaver						s							NLC
COCKCROFT, Gibson	54	Dobroyd	Warehouse clerk				m									APL
CROWTHER, John		Blind Lane	Weaver				a	d n	o							NLC
CUNLIFFE, William		Dobroyd	Sizer			b										NLC
DAVIES, George		Pavement	Watchmaker	m												SV, APL
FIELDEN, James Esq.	53	Dobroyd	Cotton manufacturer				d									SV, APL
FIELDEN, Samuel	25	Centre Vale	son of cotton manufacturer	m												APL, TH
FIELDEN, William		Shade				n m	m									
FIRTH, Matthew				m												
GIBSON, E							m									
GIBSON, James		Shade		m		b	m									APL
GREENWOOD, Barker	31	Market Street	Cotton twister				m									APL, CM
GREENWOOD, William		Pavement	Grocer	m d												SV
HAIGH, John	56	Stoneswood Bottom	Overlooker				m									SV, APL
HARGREAVES, Robert													m			
HELLIWELL, Henry	41	Hanging Ditch	Silk spinner	m		n		n	m							CM
HELLIWELL, William		George Street				n		m n	m o							
HEYWOOD, Hartley								m								
HIRST, Joseph	29	New Barn	Powerloom overlooker	m			m									WMA, APL, TH, CM
HOLDEN, John													m	m		
HOLLOWELL, F									s							
HOLT, Edmund	41	Lumbutts	Overlooker				k									WMA, TPU, APL, CM
HORSFALL, Enoch	31	Millwood	Boot & shoe maker			b	k		m k	k	k					CM
LORD, James							m									APL
MARLAND, Jonas	21	Walsden	Machine maker			n										
MARSHALL, Sutcliffe	19		Tinner				a									
MARSHALL, William	52	Dobroyd	Silk twister			k n							m			
MITCHELL, J											o					
MITCHELL, William													m			
MOONEY, James	33	Union Street	Labourer								d m	o				
MIDGLEY, Luke	24	Stony Brink	Throstle overlooker		s											NLC, CM
POLLARD, Thomas	47	Stoneswood Bottom	Carter				a									
ROBINSON, John	39	Hanging Ditch / George Street	Shoemaker										m			NLC
ROBINSON, William	41	Stones	Farmer / Surveyor	m												SV, APL
SCHOLFIELD, James	25	Roomfield Lane	Joiner			n										
SCHOLFIELD, William		North Street	Ironmonger				m									TPU, SV, APL
SHEPHERD, Henry	24	Goshen Terrace	Powerloom overlooker			m	m d									APL, TH
SMITH, William							a									
SPENCER, John									p							
STANSFIELD, James	20	Millwood	Whitesmith			n				m	m / m s					NLC
STOTT														m		
SUTCLIFFE, George		Butchers Hill	Clogger										d	m		NLC
SUTCLIFFE, James							a									
SUTCLIFFE, John		Dobroyd						n o								
TAYLOR, James		Rochdale / Todmorden	Unitarian Minister				m									
TISDALE, Joseph	37	Lineholme	Innkeeper - Railway Inn			n										
WALTON, J					s											
WHEELWRIGHT, Richard	20	Mytholmroyd / Shade	Undercarder / Bookseller										d	m	m	TH, CM
WHITHAM, Samuel	22	Castle Grove	Gardener					n	m	o	m / m	d				NLC, CM

NOTES AND REFERENCES

Abbreviations

BCL   Bradford Central Library
BPP.   British Parliamentary Papers
CRO   Calderdale Record Office, Halifax
HG   *Halifax Guardian*
LRO   Lancashire Record Office, Preston
JRL   John Rylands Library, Manchester
MSA   *Manchester and Salford Advertiser*
NS   *Northern Star*
PRO   Public Record Office, London
TA   *Todmorden Advertiser*
THA   Ten Hours Advocate
THBHA *Todmorden and Hebden Bridge Historical Almanack*
TN   *Todmorden News*
VP   *Voice of the People*
WYRO West Yorkshire Record Office, Wakefield

Introduction

1 Weaver (1987), p. 29
2 Driver (1993, pp. 120, 122) asserts that no elections took place in Todmorden in March 1837 and that the elections were effectively boycotted in 1838. This misunderstanding arises from a confusion between the Todmorden Poor Law Union and the township of Todmorden-cum-Walsden. Edsall (1971, p. 224) claims that Todmorden sold off all its cottage poorhouses in 1844 and was thereafter "in the unique position of being a Poor Law Union without workhouses". Local sources demonstrate that this is untrue, but the claim has been repeated in Wright (1988, p. 109).

1 John Fielden: Cotton Lord and Radical Reformer

Major sources used are: "C.B." (undated) for Fielden's childhood and education; Fox (1924) for Unitarianism and Fielden's religious development; Travis (1858) for local Anglicanism and rivalry between the Methodists and the Church of England. For the Fielden family and business, the sources used were: Fishwick (1884); John Fielden's own "Curse of the Factory System"; and an anonymous article on the Fieldens of Todmorden in "Fortunes made In Business". These sources are fully listed in the bibliography. Other important sources which I have used, and points of possible controversy, are indicated in the following notes.

1 Travis (1905) pp. 6-8
2 CRO: RP 1770, 1774
3 Fielden (1836) p. 39-40
4 The date at which this increase in hours took place is uncertain. John Fielden (ibid p. 41) says it happened when his father installed "the machinery that is now in use". The machinery refered to can only be the

---

spinning mule; and this would have to be before 1803, when Joshua retired from active management of the business. The mule was available from about 1790.
5 CRO: FIE 147-153
6 The John Grindrod, a maltster of the Parish of Rochdale, who witnesses a Fielden family document in 1823, was presumably her father. LRO: WCW Samuel Fielden 1823
7 Cornholme W.E.A. Branch (1986) pp. 49-54
8 Manchester Central Library, Local Studies: Samuel Crompton, statistics obtained in 1811, (transcript of original at Chadwick Museum, Bolton), f 677 C38. (The throstle was a smaller and simpler machine than the mule, often operated by women or children).
9 CRO: FIE 54-5
10 Bythell (1969) p. 238
11 Travis (1896) pp. 56, 188-9
12 Horne (1817)
13 Ramshaw (1911) p. 36
14 Weaver (1987) p. 46. WYRO: C353/132, 14 Jan 1833
15 LRO: WCW Samuel Fielden, 1823
16 Anon *An account of the riots...* (1826)
17 JRL: Fielden Papers: Attempts to regulate prices, 1826.CRO: TOD 1
18 Burnley Central Library: The memoirs of David Whitehead of Rawtenstall, unpublished typescript, p. 54
19 Weaver (1987) p. 48
20 THBHA 1869 p. 29, *Breaking powerlooms in Lancashire: recollections of an old inhabitant*
21 Travis (1905) pp. 55-6. Ramshaw (1911) p. 71

2 Working Class Life and Culture

1 i.e. the combined population of the three townships of Todmorden-cum-Walsden, Stansfield and Langfield. 1851 Census, numbers of inhabitants, BPP 1852-3 (1632) LXXXVI, vol 2, p. 238-9
2 TA 10/2/1882, obituary Joseph Hirst
3 CRO: Heptonstall Marriages. (The registers of St. Mary's, Todmorden did not record bridegrooms' occupations 1818-22)
4 *Lineholme Baptist Centenary Souvenir*, pp. 12-3
5 William Greenwood, Memorandums 1825. (Original privately owned. Transcript in author's possession)
6 John Burnett, *Plenty and Want* (1979 ed.) p. 53
7 Savage (1985) pp. 3-5
8 TA 10/9/1880, *The Nonconformist Sunday Schools of the district*
9 BPP 1835 (62) XLI p. 459; XLIII pp. 1165-1168
10 Crowther, Walsden...p. 18. THBHA 1883 pp. 13-15, 1903 p. 29
11 THBHA 1903 p. 37, 1885 p. 29
12 CRO: TM 28, Autumn 1822. "Cooper" is presumably William Cowper who was a very popular poet at this time
13 Sources for local men's friendly societies are: PRO: FS1 Yorkshire, Doc. numbers 381/1357, 833A/1401, 833A/1402, 851B/1787, 859B/1926, 859B/1927, 859B/1928, 859B/1929, 860/1944, 860/1945.

Also *Rules and orders ...Free masons' Arms, Bottoms in Stansfield*, 1825
14 Sources for local women's friendly societies are: PRO: FS1 Yorkshire, Doc. numbers 812/238, 835/1442, 838/1473, 844/1674, 851A/1777. CRO: HPC A48, STN 291. *Articles...Portsmouth female society*, 1813. *Rules...a society of females...at the Royal George*, 1816. *Rules ... the female friendly society... at New Inn, Holme...Stansfield,* 1833
15 Sykes (1982) p. 27
16 Travis (1892) pp. 139, 305
17 NS 18/4/1814
18 NS 29/3/1845
19 HG 2/2/1850
20 Lancashire and Yorkshire Co-operator No. 10 (New Series), undated. 4th Congress of delegates from co-operative societies, 1832, statistical table of co-operative societies represented.
21 Co-operative News 30/1/1937
22 Thornes (1984) pp. 61, 62, 66-67
23 PRO: FS1 Yorks. 859B/1927, *Articles... the provident society... at the house of James Crabtree at Woodend in Stansfield* (no date)
24 WYRO: C672/2/1
25 TA 20/1/1882. Travis (1896) p. 33
26 *Selections...James Standing*, p. 93
27 HG 18/9/1847
28 CRO: TT 198, 6/6/1839
29 Travis (1896) p. 40
30 Fielden (1836) pp. 79-80
31 Travis (1896) p. 29

3 The Reform Agitation

1 Sykes (1982) p. 358
2 VP 15/1/1831
3 *Rules and regulations... Todmorden Political Union*. VP 26/2/1831
4 This and following quotations from *Minutes of the Todmorden Political Union*
5 Spater (1982) p. 502.
6 JRL: Fielden Papers, Miscellaneous later additions, *Account of the Celebrations of passing the first Reform Bill*
7 TA 11/5/1900
8 JRL: Fielden Papers, Miscellaneous later additions, *Some Account of the Collateral Circumstances Connected with the above Dinner at Waterside in 1832*
9 Derived by comparing Land Tax records with lists of 1832 voters
10 The whereabouts of the records of the early Unitarian chapel in Todmorden - if they survive - is unknown. But Fox (1924) quotes extensively from them, giving the names of 46 men who were active Unitarians 1823-1828.
11 Fielden (1836), preface
12 Spater (1982) p. 613
13 Crabtree (1833) pp. 8-9
14 Factory Inquiry Commission. BPP 1834 (167) XX Sect C1 pp 228-30
15 Fielden (1836) pp. 84-5
16 Todmorden's delegate to a Manchester meeting was "J. Suthers" (Herald of the Rights of Industry, 26/4/1834). This must be James Suthers, beerseller of Toad Lane (later of the Wellington, York Street), who was secretary to the Todmorden Political Union in 1833.

4 Revolt Against The New Poor Law

1 CRO: TT 180
2 The main sources used for this account are the Todmorden Poor Law Union Correspondence (PRO: MH 12/6272-4) and the Letter Book of the Clerk to Todmorden Poor Law Guardians (CRO: TT 198)
3 CRO: TOD 2. These resolutions, made on 15/2/1837, were confirmed on 2/4/1838.
4 PRO: MH 12/6272, James Taylor to Poor Law Commission, 18/4/1838. The threat to close the works long pre-dated its implementation
5 PRO: MH 12/6272, William Sutcliffe, Hebden Bridge, to PLC, 21/2/1837
6 CRO: TT 198, 31/1/1838
7 TT 165, 6/7/1837
8 CRO: TT 165, 17/8/1837. The seven organisers of the petition for amendment were all substantial citizens, i.e.: John Sutcliffe, Mr. Thomas Eastwood, John Ingham, John Barker of Bank, James Greenwood of Harehill, William Horsfall of Underbank, and John Whiteley. Sutcliffe, Ingham, Greenwood Horsfall and Whiteley had stood for election as Guardians in February 1837, and Barker and Eastwood had been their proposers. (CRO: TT 200/1)
9 MSA 21/10/1837
10 PRO: MH 12/6272, James Taylor to PLC, 18/4/1838;
11 NS 28/4/1838
12 PRO: MH 12/6272, William Ormerod to PLC, 31/3/1838
13 PRO: MH 12/6272, April 1838.
14 PRO: MH 12/6272, Power to PLC, 9/5/1838
15 HG 7/7/1838. MSA 7/7/1838
16 PRO: MH 12/6272, printed notice calling public meeting
17 PRO: MH 12/6272, Power to PLC, 6/7/1838, reporting "3,000-4,000, and many of these women and children". MSA 7/7/1838
18 PRO: MH 12/6272, Stansfield to PLC, 6/7/1838
19 NS 14/7/1838
20 MSA 14/7/1839
21 Fifth Annual report of the Poor Law Commissioners (1839), reprinted in Cole and Filson (1965) pp. 337-338
22 PRO: MH 12/6272, Power to PLC, 2/9/1838. CRO: TT 198, 16/8/1838 to 30/8/1838
23 THBHA 1883, pp 11-13
24 Travis (1896) pp. 107-8, 120
25 NS 27/10/1838, 3/11/1838.
26 HG 24/11/1838. PRO: HO 40/38, depositions of Feather and King, 24/11/1838
27 PRO: MH 12/6272, James Taylor to Power, 16/11/1838
28 NS 24/11/1838. HG 24/11/1838
29 PRO: HO 40/38, Power to PLC, 17/11/1838
30 HG 22/12/1838
31 HG 13/4/1839
32 CRO: TT 198, 24/11/1838
33 NS 1/12/1838
34 NS 1/12/1838
35 HG 24/11/1838 (late edition)
36 PRO: ASSI 44/155, 9/3/1839
37 He sold torn-up scraps of newspaper, alleging they were the "last dying words and confession of James Blomfield Rush" (HG 28/4/1849); assaulted a wax-works proprietor and his wife (HG 24/12/1847); and was accused of wife-beating (HG 25/11/1848). He was also the father of Miles Weatherhill, who committed the Todmorden Vicarage murders in 1868.
38 HG 19/1/1839, 2/2/1839
39 HG 13/4/1839. PRO: PL 27/11, 26/132. (Some letters written by Turner during his imprisonment have recently come to light, TN 13/4/1990)
40 PRO: ASSI 41/16
41 Fifth Annual Report of the Poor Law Commissioners (1839), reprinted in Cole and Filson (1965) p. 340
42 HG 24/11/1838
43 PRO: MH 12/6272, Power to PLC, 22/11/1838, 24/11/1838, and inserts November 1838.
44 PRO: MH 12/6272, Power to PLC, 27/11/1838, 29/11/1838, 1/12/1838
45 PRO: HO 40/38, Wemyss to Phillipps (confidential), 24/11/1838
46 PRO: MH 12/6272, Power to PLC, 2/9/1838
47 PRO: MH 12/6272, Power to PLC, 8/12/1838: John Hill to Lord Morpeth, 5/12/1838. CRO: TT 198, James Stansfield to Halifax magistrates, 15/12/1838
48 PRO: MH 12/6272, John Sutcliffe of Heptonstall to PLC, 1/6/1839; Joseph Ingham to PLC, 16/7/1839.
49 CRO: TT 198, James Stansfield to PLC, 5/7/1839
50 PRO: MH 12/6272, William Bancroft to PLC, 15/7/1839.
51 PRO: MH 12/6272, Power to PLC, 18/11/1839
52 PRO: MH 12/6272, Power to PLC, 22/7/1839
53 HG 28/3/40
54 PRO: MH 12/6272, Power to PLC, 20/4/1840
55 CRO: TT 198, James Stansfield to PLC, 19/10/1840
56 PRO: MH 12/6272, Power to PLC, 7/9/1840
57 PRO: MH 12/6272, Mott to PLC, 26/3/1841
58 PRO: MH 12/6272, Mott to PLC, 28/9/1842
59 PRO: MH 12/6273, PLC to Clements, 11/4/1843; Clements to PLC 15/5/1843
60 PRO: MH 12/6273, James Stansfield to PLC, 5/3/1844
61 PRO: MH 12/6273, Clements to PLC, 24/1/1844, 26/1/1844
62 PRO: MH 12/6273, James Stansfield to PLC, 6/3/1844
63 PRO: MH 12/6273, PLC to Todmorden Guardians, 15/3/1844
64 PRO: MH 12/6273, Clements to PLC, 9/5/1844
65 PRO: MH 12/6274, James Stansfield to PLC, 7/2/1852
66 MSA 1/4/1837. PRO: MH 12/6272, Power to PLC, 17/7/1838
67 MSA 9/6/1838
68 LRO: QSP 3098/11, Notice of intention to appeal against poor rate assessment, 14/12/1838
69 HG 28/3/1840
70 VP 15/1/1831
71 CRO: TOD 1, 4/8/1838
72 PRO: PL 27/11, examination of Eli Crossley of Frith's Wood, warehouseman. HG 20/11/1838. PRO: MH 12/6273, John Sutcliffe, Heptonstall, to PLC, 8/7/1843
73 PRO: MH 12/6272, Taylor to PLC, 18/4/1838, Power to PLC, 27/11/38
74 MSA 7/7/1838. NS 28/5/1842
75 MSA 14/7/1838
76 MSA 14/7/1838

5 Chartism In Todmorden

1 NS 6/1/1838
2 NS 6/10/1838
3 CRO: TM 2/1, 18/4/1839
4 H.W. Harwood, The Midgley story: 100 years of co-operation (no publisher and undated)
5 NS 10/7/1841, 11/9/1841, 2/10/1841, 23/10/1841
6 NS 27/11/1841, 30/4/1842
7 CRO: TT 1658
8 NS 5/3/1842
9 NS 9/7/1842
10 NS 4/12/1841
11 NS 12/2/1842
12 NS 16/7/1842
13 Main source, HG 13/8/1842, 20/8/1842, 27/8/1842, 3/9/1842, 10/9/1842
14 NS 20/8/42
15 PRO: ASSI 45/66, Deposition of John Heap, 23/8/42
16 PRO: ASSI 45/66, Deposition of Thomas Marshall, 25/8/42
17 PRO: HO 45/264/1-226, John Waterhouse to HO, 15/8/1842
18 O'Connor, Chartist Trials, p. 143
19 CRO: TT/165
20 PRO: ASSI 45/66, Depositions of James Hall, William Shaw, Thomas Mitchell, William Turner, John Heap, William Hinchliffe, John Smith, Thomas Marshall, 23/8/1842 and 25/8/1842.
21 HG 20/8/1842
22 Feargus O'Connor, Chartist Trials, pp 143-145, 184-199. HG 11/3/1843
23 NS 24/12/1841
24 NS 30/7/1842
25 CRO: MISC 776/7, 776/8/1, 776/9/1
26 HG 23/12/1843
27 HG 17/12/1842
28 NS 13/1/1844, 27/1/1844
29 NS 25/5/1844
30 NS 19/8/1843, 8/8/1846
31 NS 2/2/1844
32 HG 21/1/1843
33 NS 2/5/1846
34 HG 25/2/1843
35 HG 24/2/1844, 25/3/1848, 27/7/1844, 22/4/1848
36 HG 8/7/1843
37 Todmorden Library, book of newspaper cuttings, p. 146
38 HG 2/12/1848, 12/5/1849
39 PRO: BT 41/474/2659
40 NS 18/4/1846, 1/8/1846. Ashworth (1901) p. 12
41 NS 4/12/1847
42 NS 3/6/1848, 17/6/1848, 22/7/1848
43 THBHA 1891 p. 153, 1869 p. 45. Travis (1896) p. 260
44 CRO: TT 123
45 Much of the biographical information comes from the census ennumerators' returns, or from local trade directories. Other major sources are given.
46 PRO: BT 41/474/2659
47 Travis (1896) pp. 55-6
48 HG 3/9/1842
49 PRO: ASSI 45/66, deposition of John Smith, 23/8/1842
50 NS 20/6/1840

51 HG 10/9/1842
52 O'Connor, *Chartist trials*, p. 143
53 NS 29/10/1842
54 NS 6/12/1845, 27/6/1846
55 O'Connor, *Chartist trials*, pp. 140, 144
56 TA 6/4/1900
57 NS 23/8/1845
58 TA 25/4/1884, obituary Enoch Horsfall. Travis (1896) pp. 260-264
59 THBHA 1897, pp. 27-31. TA 15/4/1897, obituary Samuel Whitham
60 NS 17/12/1842

6 Masters and Men

1 see Chapter Two, footnote 1
2 White's Directory, 1853
3 HG 10/5/1851, 31/5/1851, 14/6/1851
4 *One Hundred Years...* 1923, pp. 12-16. TA 12/12/1919
5 Savage (1985) p. 8
6 HG 1/10/1842, 15/10/1842, 10/12/1842, 25/3/1843
7 MSA 19/4/1834
8 NS 12/7/1845
9 In 1841, John Fielden gave his workers the choice between short hours at a guaranteed wage, or full-time at a variable wage. They chose the latter. (Weaver 1987, p. 235). But clearly thereafter the mills returned to the option that Fielden preferred
10 NS 1/5/1841
11 HG 21/4/1847
12 HG 19/6/1847
13 HG 17/7/1847, 8/1/1848
14 HG 9/7/1849

15 Travis (1896) p. 124
16 Foner (1967) p. 132
17 HG 19/5/1850, and subsequent issues
18 HG 20/7/1850
19 HG 31/8/1850
20 Placard in possession of Dorothy Thompson. See also E.P. Thompson (1972 ed.) p. 432
21 Travis (1896) p. 189. HG 15/1/1848

7 Towards A New Co-operative Commonwealth

1 HG 22/1/1848, 5/5/1849
2 1851 Census, Education in England and Wales, British Parliamentary Papers 1852-3 (1692) XC p. 246
3 HG 28/10/1848, 4/11/1848, 10/3/1849
4 HG 7/1/1843, 25/9/1847, 1/2/1851
5 HG 23/12/1848
6 HG 16/10/1847, 16/9/1848
7 HG 19/8/1848, 21/10/1848, 14/4/1849
8 HG 1/1/1848, 2/6/1849
9 HG 17/7/1847, obituary Thomas Greenlees
10 Charles Smith, *Centenary history of the ancient and noble order of united oddfellows, Bolton unity, 1832-1932*, Manchester 1932, p. 10
11 CRO: MISC 854
12 HG 8/1/1848
13 WYRO: C672/2/1, March 1850
14 Rochdale Library: newspaper cutting, RL170
15 CRO: MISC 854
16 West Yorkshire Registry of Deeds: RA 83-6, 12/11/1850, 13/11/1850

17 West Yorks. Registry of Deeds: LT 401-2, 15/5/1834. CRO: TT 141, TT 143, TT 110. THBHA 1884, pp. 17-21
18 CRO: MISC 854
19 PRO: FS/6 Yorks 111/534, 118/792
20 HG 20/7/1850, 17/8/1850
21 HG 14/8/1847, 21/8/1847, 18/9/1847
22 THBHA 1897, p. 31
23 Pickles (1901) pp. 3, 6. CRO: TT 110
24 PRO: FS1 Yorks 325/2117, 824/731, 826A/908
25 Pickles (1901) p. 21
26 TA 21/7/1899, 28/7/1899
27 Friendly Societies Return, BPP 1852 (39) XXVIII 349. Burnley Gazette 16/5/1891
28 Manchester Central Library, Local Studies: Friendly societies returns 1864-77 (pf 334.7 FI)
29 Co-operative Directory, 1887
30 THBHA 1897, p. 29

Conclusion

1 Driver (1993) chapter 7. Edsall (1971) passim
2 Thompson (1984) p. 62
3 Foster (1974) pp. 50-56
4 Driver (1993) pp. 123, 117
5 Driver (1993) p. 124
6 Cole (1994) pp. v-vi, 50
7 Driver (1993) p. 125

BIBLIOGRAPHY

Primary Sources

(PRO) Public Record Office, London

ASSI 44/155 North East circuit, indictments
ASSI 45/66 West Yorkshire, examinations and depositions
ASSI 41/16 North East circuit, minute book
BT 41/474/2659 Names of the subscribers to the National Land Company
BT 474/2659 National Land Company (advertisement)
FS 1 Rules and amendments of friendly societies
FS 1/325/2117 Equitable progressionists, Bridge end
FS 1/824/731 Todmorden equitable co-operative trading society
FS 1/826A/908 Equitable sincerity stores, Todmorden
FS 2/4, 2/5, 2/11 Lists of Lancashire and West Riding friendly societies registered under Acts 1793-1855
FS 6/111/534 Todmorden mutual benefit building society
FS 6/118/792 Second Todmorden benefit building society
FS 8/15/538 Todmorden flour mill society
HO 40/38 Home Office: Disturbances: Correspondence and Papers, Lancs, (Manchester and Rochdale), 1838.
HO 40/54 Home Office: Disturbances: Correspondence and Papers, (Bucks.- Lancs.), 1840
HO 45/264 Home Office: Disturbances: Correspondence and Papers, (Yorks. and Lancs.), May - Oct, 1842
HO 129/495 1851 Religious Census, Registrar's District of Todmorden
MH 12/6272-4 Todmorden Poor Law Union, 1834-42, 1843-44, 1852-55
PL 27/ A103/11 Palatinate of Lancashire, depositions
PL 26/ A103/132 Palatinate of Lancashire, indictments

(WYRO) West Yorkshire Record Office, Wakefield

C353 Fielden Archive
C672 2/1-2 Shore Baptist minute books 1823-1841, 1845-1861
QE 13/7/48 Stansfield land tax returns, 1830
QE 13/7/30 Langfield land tax returns, 1828

(LRO) Lancashire Record Office, Preston

EL 1/1 Register of Electors; Southern Division of the County of Lancaster, township of Todmorden-cum-Walsden, 1832
QDF 3/41 Hundred of Salford, jurors lists, 1831
QDL "S" Hundred of Salford, land tax returns

(CRO) Calderdale Record Office, Halifax

FIE 1-248 Fielden family records
HPC A48 Heptonstall female friendly societies membership certificates, 1810-1831
MISC 776/3 Plans of estates devised to trustees by Anthony Crossley of Todmorden Hall, gentleman
MISC 776/4 Plans of estates, roads and canals, John Crossley of Scaitcliffe, 1816
MISC 776/7-9 Todmorden Anti-Corn Law Association papers
MISC 854 Todmorden Oddfellows records, 1840-1874
MP 16/2 Map Stansfield (West), 6 chains to 1 inch, 1816
MP 17 Map Stansfield, Wood and Fishwick, 6 chains to 1 inch, 1833
MP 18 Map Todmorden hamlet, Hampson, 1823

MP 19	Map Todmorden hamlet, Robinson, 2 chains to 1 inch, 1843
MP 20	Map Walsden hamlet, Robinson, 2 chains to 1 inch, 1843
TOD 1	Todmorden-cum-Walsden resolution book, 1801-1836
TOD 2/1	Todmorden-cum-Walsden resolution book, 1836-1912
TM 2/1	Secretary's minute book of the Wesleyan Chapel, Todmorden
TM 28	Resolutions of the teachers of the Methodist Sunday school in Todmorden, 1820-1828
TR1	Stansfield rating assessment, 1835
TT 56-78	Langfield overseers account books, 1795-1833
TT 110	Langfield highways rate assessment book, 1850
TT 121	Langfield order book, 1822-1827
TT 123	Langfield voters, 1870
TT 131-2	Stansfield overseers' account books, 1802-1812, 1835-1843
TT 141-3	Stansfield poor rate assessments, 1845, 1852, 1853
TT 144	Stansfield township, poor rate 1800-17
TT 164	Minute book of Cross Stone chapelry etc. 1816-1822
TT 165	Stansfield township order book 1833-44
TT 166	Stansfield township order book, 1844-1881
TT 171	Book of resolutions of freeholders of Stansfield re. enclosure and other matters, 1812-1829
TT 178-80	Todmorden-cum-Walsden overseers account book, 1801-1838
TT 181	Todmorden-cum-Walsden poor rate assessment, 1830
TT 183	Settlement orders, removal certificates etc. 1718-1833
TT 187	Volume of notices published in Todmorden Church 1821-1837
TT 198	Letter Book of clerk to Todmorden Board of Guardians, 1837-1843

Census enumerators' returns, 1841 and 1851, townships of Todmorden-cum-Walsden, Stansfield, and Langfield.

Heptonstall marriages - microfilm

(JRL) John Rylands Library, Manchester

Fielden Papers: Loosely sorted, inc. Papers relating to the mill; Correspondence; Miscellaneous later aquisitions

(BCL) Bradford Central Library

Register of Electors; West Riding of Yorkshire, Wapentake of Morley, Townships of Stansfield and Langfield, 1832

Documents Privately Owned

William Greenwood, Memorandums, 1825
Knowlwood Mill, Strike placard

Printed Primary Sources

Government publications

1841 Enumeration Abstracts, BPP 1843 (496) XX11, (496) XX111; 1844 (587) XXV11
1851 Enumeration Abstracts, BPP 1851 (1399) XL111, (1631) LXXXV; 1852-3 (1632) LXXXVI, (1691) LXXXV111, (1690) LXXX1X, (1692) XC
Abstract of Returns relative to the state of education in England and Wales, BPP 1835 (62) XLI, XLIII
Minutes of Evidence before the select committeee on manufactures, commerce and shipping, BPP 1833 (690) V1
Factories Inquiry Commission. Supplementary report on employment of children in factories, part 2, BPP 1834 (167) XX Section C1 (Yorkshire)
Children's Employment Commission. Appendix to first report of commissioners for mines, Part 2, Reports and Evidence from Sub-commissioners. BPP 1842 (382) XVII

Newspapers and periodicals

Burnley Gazette
Co-operative News
Halifax Guardian
Herald of the Rights of Industry
Lancashire and Yorkshire Co-operator
Manchester and Salford Advertiser
Northern Star
Todmorden Advertiser
Ten Hours Advocate
Todmorden and Hebden Bridge Historical Almanack
Todmorden News
Voice of the People

Directories

1818-20		Lancashire general directory
1824-5	Pigot	
1825	Baines	History and directory of Lancashire
1828-9	Pigot	National commercial directory
1830	Parson	Directory of Leeds etc.
1834	Pigot	National commercial directory
1837	White	Directory of West Riding
1842	White	Directory of the clothing district
1843	White	Directory of the clothing district
1845	Walker	Directory of Parish of Halifax
1847	White	Directory of the clothing district
1853	White	Directory of Leeds etc.

Contempory Writings, Pamphlets, Rules, etc.

Anon., An account of the riots in the North of England, J. Moore, London 1826
Articles, rules and orders to be observed and kept for the good government and guidance of a female friendly society called the Portsmouth female society held at the house of John Whitaker, sign of the Roe-buck Inn, at Portsmouth in Cliviger, Burnley, 1813
Crabtree, George, A Brief description of a tour through Calder Dale Huddersfield 1833
Fielden, John, The Mischiefs and iniquity of paper money, London, 1832
Fielden, John, The Curse of the Factory System, Milner, Halifax, 1836
Horne, Melville, A Word for my Country; or an Address to the Parishoners of Crosstone, and All Whom it May Concern, London, 1817
Minutes of the Todmorden Political Union, Todmorden, 1907
Ratcliffe, William (compiler), A list of all the lodges comprising the Manchester Unity of Independent Oddfellows, for 1846-7
Rules and articles belonging to the female friendly society holden at Mrs. Mary Horsfall's, innkeeper, New Inn, Holme in the township of Stansfield, Todmorden 1833
Rules and Orders of a friendly society meeting at the house of David Hollinrake, Free Masons' Arms, Bottoms in Stansfield, Todmorden 1825
Rules and orders to be observed by a society of females holden at the house of Mr. John Haworth, the Royal George in Todmorden. Todmorden, 1816
Rules and regulations for the government of the Todmorden Political Union, Feb. 1831

Printed Maps

1848	O.S.	Lancashire, 6 inches to 1 mile, sheet 73
1852	O.S.	town plan of Todmorden, 5ft to 1 mile
1853	O.S.	Yorkshire, 6 inches to 1 mile, sheet 229

Secondary Sources

Anon., Fortunes made in business, Vol.1, London 1884
Anon., Leaves from an old church book; historical notes of Bethel Baptist Church, Lineholme, Reprinted from the Todmorden Advertiser, 1901.
Anon., Historical Sketches of the Inghamite Churches, Colne, 1814
Armitage, H., The Rawden family, Trans. Hfx. Antiq. Soc. 1967
Ashworth, T. Edwin, An account of the Todmorden Poor Law riots of November 1838 and the plug plot of August 1842, 1901 (unpublished)
Baines, Edward, History of the County Palatinate and Duchy of Lancashire, Vol. 2, 1836 edition
Boeckstyns, Ann, "Honest" John Fielden, the Ulysses of the factory movement, unpublished thesis, City of Manchester College of Higher Education, 1978.
Briggs, Henry, History of the Roomfield Baptist Church, 1908
Bythell, Duncan, The Handloom weavers, Camb. Univ. Press, 1969

Catling, Harold, *The spinning mule,* Lancashire Library, 1986

"C.B", *Unitarian social reformers no. 2,* Lindsay Press, (no date)

Cole, G. D. H., *Chartist portraits,* Macmillan, 1965

Cole, G. D. H., and Filson, A. W., *British Working Class Movements: select documents 1789-1875,* Macmillan, 1965

Cole, John, *Conflict and co-operation: Rochdale and the pioneering spirit, 1790-1884,* Kelsall, Littleborough, 1994

Crowther, J., *Walsden a century of change,* Todmorden, (no date)

Dalby, G.R., *The Chartist movement in Halifax and district,* Trans. Hfx. Antiq. Soc. 1956

Driver, Felix, *Power and pauperism; the workhouse system, 1834-1884,* Cambridge Univ. Press, 1993

Edsall, Nicholas C., *The Anti-Poor Law movement, 1834-44,* Man. Univ. Press, 1971

Fishwick, Henry, *Genealogical memoir of the family of Fielden of Todmorden,* London, 1884

Foner, Philip S. (editor), *The autobiographies of the Haymarket martyrs,* New York 1967

Foster, John, *Class Struggle and the Industrial Revolution,* Weidenfeld and Nicolson, 1974

Fox, A. W., *Annals of the Todmorden Unitarian congregation, a centennial sketch,* Todmorden 1924

Holden, Joshua, *A Short history of Todmorden,* Man. Univ. Press, 1912

Holroyde, H., *Textile mills, masters and men in the Halifax district, 1779-1851,* Trans. Hfx. Antiq. Soc., 1979

Holt, Raymond, *The Unitarian contribution to social progress in England,* Unwin, 1938

Kirby, R. G. and Musson, A. E., *The Voice of the people; John Doherty, 1798-1854, trade unionist, radical and factory reformer,* Man. Univ. Press, 1975

Knott, John, *Popular Opposition to the 1834 Poor Law,* Croom Helm 1986

Law, Brian R., *The Calder millowners and the Rochdale canal,* Trans. Hfx. Antiq. Soc., 1954

Lineholme Baptist Church centenary souvenir, 1815-1915, Todmorden, 1915.

Mather, F. C., *Public order in the age of the Chartists,* Man. Univ. Press, 1959

Mitchell, B. R. with Deane, P., *Abstract of British historical statistics,* 1962

Newell, Abraham, *Eastwood and the Eastwood family,* Trans. Hfx. Antiq. Soc. 1916

Newell, Abraham, *Stoodley in Langfield,* Trans. Hfx. Antiq. Soc., 1918

O'Connor, Feargus, *Chartist Trials* (undated)

One Hundred Years, 1823-1923, Wilson Brothers, 1923

Ormerod, William, *The Crossleys and Scaitcliffe,* Trans. Hfx. Antiq. Soc., 1907

Pickles, Fred, *Jubilee history of the Bridge End Co-operative Society Ltd., 1847-1901,* Manchester, 1902

Priestley, A., *120 not out, the history of Todmorden Church of England School*

Ramshaw, C. G., *Concerning Todmorden Parish: A Bit of Local History,* Todmorden, 1911

Savage, Mrs. E. M. (editor), *Sam Banks, his life and times,* Todmorden Antiquarian Society 1985

Savage, Mrs. E., *The Development of Todmorden, 1700-1896,* Todmorden Antiquarian Society, 1987

Selections from the works of James Standing, Todmorden c. 1898

Spater, George, *William Cobbett: the poor man's friend,* Camb. Univ. Press, 1982

Sykes, R. A., *Popular Politics and Trade Unionism in S.E. Lancs, 1829-42,* unpublished PhD thesis, Univ. of Manchester, 1982

Thompson, E. P., *The making of the English working class,* Penguin, 1972

Thompson, Dorothy, *The Chartists; popular politics in the industrial revolution,* Wildwood house, 1984

Thompson, Dorothy, *Women and Nineteenth-Century radical politics: a lost dimension* (in Juliet Mitchell and Ann Oakley [editors], *The Rights and wrongs of women,* Penguin, 1976)

Thornes, R. C. N., *The early development of the co-operative movement in West Yorkshire, 1827-1863,* Unpublished D. Phil. thesis, University of Sussex 1984

Timmins, Geoffrey, *the Last Shift; the decline of handloom weaving in nineteenth century Lancashire,* Man. Univ. Press, 1993

Travis, John, *Local historical notes,* Todmorden, 1905

Travis, John, *Notes (historical and biographical) mainly of Todmorden and district,* Rochdale, 1896

Travis, John, *Todmorden; its churches and other matters connected therewith,* Todmorden, 1858

Ward, J.T., introduction to reprint of Fielden, John, *Curse of the Factory System,* Frank Cass and Co., 1969

Weaver, Stuart Angas, *John Fielden and the politics of popular radicalism,* Oxford Univ. Press, 1987

Webster, Eric, *19th century co-operatives,* Trans. Hfx. Antiq. Soc. 1983 and 1984

West, John L., *The Taylors of Lancashire, Bonesetters and Doctors, 1750-1890,* Worsley, 1977

Wilkinson, Ralph, *Unto the Hills: the story of Methodism in Lumbutts, 1837-1987,* Todmorden 1987

Wilson, Joshua H., *A short memoir of Alice Wilson,* Manchester, 1877

Wood, Herbert, *Congregationalism at Eastwood: 250 years of local history,* 1940

Wright, D.G., *Popular radicalism: the working-class experience, 1780-1880,* Longman 1988

York Street Wesleyan Sunday School Todmorden; the vista of a century, Todmorden, 1921

INDEX

Note: Not included in the index are the list of Todmorden Subscribers to the National Land Company (p. 72) and the Appendix "Todmorden Chartists and their Recorded Activities" (p. 98-9)